The Only Good Snake . . .

THE ONLY GOOD SNAKE . . .

Tales from a Rattlesnake Whisperer

David E. Jensen

Published by AO Press

Austin, Texas

Softcover ISBN: 978-1-964078-47-2

For my family, who patiently put up with my snake addiction. And for my herping friends, past and present, for your knowledge, support, and enthusiasm.

CONTENTS

Introduction   ix

Chapter 1: Snake in the Grass   1

Chapter 2: Skull Valley   18

Chapter 3: What the Heck is Herping?   35

Chapter 4: Snake Stuff   53

Chapter 5: Gearing Up   68

Chapter 6: The Money Conundrum   85

Chapter 7: The Museum   100

Chapter 8: In Defense of Rattlesnakes   113

Chapter 9: Heads and Tails   127

Chapter 10: Friends in Low Places   144

Photographs   159

Chapter 11: Buzzer Butts and Beemers   167

Chapter 12: Hollywood Calls   179

Chapter 13: The Venom Factor   192

Chapter 14: Journey to Snake Road   208

Chapter 15: Media Matters   221

Chapter 16: Legends and Lies   234

Chapter 17: Right vs Happy   249

Chapter 18: Fear and Loathing   258

Chapter 19: The Off-Season   276

Chapter 20: It Takes all Kinds   288

Epilogue   309

Acknowledgements   321

"When you're a snake,
it's hard to get the upper hand,
get a leg up, a step ahead, hold a grudge,
have a chip on your shoulder,
or stand up for yourself."

—Dave Jensen

INTRODUCTION

"Snakes are living brushstrokes, beauty in motion, sculpted by nature to keep the wild in balance." –Sylvia Knox, former reptile curator

"The only good snake . . ."

It's a phrase I've heard a lot in my life, but it's only half a sentence. How someone completes the other half speaks volumes about their understanding and perception of snakes, their level of indoctrination (good or bad), and how they choose to utilize the knowledge they have regardless of whether it's right or wrong.

If you ask the average person for their opinion about snakes, the results will range from unbridled excitement to utter revulsion, although it usually falls somewhere on the broad spectrum in between. As a confirmed snake lover, I fall into the first category. I fell in love with snakes as a kid, and the kid within me still gets excited at the prospect of finding or catching a snake.

Keeping snakes as pets, and later, saving them from the perils of human malice, misconception and fear, continued to fuel this excitement well into my later years. Since the age of 10, I've kept snakes as pets with only brief interludes of snakelessness — a condition I quickly remedied. After all, a house isn't truly a home without at least one snake in it.

Snakes did not comprise my entire life, but they definitely provided the structural framework for it. Non-snake lovers may not understand that for me and for many of my closest friends, snakes are nature's prescription for joy in a cynical, chaotic, and sometimes joyless world. Snakes have long been my go-to animal for discovering the infinite panoply of life and the interwoven intricacies of the natural world, while providing a valid excuse for immersing myself in raw nature as often as possible.

This is not some awkward confession or an admission of weirdness. Or maybe it is. All I know is that since I was a kid, snakes have inspired in me an all-consuming empathy and admiration, stemming perhaps from their seemingly incongruent form, which appears at first glance like nature's cruelest joke being played out on an animal too disadvantaged to fight back. But snakes, not to be outdone, accepted the challenge, becoming some of the most well-adapted and ecologically vital animals on the planet. As masters of adaptation, snakes evolved to occupy a variety of niche environments, habitats, and climates, allowing them to thrive in all but the harshest of conditions.

One hundred million years ago, snakes gained an evolutionary head start on many of their four-legged competitors, giving them the upper hand, so to speak, in the race to conquer diverse habitats across the globe, making them vital emissaries of successful evolutionary compliance.

Today, snakes are among the most dominant reptiles on the planet — a testament to natural selection, biological imperative, and the incredible diversity of life on this blue and bountiful orb. Snakes are found virtually everywhere except Antarctica, Iceland, Ireland, Greenland, New Zealand and Hawaii. For me, there is no allure to living in any of those snakeless places. (There is no allure for living in Antarctica with or without snakes.)

I'm comfortable around snakes. More than comfortable, really. Stick me in a room full of people, no matter the venue, and my comfort level drops like an anchor in deep water. I've never been diagnosed with a social anxiety disorder, but my symptoms indicate that consorting with too many unknown members of my own species makes me uneasy.

It's not that I'm socially inept. The truth is I can strike up a conversation with almost anyone from a Supreme Court judge to a park bench wino. We may not reach bilateral consensus, but we'll definitely find common ground on a path of civil discourse. However, it's more of a social necessity than a required skill. The ability to do something is not the same as wanting to do it. It is certainly not the same as enjoying it. But drop me into a pit of snakes and I'm as comfortable and content as a rattlesnake at a rodent ranch.

If you love snakes like I do, have you ever wondered why? Why do you run toward them when others are running away?

What makes you feel compassion toward a creature that has been the focus of fear throughout history? How did you escape the mass delusions, the social stigmas and the skeptical attitudes that shroud the reputation of the humble serpent?

Introduction

Why do you look for them in nature, keep them in your home, and do your best to help others understand and appreciate them?

I have asked myself these questions over the years, and there are a multitude of reasons.

This book is an accounting of my personal infatuation with snakes, and later, snake relocation for the safety of snakes and humans. After all, everyone needs a passion in life — that one thing that arouses our curiosity, stimulates our senses, and inspires joy in a world that works overtime to stomp out the flickering fires of happiness that illuminate our souls and bring us bliss. For me, that passion has always been snakes.

I don't know why destiny tasked me with this interest, why I gravitated at an early age toward a creature that most people find disagreeable, or why I feel such empathy toward an animal that far too many people would go out of their way to avoid or even kill, mostly because they don't know any better. But it's the hand I was dealt, so who am I to question fate?

My parents probably wondered what they did to end up with a snake kid, but they didn't discourage my interest.

As a girl, my mother was a tomboy, catching bees and black widow spiders in bottles. I'm not sure if she ever met a snake, but she certainly had no aversion to them. This fact came in handy later on when her tolerance was tested.

After all, how many moms let their sons bring home garter snakes, gopher snakes, rattlesnakes, iguanas, tegus, tarantulas, and a Gila monster? When I wanted a boa constrictor at the age of 12, she was the one who went and got it for me.

My dad probably never saw a snake outside of a zoo until I started finding them on our desert outings. He certainly had no problem with them, and fortunately for me, no problem having them in his house. Not in the beginning, anyway.

My parents' unbiased perspective about snakes left me untainted by the animosities and false perceptions so many parents inflict on their children, deliberately or otherwise; a fact for which I am extremely grateful. My initial opinions of snakes were as blank as bedsheets, although a definite pattern was forming.

For me, there is beauty in the serpentine form that defies conventionality. Whether you believe in evolutionary theory or a supreme creator or both, those who can see beyond the confines of personal prejudice and cultural bias know that everything in nature is essential and that nothing in nature is a mistake. This is certainly true of snakes, despite the antagonistic insinuations of Genesis, Hollywood, and reinforced cultural conditioning based largely on ignorance, superstition, and unjustified hostility. These are the forces that have shaped most people's perceptions, not only of snakes, but their intolerance of everything, up to and including a closed-minded worldview.

In a story I wrote for a college writing class many years ago, I described a snake as *elegant*. When I was asked to read the story to my fellow students, their reactions were less than cordial.

"Snakes aren't elegant!" someone said in a tone of disgust. "They're revolting!"

"You need to find a different adjective," said another.

"Have you ever met a snake?" one of them asked.

"One or two," I replied.

Beauty, it is said, lies in the eye of the beholder, and it may be sufficient to assume that those who fail to recognize beauty in any of its myriad forms are unqualified to define beauty based on their own narrow perception of what innate beauty really is.

Many species of snakes are stunningly beautiful, rivaling any other creature in nature's vast tapestry, including birds, butterflies, and fishes. As the wise Chinese philosopher Confucius observed, "Everything has beauty, but not everyone sees it."

Sadly, Confucius is right about this, as he was about most things. As with many of life's virtues, an intrinsic perception of beauty is a gift not everyone possesses or ever acquires. However, if any human being claims to see beauty in a rose or a sunset, but is incapable of seeing it in an insect, spider or snake, can we accept that person's concept of innate beauty within the confines of their own limited and seriously subjective internal views? Or do we let them off the hook by considering them innocent victims of social brainwashing and a substandard personal awareness?

Similarly, if a person claims to love animals, but draws a line at the scaly or slimy ones, are they truly an animal lover? Can someone claim to be a true animal lover if they only love the cute and fluffy ones? Maybe they're just bird and mammal lovers, and that's okay as long as they acknowledge it.

Go to the reptile house at any zoo on any given day and listen to the shrill denunciations of the average crowd of onlookers. "Yuck!" says a woman, twisting her face in a distorted grimace as she looks at a harmless king snake. "Gross!" says her young daughter as she scrunches her face and pretends to shudder, imitating her mother's disdain.

Sadly, the mother is projecting her own prejudices and fears onto her child, instilling in her an enmity toward something that could just as easily be a source of beauty, respect, and fascination. Yet, despite their conjoined animosity, they can hardly take their eyes off these compelling creatures.

Perhaps Gandhi said it best: "The good man [and woman]" he said, "is the friend of all living things." You don't have to love something in order to respect it, and it doesn't make sense to hate something enough to want to kill it. Try to appreciate every living thing for what it is and understand that it exists for a purpose, even if you don't know what that purpose is, especially if it doesn't affect you directly.

When I was a boy, my own dear grandmother, a confirmed snake-hater her entire life, was enthralled by watching my pet boa constrictor, Caesar, swallow a large rat.

"Oh my!" she'd exclaim, as the eight-foot snake swallowed a meal several times the diameter of his own head. "Isn't that interesting?"

Grandma wouldn't touch a snake, but she still managed to find some aspect of them enthralling. We should all be enthralled by the wonders of nature.

As a freelance writer most of my adult life, I have written frequently about snakes in an effort to educate the masses about the inherent qualities and overlooked benefits of snakes in a world that, despite all facts to the contrary, and with infinite access to knowledge, still manages to condemn them. Clearly, in the information age, remaining ignorant about any topic is a conscious choice.

Aldo Leopold, author of *A Sand County Almanac*, said, "The last word in ignorance is the man who says of a plant or animal,

'What good is it?' If the land mechanism as a whole is good, then every part of it is good, whether we understand it or not."

Most of these attempts to educate and inform have fallen short of the goal, largely because the very audience I wrote them for — those who dislike snakes — aren't inclined to read them. This makes sense I suppose; sort of like writing vegetarian recipes for meat lovers. In the end, I accomplish nothing more than preaching to an already converted choir.

I have incorporated some of those writings here. Most of these works do not appear in their original form, having been chopped and blended into the mix, adding spice and flavor where it was needed most. In some cases, these writings helped to trigger details and memories that may have otherwise been forgotten in the intervening years.

It's important to me that I record these events for posterity because some day when I'm old and decrepit, I'll be telling these stories at the Senile Acres senior living center and no one will believe me.

The people I describe in these pages are all real, or at least they were when I met them. I assume they still are. Some are composites of multiple individuals stuffed into a single generic character (or caricature, as the case may be). As customers of mine, I met most of them for only a few moments as I retrieved an unwelcome rattlesnake from their yard. For that reason, I remember hardly any of their names, so they've been given new ones, if I made any attempt to identify them at all.

Family, good friends and long-time acquaintances are referred to by their first names only. This isn't because they're ensconced in the witness protection program or on the lam for crimes against humanity. No, they are simply good folks who deserve their privacy in a world where privacy is at a premium and our identities and whereabouts are too easily discovered and just as easily exploited. I know who they are, they know who they are, and soon, so will you.

Unlike other memoirs, this one doesn't dive into tragedy or sensationalize personal struggles. It's not an exposé of a near-death experience, a triumph over addiction, or a bounce-back from childhood trauma. Nor is it an attempt to immerse readers in religious dogma, dubious belief systems, moral conundrums, or ethical relativism. It is merely a compendium of thoughts, memories and actions concerning my innate fascination and interaction with snakes over many years, and I thank you for taking the time to read it.

You also have a right to know that I am not a professional herpetologist, nor do I possess a degree in the biological sciences or any related field. While much of my knowledge of snakes was gained through firsthand observation, experience and study, I acknowledge the insights of qualified mentors who helped me fill the vast chasms of my ignorance with understanding. It is my hope that you find this book not only informative but entertaining as well. Whether you presently appreciate snakes or not, I hope you can expand your understanding of them in these pages and beyond.

This is not a "snake book" by the usual definition, even though snakes are definitely at the heart of it. Because I'm not a scientist or researcher, it is not my intention to overwhelm readers with an unreasonable number of references to morphology, anatomy, physiology, taxonomy, nomenclature, or distribution of species. For that reason, I have kept scientific references to a minimum, including them only where they add to the narrative or help to clarify a concept.

Scientific names of animals are included where relevant in reference to specific species. This is because the common names of most animals as used by laypersons (and even enthusiastic amateurs like me) may refer to different animals in different locales, often having no bearing on the true taxonomic identity of a species. Too many common names are unique to particular demographics or regions and may not be representative of a given species within its natural range.

Although snakes have always played a defining role in my life, they were never the sole focus of it. For example, I didn't earn a living working with snakes, nor did I place my interest in snakes above career or family obligations. Even when I ran a business dedicated to the relocation of urban snakes, it was a backburner endeavor — a side hustle — a passion-driven, extracurricular avocation outside my full-time job and not a means of earning a living. As mentioned previously, we all have that one peculiar motivation that keeps us sane, and while I don't personally see myself as eccentric or obsessed, opinions may vary depending on who you ask. (You should be aware, however, that all my friends and family members are pathological liars.)

Some of the anecdotal material presented here is based on youthful exploits, and later, on the many unusual circumstances I encountered as a rattlesnake removal expert, along with my insights into human nature. I hope my understanding of snakes (and to an only slightly lesser extent, my fellow humans) is evident in this book, and that I can convey to readers a sense of the enthusiasm and excitement I experienced during a lifetime of learning about and dealing with snakes.

It is my desire that you find something of value within these pages. At the very least, I hope you find yourself actively engaged for a while. If I've done my job well, you might come away with a greater appreciation of our serpent friends. Readers who want to know more about topics that pique their curiosity are encouraged to pursue their own quest, whether it concerns snakes or any other subjects that ignite a personal desire for knowledge and adventure.

Shrouded in mystery and steeped in superstition, snakes are champions of conceptual nonconformity. An absence of limbs makes it hard for humans to relate to snakes, so we distance ourselves, unwilling to make an emotional connection with a creature so different from us. But snakes are creatures like any other; they have red blood, they breathe air, they feel pain and fear, and they have a full-time job just surviving in a world that holds them in contempt based largely on a biblical tale of a talking snake. But that's someone else's story.

This is my story.

–David E. Jensen

CHAPTER 1

Snake in the Grass

"Every great story seems to begin with a snake." –Nicholas Cage

One day, a year or two out of high school, I received a call at my first full-time job. A coworker answered the phone. "It's for you," she said, handing me a receiver attached to a long, coiled cord. My mother's voice was on the other end of the line. "There's something going on in your room," she announced angrily, "and you had better come home and fix it. Right now!"

Telling my boss I had a family emergency, I drove home as if I was leading the Indianapolis 500. Mom was waiting for me. "There were noises coming from your room," she said, "and things were falling and breaking. I was too afraid to open the door."

I was afraid to open the door too — afraid of what I might find. I slowly turned the knob and reluctantly peered inside. My bedroom, once clean and organized, with tidy cages arranged on shelves and dressers, now looked like the aftermath of a hurricane.

My nightstand had been swept clean of its alarm clock and lamp. Books had been pulled from shelves. Potted plants, once lined up neatly in the windowsill were now strewn about the floor and on my bed. Shards of glass from shattered terrariums were embedded in the carpet along with damp potting soil. Leaking cologne bottles gave off a pungent aroma. My room was a disaster area. But at least it smelled good.

Earlier that summer, an older friend of mine named Eldon had taken a job supervising a pineapple picking crew in Hawaii. He had an impressive trio of reptiles and needed someone to care for them in his absence. After getting approval from my parents, Eldon gave me cash in advance to cover the cost of food and I became the manager of a reptile boarding house.

Eldon's collection consisted of a 12-foot Burmese python named Thor, an eight-foot Indigo snake named Merlin, and a dignified and somewhat entitled green iguana named Ezekiel. "Zeke" was easily five feet long from his regal snout to the tip of his buggy whip tail. He wore a crest of flexible spines on his head and a row of soft spikes adorned his arched back, giving him a dragon-like appearance. A large dewlap hung from his throat like a banner, and a pattern of chevrons adorned his sides and back like blue tattoos on rough green hide. He was a small but majestic dinosaur.

At the ripe old age of 12, I saved my lawn mowing money for a few weeks, bought a baby South American boa constrictor and named him Caesar. Over the next nine years, Caesar grew like a horizontal beanstalk; a stout, handsome serpent that was slowly eating me out of house and home, finally becoming too expensive to feed and too large to contain in my cramped basement bedroom. Caesar had grown from a chubby little snake that could wrap around my wrist into a ravenous, 10-foot-long snake that could inhale rats like a vacuum cleaner sucks up dust bunnies.

He quickly learned that by flexing his muscular body between the back wall and the front doors of the cage Dad and I had built for him, he could pop the deadbolt that was supposed to make it escape proof. More than once in the middle of the night, I was awakened by the *sproing* of the latch and the sound of the double wood-framed doors with glass panes as Caesar casually flung them open from the inside.

"Caesar," I'd mumble groggily, "not again." Then I'd get out of bed, closing and re-latching the doors before he could go exploring. By this time, my menagerie had expanded to include a few more snakes, a belligerent iguana named Chunky (along with two calmer cage mates), a tegu, a red-footed tortoise, and a tiger salamander in a semi-aquatic tank. I was lucky there was still space in my room for me.

On that fateful day, they were all loose in my bedroom. Six snakes patrolled the carnage, crawling and climbing and having the time of their lives. Caesar and Thor were the ringleaders of this chaotic circus. Both had escaped, rearranging the room and freeing their fellow inmates like a scene from a bad prison movie. Zeke and Chunky surveyed the disaster from atop their perch on

2

the curtain rod, watching in horror as snakes big enough to eat them cruised back and forth in the pandemonium below.

None of the animals was injured, but the cost of cages and cleanup took a toll on my already strained budget. Summer ended and Eldon came to reclaim his critters. I had sent him pictures of the incident and he offered restitution, but it wasn't his fault.

When he was only five-feet-long, Caesar shimmied up the heat duct from my basement bedroom to hang out in the joists between the basement ceiling and the upstairs floor. I tried everything I could think of to lure him out of this improvised lair, but he was having none of it.

After a couple of weeks of worry on my part and frustration on my dad's part, Dad finally had to cut out a section of the ceiling to extricate Caesar. Neither my dad nor Caesar was very happy about it. This led to us building Caesar a new and more secure enclosure.

When he was larger, Caesar got away from my little sister while she was holding him on the living room sofa, winding his way into the springs where he made himself quite comfortable. I freaked out. "Don't sit on the couch," I admonished my family, "you'll squish Caesar!"

We decided to tip the sofa onto its front so that none of us would forget and sit on it by mistake. One day, two women from the neighborhood came to visit my mom and she invited them in. They looked quizzically at the sofa as my mom tried to explain why it wasn't usable. "David's snake is in the sofa and . . ." They didn't wait to hear the rest of the sentence. Jetting out the front door like their pants were on fire, they left without saying goodbye, calling first before they came back a month later.

After a week of patiently waiting for Caesar to get hungry or thirsty enough to exit the sofa on his own, Dad decided that we had been inconvenienced long enough. By this time, Caesar had made his way into one of the arms, so dad, being the handy guy he was, unupholstered the end of the sofa, removing staples, fabric, foam, stuffing, and finally, a friendly but somewhat confused boa constrictor. After the sofa incident, I received a stern warning about further escapes and being more responsible.

The Only Good Snake . . .

Eventually, a parental ultimatum was issued: Caesar had to go. I placed an ad in the newspaper, selling him to a man who wanted a new male boa as a mate for several females. Having his own harem sounded like a great life for Caesar, and I bade him a reluctant goodbye.

It happens all too frequently with large constrictors like boas and pythons. People fall in love with the idea of having an exotic snake. They purchase an irresistibly cute baby snake, not thinking of its potential to eventually consume more room and resources than might be feasible. With proper care, these animals can easily grow a foot a year. In a disturbing trend, reptile rescue organizations are often inundated with big, beautiful snakes that simply got too big or too unpredictable to still be good pets. This may explain the current infatuation with ball pythons, which remain a reasonable size and are extremely docile.

My infatuation with snakes began innocently enough. It was an unforeseen consequence of a chance encounter in my neighbor's neglected yard when I was 10. I spotted the snake from a distance, cruising slowly among the yellow remnants of a once-green lawn. There was something mesmerizing about its movements, which were smooth as muslin and fluid as water.

Intrigued, I stepped closer to the wary reptile. At my approach, its unblinking eyes locked onto me in a baleful glare, as unyielding as the copper rivets on my new blue jeans. Black pupils in amber eyes reacted in a mix of fear and defiance, following my every move. The agitated serpent writhed and coiled in a display of steadfast ferocity, striking occasionally, mostly for effect I assumed, considering that I was well out of biting range. The intensity of her unflinching gaze spanned the distance between us like an invisible tractor beam, slowly pulling me in. I was enthralled. In that moment she was the most incredible creature I had ever seen!

She must have crawled in from the weedy fringes of the abandoned alfalfa field west of my parents' home in the rural community where I spent the halcyon summers of my youth in the pursuit of mischief, fun, and adventure.

Snakes were not overly common where I grew up, certainly not to the extent that they should have shaped my life in any

4

meaningful way. Aside from the frenetic garter snakes with their yellow racing stripes that patrolled the ditch banks where my friends and I played Army and Capture the Flag, snakes were not something I gave a lot of thought to.

These prolific little snakes were plentiful, and all of us, snakes and boys alike, were ever on the lookout for fish and frogs in the murky waters of the old canals and ditches. These final frontiers of our collective boyhoods were in steady decline, bucolic sacrifices to the ravenous development of the encroaching suburban neighborhoods that were devouring them, ours included.

Oh sure, I had seen snakes in the desert with my dad and little brother. These were whip snakes and racers mostly (although I didn't know that at the time), and a rattlesnake once or twice, usually at a distance. I expected to see snakes there. I looked forward to it. But here I was on my neighbor's front lawn, within sight of my own house, having a one-on-one encounter with a snake I hadn't seen up close before and a creature I knew nothing about except that it was harmless. I was thrilled by this discovery!

This snake was more attractive and much larger than the garter snakes I was so overly familiar with. A background color of tawny brown was overlaid with irregularly spaced black patches that ran down her back like thick painted rungs on a long, flexible ladder. It was the type of random symmetry found only in nature. The bars stretched wider near the tail where they appeared more like bands extending longitudinally across her body before disappearing down the sides. Between these bands, the tan coloration transmuted into a deep salmon color. On her face was a black Zorro mask that crossed over her eyes and connected on top of her head, giving her a bandit-like appearance. Her scaly skin was shiny as a glazed donut and her lidless eyes were bright and alert.

As I got closer still, the snake became even more agitated, expelling bursts of air from her long, lissome body, causing her to deflate quickly and noisily like a leaky bicycle inner tube under high pressure. By flattening her narrow head, she could appear larger and more menacing than she really was, and by forcing air from her trachea through her epiglottis, she could produce hissing and farting noises that I found both humorous and endearing. Her mouth remained partly open, allowing both air and sound to escape. After each loud expulsion of air, she would re-inflate herself and repeat the process. She mostly struck in my general direction, although random strikes at nothing in particular were common and made me wonder if she needed glasses.

It was a truly impressive performance, almost worthy of an Oscar. But as I would learn later, she was not acting, nor was she being aggressive. She was in a confrontation with a large, imposing, potential threat to her safety, having no idea what my intentions were, only striking when I got too close, and never closing the gap between us. She most certainly was not the provocateur in this scenario. I was.

I hovered over her with rapt fascination, knowing she could bite me and that she probably wouldn't hesitate to do so if I didn't respect her boundaries. Still, something within me suspected that this was all a show for my bemusement and that this amazing creature was incapable of inflicting any serious harm. But I had no desire to donate any amount of blood, just in case.

People talked of "blow snakes," and I could only conclude that luck had sent one my way. This one was about three feet long. The back two thirds of her agile body was partially raised off the ground like a coiled spring, while the bitey end was facing me, poised in a rigid S-curve that extended straight as an arrow when she struck. Hissing, lunging, and vibrating her nervous tail, she seemed rather formidable at first. She did her best to scare me, and I should have been intimidated, I suppose. Most people would have been. In fact, most people, including most adults, would have run the other way. This is what the snake was hoping for, of course, wanting nothing to do with whatever threat I may have posed to her. She couldn't possibly have known in that moment that I was her greatest ally and biggest fan.

Wanting so badly to pick her up, but not wanting to get bit, I jockeyed for the best position, hoping to gain a tactical advantage. If I moved left, she moved right to face me. If I moved right, she swung to her left, her flexible contra posture keeping me constantly in her field of vision. If I tried to get behind her, she simply pivoted her flexible body around, smooth and precise, as if swiveling on ball bearings. Her all-seeing eyes followed my every movement. Attentive as a guard dog, she continued to hiss like an air hose while rapidly shaking her nervous tail in the dry summer grass.

Convinced that I could outsmart this clever critter, I leaned over and waved my left hand in front of her face, wiggling my fingers for added effect. I made sure to stay out of striking range. I noticed that she could strike a little further than the S-shaped curve in her neck could extend, but in moments of true agitation, she could strike with enough ferocity to propel her entire body forward several inches. Making a mental calculation of this fact, I made sure to keep my hand at least 18 inches away from her face at all times.

Once her attention was fixated on my left hand, I reached behind her with my right hand, scooped it gently underneath her middle, and slowly lifted her off the ground. Her coiled form was tense as a cable and her muscles were rigid. Once airborne, however, she seemed more confused than angry. She was flying!

I slid my left hand under her taut body. She was cool and dry and her belly was smooth to the touch. Supporting her weight with both hands, I boldly placed her around my neck. The only target she could possibly focus on now was my face — a prospect I hadn't considered until that moment. No matter, I had just caught my first real snake and hadn't lost any blood in the process. I was a natural!

As she calmed down, her flatulent-sounding expulsions subsided, becoming fewer and farther between. Finally, after being outsmarted by the large and formidable creature I was, she gave a final huff of indignation before resigning herself to her fate.

I didn't know it then, but this technique for picking up angry snakes has been used by both amateur and professional snake catchers since the beginning of time.

In years yet to come, I would use this technique thousands of times to capture harmless snakes, mostly without incident. Occasionally though, either by miscalculation or carelessness, a deftly clever snake would get the better of me and draw blood. No big deal. A bite from a harmless snake is no more dangerous than a prick by a thorn bush or a nick from a paper cut. A quick cleaning with soap and warm water is all that's required.

The Only Good Snake . . .

Within minutes after capture, my new serpent friend relaxed to the point of exploring my neck and shoulders, poking her snout in my ears and hair, and tasting my scent with her black and bifurcated tongue. She was already a pet!

Hanging like a braided leather whip from my suntanned neck, she rode suspended above my chest, her plated head bobbing up and down in rhythm to my confident stride. Like flipping a switch, a connection had been made. With very little effort, I had befriended a wild beast! Her unblinking eyes and tireless tongue fed a steady stream of information to a primitive yet cognizant brain.

I hurried home, excited to share this adventure with my family. Placing the snake in a cardboard box, I punched air holes in the lid and secured it with a rubber band or two. Needing to expand my knowledge beyond this primitive beginning, I had to know more, but the year was 1969 B.C. (Before Computers), so I begged my mom to take me to the library. She encouraged my new fascination and I checked out a stack of snake books.

Research would reveal that my snake was a Great Basin gopher snake, a common denizen of the entire Intermountain West, making it Utah's most ubiquitous snake species. In the local vernacular, gopher snakes are known as blow snakes, although you will never find that designation in any field guide. It is strictly a regionalism. Their defiant display in the face of danger is an attempt to convince a predator that they are rattlesnakes — a creature not to be trifled with.

Sadly, their provocative posture and defensive demeanor only serve to convince the uneducated that they really are rattlesnakes. Consequently, far too many gopher snakes are savagely dispatched by people who don't know any better.

Great Basin gopher snakes, I learned, were just one of several subspecies of large, handsome constrictors that are common all across North America. In the west, they're called gopher snakes; east of the Continental Divide, they are known as bull snakes; and east of the Mississippi, they are categorized as pine snakes. In total, there are six subspecies comprising the genus *Pituophis*, including the Pacific, San Diego, Santa Cruz, Great Basin and Sonoran gopher snakes, the bull snake, and four distinct subspecies of pine snakes.

From that moment on, I was hooked. I started reading everything I could about serpents and my room soon filled with terrariums, field guides, and shed skins that I treated like rare treasures. What began as a passing curiosity quickly grew into a passion that slithered into every corner of my life. The more I read about snakes the more I wanted to know. I looked for snakes on TV. I read books by Ross Allen, Lawrence Klauber, Clifford Pope and Robert Stebbins — the notable herpetologists of the day — and they became my heroes. Absorbing information like a thirsty sponge, I looked for snakes everywhere I went, checking them off in my *Field Guide to Western Reptiles and Amphibians* by Robert Stebbins. And I memorized the scientific names of all the snakes in Utah.

One day I crossed paths with a plump Wandering garter snake that was resting near a ditch bank. Back at home, I placed her in a terrarium decorated with sticks, leaves, rocks and a water dish, then sat back to admire this new addition to my meager snake collection.

By the next morning, my single garter snake had magically produced 23 miniature garter snakes! This is how I learned that garter snakes give birth to live young. I must have overlooked this fact in my research. In my own defense, I didn't know she was expecting. I just thought she was fat! For my inquisitive young self, it was a revelation that left me spellbound.

The 1960s and '70s were a great time to be a kid. Utah was less cosmopolitan back then and our fun was homegrown, free from today's digital distractions. The virtual world didn't exist yet. We lived in the real world and we made our own fun.

Situated in the northwest quadrant of the Salt Lake Valley, our middleclass neighborhood was surrounded at that time on two sides by undeveloped land. This long-abandoned agricultural acreage, crisscrossed with irrigation canals and the bleached skeletons of deceased barns and corrals, had lost the development battle and now sat sallow and overgrown with waist-high weeds, awaiting the bulldozers and backhoes that would ensure its demise.

The Only Good Snake . . .

Like an insatiable monster, the resulting building boom would eventually consume every remaining square inch of undeveloped land in the valley, including productive farmland, supplanting it with suburban tract houses, strip malls, and intrusive big-box stores with their acres of asphalt parking. It's an ongoing real estate developer's deep-pocket dream and an environmental nightmare for the native plants and animals that once called it home.

This race toward unregulated population growth continues unabated to this day, decimating valuable farmland as well as critical habitat for a variety of wildlife species, all for the sake of rampant, unchecked urban sprawl — a trend local politicians and the Chamber of Commerce eagerly extol because it boosts the tax base and brings new voters — more sheep to be fleeced. However, that wasn't part of my personal reality at the time.

As kids, we don't have the luxury of choosing our own destinations or faraway adventures. I had to take advantage of every family outing, vacation or scout camp to expand my snaking exploits beyond my rather minuscule geographical range. Many of today's kids aren't as fortunate as I was. Every neighborhood used to have at least one vacant lot where kids could jump dirt hills on their bikes or build forts out of discarded grocery store pallets, inventing their own games and getting good and dirty in the process.

The only places left for urban kids to play now are municipal parks and recreation centers where the grass is cultivated, cut, poisoned with chemical fertilizers, pesticides and herbicides, and the playgrounds are cushioned with wood chips, rubber mats or shredded tires. These weed-free, mud-free, wildlife-free zones of civilized nature contain none of the elements of adventure that could provide a modern kid with an encounter like the one I had.

For me, catching that snake was a life-changing experience, but it wasn't extraordinary. Kids lucky enough to engage with nature on a regular basis experience the world through their senses, fostering curiosity, creativity, and joy. From splashing in puddles to climbing trees, watching bugs or catching snakes, these moments shape a child's growth in profound ways.

1 | *Snake in the Grass*

Children are natural sponges, soaking up knowledge and repeating what they've learned like talkative parrots. This is why it's imperative that we teach our children from the best books and set the example that learning is not a chore, but rather, a wondrous, lifelong enterprise. Adults could learn a lot from their children if they'd only listen to them more, and children benefit when adults take the time to teach them about the stunningly beautiful world around us.

Spending time outdoors also nurtures a sense of wonder, encouraging children to care for the environment, while the calming effects of nature reduce stress and anxiety. Whether it's the tactile satisfaction of building forts from branches or passively listening to the songs of birds, these interactions create lasting memories and deepen a child's connection to the natural world. The real world.

This is especially important in today's world, where nature is often replaced with gadgets, where immersion in virtual worlds has become a counterfeit replacement for authentic adventures and genuine imagination. Hands-on experiences with plants, animals, and ecosystems establish a lifelong appreciation for the natural world. Kids who interact with nature often grow into environmentally conscious adults, and the world could use more of them.

Spending many years as a Boy Scout leader provided me with opportunities for teaching youth. As a counselor for the Reptile Study Merit Badge, among others, I was able to impart invaluable information to young men who were required to learn through hands-on observation. In addition to observing animals in the wild, keeping an animal for 30 days and documenting its behavior was a primary requirement for earning the badge. A boy could choose any type of reptile or amphibian for this purpose, but most of them wanted to keep a snake. Who could blame them?

I was disappointed by the reactions of those parents who forbade their sons from having this learning opportunity because they didn't want a caged snake in the house — not even for a mere 30 days. By placing their own needs, fears, and prejudices ahead of the learning opportunities of their sons, these parents denied both their sons and themselves the benefit of a unique learning experience.

Why would a parent prioritize their own momentary discomfort over a child's joy of discovery? Why deny them an experience that could blossom into a lifelong passion — even as a quiet hobby or passive curiosity? Worst of all, why pass down fear to new generations like a family heirloom?

The snake prohibition was in effect no matter how badly the boy wanted to earn the badge simply because the parent wasn't willing to set aside his or her own discomfort in order to benefit their child. (I do understand that any phobia, no matter how irrational it may appear to an observer, is very real for the person who carries it. Just the same, I find it hard to be empathetic when the object of that fear is completely harmless and logic can find no leverage.)

I am happy to announce that out of those parents who did allow their sons to keep a snake, there was a 100 percent survival rate of both snakes and mothers. (In all honesty, one snake did escape in a house, causing much distress and doing nothing to increase the mother's appreciation of them. Oops!)

Several times each year, I was asked to give snake shows to groups of 10- to 14-year-old girls before they went to summer camp. They were always polite and respectful — much more so than boys their age. As we talked, sitting cross-legged on the floor, I learned that one of them had a pet ball python. The youngest girl, who wouldn't hold even a small snake when we started, was proudly carrying a six-foot snake around her neck by the time we were done. This was my payment and my reward.

I always told the girls and their leaders that if they didn't want to see snakes at camp, they should walk with heavy steps because snakes feel vibrations through the ground. I can imagine troops of petite little girls tromping through the woods like Trojans storming into battle, terrifying every unfortunate snake in a hundred-yard radius.

Children who absorb information will know it their entire lives and will perpetuate it by sharing it with others, including children of the future. In this way, perhaps each successive generation can become smarter and more compassionate by displaying a demonstrable knowledge of nature and an empathetic embrace for the earth and all her creatures.

In the late '80s, someone brought me a large, venomous lizard known as a Gila monster (in violation of several state and federal laws). I called him Puff, because just like in the song of the same name, he was most definitely a magic dragon. After a short-term observation period, I returned Puff to his native stomping grounds in Snow Canyon State Park in the southwest corner of the state.

Shortly thereafter, I wrote my first reptile-related article about the experience. It was published in a local outdoor sports magazine under the title *Month of the Gila Monster*. It was the first in a litany of reptile and environmentally themed articles that continues to this day.

As years passed, I began talking about snakes to anyone who would listen in an attempt to replace fear with facts, hoping that even people who hated snakes would no longer kill them out of ignorance. I understand snakes — their instincts, behaviors, motivations and attitudes — more than I understand human nature. These many years later, I am still amazed by an animal that can crawl, swim, dig, climb, capture prey, and, in some cases, glide through the air, all without the benefit of limbs, fins or wings.

Snakes got a raw deal in that whole Garden of Eden fiasco, and they deserve better. I decided early on that I'd be their PR guy. Even as a kid, I was fascinated by the fact that snakes were both worshipped and feared across different cultures, showing up in the myths and legends of some of history's greatest religions and civilizations. Even today, they're too often cast as villains in a world that doesn't take the time to understand them or their importance to humanity.

Snakes occur on six of the seven continents, ranging from the semi-frozen tundra of Northern Canada to steamy equatorial jungles and most of the world's oceans. Their contributions to maintaining the balance of nature are immeasurable. With their ancient lineage and the fact that they are the living, breathing, modern-day descendants of extinct prehistoric beasts, I admire their stealth, beauty, mystique, and diversity.

The Only Good Snake . . .

While most people will never consider it, snakes make great pets. I have kept snakes as pets for more than 55 years now, and they provide an equal or greater amount of aesthetic enjoyment than any aquarium filled with tropical fish. (Have you ever tried to hold a pet fish?)

Snakes don't claw the drapes or leave hair on the furniture. You don't have to fence the yard, get them licensed or have them vaccinated. They don't poop on the lawn or bite the mailman or bark and keep the neighbors awake. As I would later learn, however, it doesn't keep some of the more paranoid neighbors from complaining about them as though the snakes in my house somehow pose a threat to their mental health, general well-being, public safety, and even their progeny. (We must protect the children!) This is absurd, of course, because kids and snakes go together like peanut butter and jelly.

I owned a small rental house for many years. All I ever asked of my tenants was that they call me "His Lordship," at least when I was on the property. Five-year-old Caden almost got it. He called me "landlord."

One day I took Durango, a pet bull snake, to the house. Caden and his mom Carmen met me on the patio. Caden was reluctant to hold a snake at first. His mom did her best to encourage him, but he stood firm, arms folded and face twisted in silent rebellion.

Carmen placed Durango around her own neck like a feather boa and began to dance around. It was the perfect psychological ploy. Not to be outdone by his mother, Caden suddenly wanted to hold Durango. Carmen gently placed the snake across Caden's shoulders and showed him how to support and guide the head, giving him complete control. As Durango sniffed and prodded Caden's arms and shirt with his curious nose and tongue, Caden's stoic face exploded in a gigantic smile.

"Well Caden, what do you think of that?" Carmen asked.

Puffing out his chest in pride, Caden responded enthusiastically, "It's fantastic!"

Children should be taught not to fear snakes, but rather, to admire wild snakes from a distance. There are enough things in the world for kids to be afraid of and snakes shouldn't be one of them. But teaching them to avoid a potentially dangerous situation will keep them safe.

Snakes still show up in the heart of suburbia, but the reactions are often different from when I was a kid. Today, adults are consulted; someone who knows nothing about snakes concludes that it's "poisonous," people freak out, someone calls the police (ridiculous, I know), and the snake is often killed because no one understands the benefits it provides or appreciates such a unique opportunity.

Years later, when I started a rattlesnake relocation business, I could always tell when a rattlesnake was happy to see me because it was often wagging its tail. It was all I could do to keep from patting them on the head when they did this.

In all seriousness, however, the rattlesnake's rhythmic salutation was never meant as a threat, but rather, as a friendly warning. A formal greeting. An anthropomorphic projection of primitive personality. They are known as the most considerate of all snakes for a reason. After all, no other venomous snake extends such a courtesy with so much enthusiasm.

My team and I relocated dozens of snakes each summer for residential and commercial clients, schools, state facilities, and multiple police departments. We also performed yard inspections, recommended snake remediation procedures, acted as media consultants, and were hired as on-set snake wranglers for movie and TV productions, commercials, weddings, and other outdoor events.

As professionals, we charged a nominal fee for our services, and our customers were always grateful for the peace-of-mind we provided and for being able to let the dog and the kids play in the yard again. Best of all, they didn't have to kill a snake, which is illegal, and for me was the whole point of the venture.

I met hundreds of rattlesnakes, and almost without exception they were all glad to see me, because, upon my approach, they would invariably wag their tails like excited puppies.

Mostly though, it was homeowners who were thrilled to see me because they were concerned about having a rattlesnake monopolizing their backyard, garage, swimming pool or patio, putting those areas off limits and causing great consternation.

The Only Good Snake . . .

It could be hard to convince those people that the snake that chose to spend quality time with them didn't seek them out, nor did it mean them any harm. It was merely enacting a ritual as old as time, when, unlike the chicken that crossed the road, it could go where it pleased without having its motives questioned. There was no existential crisis. No ominous intent. It was just an introverted animal looking for a meal or a drink of water on a sweltering hot, bone-dry day. On the other hand, it may have simply been curious about these strange new surroundings.

Present day conflicts between snakes and humans are not instigated by the snakes, which are merely doing what snakes do. Instead, an invasion of modern-day humans has resulted in friction between man and beast. Human expansion has turned peaceful coexistence into a full-blown turf war where snakes are accused of trespassing on the very land where they evolved. Where once they could fulfill their rightful existence in nature's grand plan, humans have imbued them with powers of malevolent intent and threatened them with extermination. The conflict is real, and while there are no actual villains, a mediator is often required to broker peace between the parties.

That's when my phone would ring.

With a deep empathy for snakes that extends far beyond the undeserved accusations of malicious evil, I see them as sovereign beings on a sentient journey. Their choices aren't random — they're encoded in millennia of evolutionary wisdom. They navigate landscapes with quiet certainty, not seeking attention or approval, but merely fulfilling rituals written long before we paved over their ancient domain and called it progress.

My role as relocator, ambassador, and peace broker was never about taming nature. Wildness doesn't need to be tamed, just understood. A rattlesnake doesn't wag its tail because it's excited; it rhythmically warns, "I am here. Respect the boundary." And maybe, just maybe, that's a message we humans should heed more often — not only with snakes, but with everything else we've tried so hard to bulldoze out of existence.

Snakes have an important job to do, controlling rodent populations and preventing the spread of several lethal diseases. This is their service to humanity. If you're fortunate enough to see a

16

snake in your travels, neighborhood or yard, teach your children about it, take its picture, then leave it alone to do the job nature intended. It's good karma, and the snake gods will smile upon you!

CHAPTER 2

Skull Valley

"Spend your life doing strange things in unusual places with weird people." –Unknown

Long before Steve Irwin became the world's foremost animal authority and influencer, a man named Marlin Perkins held that title. As host of a Sunday night TV show called *Wild Kingdom*, Marlin was largely responsible for my love of wild creatures and exotic places. I made up my mind at around eight years of age that I would visit Africa one day if I had to swim. I did make it to Africa some 40 years later, spending 14 glorious days in a paradisiacal wonderland. Everything I saw and did was a pinch-me moment because it all seemed so surreal. It was the best two weeks of my life. Before that dream came true, however, I had to seek adventure closer to home.

Those early adventures consisted of driving remote roads in Utah's west desert in the middle of the night, catching snakes that had gotten too comfortable warming their bellies on lonely asphalt and moving them away from the carnage of infrequent but deadly car traffic. The best place for this was the 38-mile stretch of road that cuts through Skull Valley and leads to the military base at Dugway.

Skull Valley is an enigmatic place — a riddle wrapped in a conundrum tucked in a mystery. Topographically, it is a sprawling, unimpressive swath of flat, weedy desert trapped between two mountain ranges on its long sides, with Interstate 80 and the south shore of the Great Salt Lake as its northern boundary and the Dugway Proving Grounds to the south. Scenically, it's about as appealing as an armpit.

Dugway is a U.S. Army installation, better known to non-Utahns as Area 52 due to the likelihood of it being the military's newest repository for alien technology. Supposedly, after Wright-Patterson Air Force Base in Ohio became the central focus of impassioned UFO buffs, whatever the government was allegedly hiding found its way to Dugway instead.

2 | Skull Valley

When I was 16, my younger brother Gary and I would sleep in the backyard on summer nights with one or two of our friends. We'd get up after mom and dad were asleep, jump in my car and drive out west to cruise for snakes on the Skull Valley road.

In the languid warmth that rises from the pavement after dark, the road gives back the heat it stole during the day. Snakes that came across this alien surface would sometimes pause and linger there, often at their own peril.

As a teenage driver with a newly minted license, it didn't take me long to discover the convenience of putting Gary and his friend Keith on the hood of my orange '68 Chevy as I drove slowly along desolate ribbons of blacktop in the summer darkness.

Dad sold me the old family car cheap. It was a silver 1968 Chevelle station wagon with a 327 V-8. I outfitted it with the latest technology — an 8-track tape player — and had it painted an overwhelming shade of orange called Vitamin C. As a big car, the color was a testament to bad taste, but I loved it. Dad dubbed it "The Great Pumpkin."

Dangling their legs in front of the Pumpkin's grill, Gary and Keith could jump off and instantly grab any snake that appeared in my headlight beams. To my great satisfaction, I discovered that by simply tapping the brake pedal, I could launch my brother and his friend off the hood and onto the roadway any time I wanted. This kept them more alert than they may have been otherwise.

Mom didn't know it, but I used to 'borrow' pillowcases out of her linen closet to use as snake bags. We'd move snakes off warm pavement so they wouldn't get run over by other cars. We weren't able to save them all, of course, but we snatched a lot of snakes out of the path of potential danger (mostly gopher snakes and Great Basin rattlesnakes), preventing them from becoming road pizza. And we had a hell of a lot of fun doing it!

Too often, we'd see snakes that had already been run over, sometimes deliberately, since many of them were on the shoulder of the road, causing me to wonder about the type of person who would swerve to hit a snake at 60 miles an hour. Is their contempt for snakes so great that they are willing to risk their own life to kill one, and if so, why?

The Only Good Snake . . .

We usually saw gopher snakes, Western yellow-bellied racers, or the elusive Desert-striped whip snake — all harmless species — but occasionally providence would place a Great Basin rattler in our path. This was always cause for excitement. We'd lift these venomous serpents carefully and against their will with sticks, drop them into one of mom's clean pillowcases, tie the open end securely, and drive them closer to the foothills and away from danger. Overhead, a million stars winked in approval.

We always made sure to be back in our sleeping bags before Dad left for work in the morning. And of course, I always made sure the pillowcases were folded and placed neatly back in the linen closet so Mom wouldn't know.

That was a long time ago, but the tradition continues. Even when I couldn't drive at night anymore, few things were as fun a spending time on dark desert roads, moving snakes, listening to tunes, and sharing great conversation with good friends. You never know what you might find.

Over the years, Skull Valley has become my go-to escape zone. Some of my fondest memories revolve around the many times my dad took Gary and me to the desert when we were very young. Dad would load his Honda 350 into the back of an old Datsun pickup truck and we'd be Skull Valley bound! Once there, he would leave us near any one of a hundred talus slopes or rock outcroppings that cover the lower slopes of the Stansbury Mountains like a modest skirt. We'd fend for ourselves while he took off on his motorcycle for some much-needed personal time.

Although he never left us for very long, in today's paranoid, wacked-out world it would probably be considered child abandonment to leave two kids alone on a rock pile in the desert . . . but we loved it! With our green Army surplus canteens and a sack lunch, we were happy as two little pigs in a mud puddle.

Gary would look for fossils and interesting rocks, and together we'd harass the local reptile population, sometimes filling a pillowcase with Desert-striped whip snakes. These slender, agile snakes would reveal themselves by rising up and peering over the top of the wilted grasses that covered the slopes, looking like periscopes on a submarine. After catching our fill, we'd release them, marveling at their grace and speed as they rippled and vanished back into the yellow grass. We'd scramble over jagged layers of sedimentary rock to catch the hyper-alert and lightning-fast collared lizards and fence lizards that hid from us in the crevices. It proved to be the foundation for passions we both enjoy to this day and I still appreciate those early opportunities to be close to nature.

Two decades later, I would take Boy Scouts to Skull Valley and expose them to the same adventures I enjoyed at their age. I'm still friends with a lot of those kids, and although they're scattered far and wide with families of their own, they still text me photos of the snake, lizard or frog they found. "Saw this and thought of you!" they'll say, and it's rewarding to know that they're passing those same moments of wonder along to their own children.

In April 2019, Bryan, who now lives back east, sent this message on Facebook: "We spent all last weekend weeding our overgrown new yard, during which time we came across about 15 snakes. My wife was terrified, but I remembered what Uncle Dave always said: 'The only good snake is a live snake,' and I gently relocated them to the woods behind the yard. Thanks Dave, for helping me see the good in all living things!"

(The scouts always called me Uncle Dave. In fact, most people call me Uncle Dave to this day. It became my official moniker long before I was an actual uncle. I'm not sure how it started or why, but it's who I am.)

Nine snake species inhabit this and other desert basins ranging from Idaho on the north, southward to the town of Delta, and westward into Nevada. These include the Great Basin rattlesnake (*Crotalus oreganus lutosus*), Great Basin gopher snake *Pituophis catenifer deserticola*, Desert-striped whip snake (*Masticophis taeniatus taeniatus*), Western yellow-bellied racer (*Coluber constrictor mormon*), Northern night snake (*Hypsiglena chlorophaea deserticola*), Long-nosed snake (*Rhinocheilus lecontei*), Regal ring-necked snake (*Diadophis punctatus regalis*), and the elusive Utah milk snake (*Lampropeltis gentilis taylori*). Of these, the gopher snake is the most abundant, followed closely by the racer and the Great Basin rattler. In places where water is available, you can often find the Wandering garter snake (*Thamnophis elegans vagrans*), a subspecies of the Western terrestrial garter snake (*Thamnophis elegans*).

(In the mid-to-late 1800s, numerous migrations of settlers looking for a better life in California passed through Skull Valley, including the ill-fated Donner Party in 1846. The yellow-bellied racer, also known as the Mormon racer, was given the species name *mormon* because the Mormon pioneers, who arrived in Utah in 1847, were the first non-native people to see it.)

Granted, the diversity isn't great. There are places in the country, namely the southwestern and southern states, where dedicated herpers can find many more species. Texas, for example has 105 species and subspecies of snakes. In addition to Skull Valley, we drive other roads, but no matter where we go, we can count on finding the same five or six snakes over and over again. It's like going to an ice cream store that only has five flavors. But you'd rather have those five overly familiar flavors than not have any ice cream at all.

Once, after a night of camping near Horseshoe Knoll, five of my Scouts accompanied me on a morning hike. While the younger boys remained in camp to work on merit badges with the Scoutmaster, we traversed the rocky, juniper covered west-facing slopes of the Stansbury Mountains, excited to see and catch a rattlesnake, gopher snake, whip snake, racer, and ring-neck, all in the space of a few hours. The boys excitedly inspected each new animal, plant, or fossil discovery as I tried my best to answer their many questions.

The day had already provided us with glimpses of a small deer herd, a doe antelope with twin fawns at her flanks, sharp-eyed hawks and eagles circling on thermal updrafts high overhead, shiny black ravens that scolded us from the branches of juniper trees, tiny burrowing owls with scholarly faces peering inquisitively at us from their comfortable burrows, a pair of coyotes, and a lone red fox on a quest for his breakfast. It was a truly magical morning and one I hope those kids remember for the rest of their lives.

I always forbade the boys from bringing electronic toys or music players on campouts. Despite their feeble protests, they were better off without those distractions. The current generation of kids is lacking a true connection with nature, having been diverted from real-world adventures and immersed instead in an artificial world of virtual reality, phony achievements, imaginary life forms, and fake heroes.

A recent study showed that urban kids could identify more corporate logos than animals and plants found near them. It's a sad reflection on modern priorities that far too many kids today have no idea how to spend time in nature without the throttle-twisting clamor of an ATV or a wave runner beneath them, or at the very least, some blinking, bonking, electronic time-wasting device that further separates them from what really matters. If you're not doing this already, unplug your kids and send them outside to play without these things. Who knows, they may thank you some day. Maybe even today.

Human beings don't typically fight for things we don't love. If children don't learn to love nature by experiencing it firsthand, chances are they won't see the need to protect special places and creatures when they're at risk by those who would exploit them. Depriving children of a connection to the natural world should be considered a form of emotional and intellectual abuse, because there's no better teacher than Mother Nature, and not all classrooms have four walls.

That's not to say that every experience in nature is a pleasant one.

One of my best and oldest snaking friends is John. We met at the old Utah Association of Herpetologists (UtAH) meetings back in the '70s. I was 16 and John was about 15 years older. We started making regular forays to Skull Valley when his kids were little, and for John and me, those trips continue to this day.

As a gun guy, John would take a small arsenal of weapons, and I, with a dad who was a gunsmith, would bring my own sidearm and a small caliber rifle or two. We'd spend the morning looking for snakes and lizards while the remainder of our time was spent in target practice on the many cans, bottles, discarded microwaves, computer monitors, and other refuse dumped there for target practice by the locals. If we were having a slow snake day, we could still occupy our time shooting, so there was never a wasted trip.

The Only Good Snake . . .

Correction: there was *one* wasted trip.

One cool spring evening back in the late '80s, John and I headed to Skull Valley with his four young boys. Arriving just before sundown, we got out of the car at Simpson Springs with high hopes of finding a snake or two on the crawl before cruising the road. But anticipation turned to instant regret. The thick drapery of bug guts on the windshield should have been a clue that we may have been in the right place, but it was definitely the wrong time.

We had no sooner shut the car doors than we were enveloped by dark and ravenous clouds of blood sucking vampire mosquitoes and gnats. Known as 'no-see-um's,' a single gnat is practically invisible, but in a swarm the size of a car, they present a formidable foe. Giant, insatiable mosquitoes with proboscises the size of soda straws immediately infested our hair and clothes, poking and piercing our skin and engorging themselves on every square inch of exposed flesh. Darting and buzzing into our eyes and ears, they even invaded our collars in their quest for blood. There was no doubt in my mind that they intended to exsanguinate us, and that they easily could have.

Swatting and flailing against this noxious horde of flying suck-monsters, we scrambled back in the car and left. Back on the pavement, we opened the windows and turned on the AC in hopes of blowing some of them out of the car, but to little avail. The boys cried as we angrily swatted mosquitoes from ourselves and each other, smashing bug guts on our clothing, the windows and the upholstery for the entire 50-mile trip back home.

On another occasion, I was with John when we found the biggest rattlesnake either of us had ever seen. Great Basin rattlesnakes are not large snakes and their venom is at the lower end of the toxicity spectrum. Just the same, getting bit by one will ruin your whole day and part of the next one too, yet bites are virtually never fatal with proper care. Despite seeing at least one rattler almost every time we went out, it never got old. These enigmatic snakes are a thrill to behold, and finding one unexpectedly was always a treat. To this day I affectionately call all rattlesnakes "buzzer butts."

2 | Skull Valley

Shortly thereafter, on a balmy summer night, we had already driven the length of the valley in both directions without seeing much. I was driving us slowly along one of the dirt roads that run parallel between the foothills and the paved road at the north end of the valley where the solar farm sits today.

All of a sudden, in my headlight beams appeared a massively big buzzer butt. The literature claims that these snakes can reach lengths up to 60 inches, and they may in some locales in the southern part of the state. But this was an extraordinarily large snake for Northern Utah, where the active season is much shorter. Most Great Basins average 30 to 48 inches in length, but this one was easily 60 inches long.

In his excitement, John frantically fumbled for the door handle; eventually escaping from the car like it was on fire. I grabbed my snake stick, switched on my headlamp and got out. We walked to the front of the vehicle where the snake lay coiled on the dusty double-track, rattling nervously.

"Look at the size of that snake, John!" I exclaimed. John's mouth was open and his eyes were glued on the snake. In the middle, she was as big around as my wrist, and toward her posterior she was even bigger. "She's a gravid female," I observed, and John nodded. (Gravid is the reptilian term for pregnant.)

"Look how beautiful she is," John said, as though he was beholding a vision, and I concurred. I don't like to bother wildlife other than to take its picture or move it off a road, but I had to pick this big girl up if only to see if she was really as long as she looked.

She tracked me with an elliptical gaze, but I don't recall her ever striking. Using my snake stick, I pinned her with minimal effort. I placed my right index finger and thumb in the notch between her broad head and narrow neck. Lifting her off the ground, I handed her lower half to John as we stretched her out along the bumper of my car. The average car is roughly five feet, eight inches wide, and she was indeed five feet long, if not more.

Before I could set her down, she made a disconcerting little twist maneuver in my hand, attempting to wrench herself free and possibly sink a fang into my thumb. I didn't blame her. She didn't deserve this treatment and she'd had enough. I placed her gently on the ground and let go of her neck. She side-slithered away from me in that ingratiating way that rattlesnakes do, escaping while still facing their tormentor. After using this tactic for four or five feet, she maneuvered her stout body straight into the sagebrush and vanished from view. I apologized for bothering her and looked forward to one day meeting some of her babies.

This was long before I ever began relocating rattlesnakes, and although I've caught hundreds of them since that time, I have yet to see another Utah rattlesnake as big as that one.

In years to come, I would create some truly epic and mosquito-free memories, such as the time I was sitting in my car at three in the morning when a high-ranking uniformed female Army officer on her way to the base stopped to see if I was okay. Due to the lack of a true shoulder, my car was jutting halfway into the southbound lane of the two-lane road and my flashers were on.

She pulled her military Jeep next to my car, turned on her dome light and rolled down the passenger-side window. I rolled down my window. "Are you okay?" she asked, a note of concern in her voice. She was blonde, attractive, and due to her rank, undoubtedly armed. Why else would she stop to help a strange civilian on a desolate road in the middle of the night?

"Hi!" I said, with perhaps a tone of surprise in my voice. "Yeah, I'm fine. I just moved a rattlesnake off the road and I'm looking at the pictures."

There was a moment of silence as she tried to ascertain exactly what kind of weirdo she was dealing with.

"Interesting," she exclaimed. She said the word slowly, breaking it down into syllables as though trying to make sense of what I had told her. Then she drove away, her taillights shrinking in the blackness. And that was it. I couldn't help but chuckle as I imagined her recounting the incident to her fellow soldiers when she got to the base.

One of my most deeply ingrained memories also took place on that road many years before. I don't recall why I was in Skull Valley in the middle of the day as it was too hot for snakes to be active. To cool off, I suppose. I had just spent time in an inviting body of water known as Horseshoe Springs — a natural, semi-brackish oasis not far off the main road.

As I dried off in the car on the mostly barren stretch, heat waves created a shimmering mirage above the sunbaked asphalt like a fever dream. That's when I spotted a large rattlesnake shaded by the desiccated weeds on the right-side shoulder just ahead of me. I stopped, turned on the flashers, and got out of the car wearing nothing but a Speedo-type swimsuit and flip-flops. (I had a decent physique at the time, but I must have left it in an old shirt because I haven't seen it since.)

Lacking a proper snake stick (don't ask me why), I caught the snake by the tail and was about to walk it into the sagebrush when a car pulled up to see if I needed help. It was a station wagon with a family in it. I turned to face them, mostly naked and still holding the rattlesnake. I assured them I was fine and thanked them for stopping. They didn't hear a word I said, because in their haste to get away, dad squealed the tires, leaving skid marks on the pavement and the smell of burning rubber hanging dense and noxious in the thick August air.

Some people have no manners at all. But I saved that snake from the very car that may have run it over if I hadn't been there. It wasn't my finest teaching moment, but the way I see it, if we can't educate our fellow travelers in this life, we can at least entertain them or make them wonder.

I have caught hundreds of snakes in Skull Valley over the years, making it the most abundant repository for snakes I've found within a reasonable distance from home, due mostly to a paved road that bisects prime habitat.

Thirty years ago it wasn't uncommon to find four or five snake species in a single outing, but since then, the collective human consumption of resources, including over-grazing by cattle, has decimated the range and destroyed the habitats of the wild things that live there. Making matters worse, range fires, vehicle carnage, the testing of biological agents, air pollution from a nearby magnesium plant, climate change, and even poaching, have all wreaked havoc on wildlife populations in the valley, making it harder with each passing year to find animals in the same numbers as when I was a kid.

It's not uncommon to visit the west desert and see every gun totin', ATV drivin' redneck and his progeny on their little toy cars.

These machines and their riders should be relegated to designated areas where they can't damage our public lands.

Fires regularly consume the tinder-dry grasses and juniper-covered hillsides, scorching essential habitat and turning it into an uninhabitable hellscape, often taking years to recover. There seems to be an abnormally high percentage of folks who aren't exactly the sharpest knives in the drawer. Some fires are natural, but stupid, careless human beings on ATVs, shooting at exploding targets, or failing to extinguish campfires properly, start many of them. This sector of the population sees public land as their personal playground, resenting any imposition of bureaucratic restriction or personal responsibility, and they often react like impudent children as a lowbrow form of protest.

I've seen entire hillsides ravaged by the unconscionable scourge of poaching. Those selfish bastards have no compunction about taking as many animals as they can from an area, surreptitiously selling them for personal gain and leaving an ecological dead zone in their wake. This can make propagation a decades-long and sometimes non-recoverable process.

This is in stark contrast to the Goshute Indians who were the first human inhabitants of this uncompromising land, migrating here from the Death Valley region of California about 1,000 years ago. The word Goshute means "dust people" or "desert people." As hunter-gatherers, they made respectful use of all available resources for their survival, scratching a livelihood out of the Great Basin's unfriendly terrain by eating seeds, grasses, roots, pine nuts and small animals. Fish were caught in the local springs and in Utah Lake to the south and the Jordan River to the east. Living in loosely connected groups, their numbers were few and their impact on the land was negligible. Caves throughout the region bear record of this resourceful civilization in the form of 700- to 1000-year-old pictographs, arrowheads and animal bones, along with numerous beaded and woven artifacts.

Conflicts between the Goshute tribe and white men began shortly after the arrival of Mormon Pioneers in 1847. Early efforts by the federal government to remove the Goshutes from their native lands were unsuccessful, and it wasn't until 1912 that a reservation was finally established, granting the tribe ownership of the land and forcing them into an unfamiliar agricultural lifestyle. This situation wasn't compatible with their ancestral ways or with their ability to be self-sufficient, especially in a place like Skull Valley. For this reason, tribal members today suffer high unemployment and poverty rates.

Goshutes are comprised of two groups — the Confederated Tribes of the Goshute, and the Skull Valley Band of Goshute. The latter group once laid claim to 17,920 acres of reservation land in Skull Valley in Tooele (pronounced *too–willa*) County. Today, fewer than 150 Goshutes live on only 160 acres of desolate reservation land.

Unable to support themselves by farming, modern Goshutes turned to other sources of income. In 1976, they leased a section of land to Hercules Aerospace for use as a rocket motor testing facility known as the Tekoi Rocket Test Range.

If you spend enough time in Skull Valley, you're bound to see things you can't explain. While not visible from the public road, there is an abandoned facility with a yellow shed that was once used to test rocket motors capable of delivering a retaliatory nuclear strike in the event of a Soviet missile attack. It is off-limits to all but an intrepid few who dare to breach the NO TRESSPASSING signs, although I don't believe it's still under surveillance.

About the size of a large garage, and encircled by lightning rods, the shed and other structures look oddly out of place amid the sagebrush and cheat grass that surrounds them. Abandoned and virtually forgotten for decades, this derelict monument is a remnant of nuclear proliferation and Cold War collaboration.

Tekoi was a solid fuel rocket motor test and calibration site operated by Hercules under contract by the U.S. Military, and was operational throughout the 1980s and '90s. In the early '90s, Alliant Techsystems (ATK) purchased Hercules.

Both Hercules and ATK were vital military suppliers of solid fuel rocket motors capable of delivering Inter-Continental Ballistic Missiles (ICBMs) from underground silos and nuclear submarines during the U.S./Soviet nuclear arms race, guaranteeing not only mutually-assured destruction of both countries in the event of a nuclear attack by the Russians, but total global annihilation. Like the movie *War Games* but without the happy ending.

Located on Goshute tribal land about 10 miles north of Dugway, Tekoi is a relic of the U.S./Soviet disarmament agreement known as StART (Strategic Arms Reduction Treaty) which was signed in 1991 by George W. Bush and Mikhail Gorbachev.

Because of Soviet involvement, the most peculiar aspect of the Tekoi site is the signage at the gate, which is in Russian.

Prefabricated houses at the site, according to one source, "were shipped from Russia for the Russian inspectors, and were complete with Russian furnishings and electricity scrubbers," to ensure that the Americans hadn't planted listening devices in the walls with the intent of eavesdropping on their Soviet counterparts.

ATK's lease expired in 1999, and control of the land reverted back to the Goshute Tribe. It remains mostly unchanged today except for the slow intrusion of desert vegetation and the ravages of time.

A concrete barricade now blocks the padlocked gate. This is unfortunate, because, in addition to the aboveground structures, there remains the probability of an underground control center awaiting exploration.

In a later attempt at economic independence, the Goshutes attempted to secure a lease to store spent nuclear fuel rods from the nation's nuclear plants, but as a long-term solution, that venture also became untenable due mostly to opposition by the state legislature.

Another Skull Valley anachronism is Iosepa, a Hawaiian word meaning *Joseph,* after Mormon Church President Joseph F. Smith. Iosepa is a cemetery containing the graves of 19th century Hawaiian and Polynesian Mormon settlers who were sent here by the church from a temperate paradise in a cruel and ultimately failed attempt to colonize the area and make the alkaline soil of Utah's west desert prosper and "blossom as the rose." Surely, their spirits still wander this place, longing for their tropical island homes.

The cemetery is especially inviting between midnight and 3 am. Watch out for the black widow spiders that weave their webs at ankle height in the stubby grass, and the scorpions that lie invisible near the entrances of burrows, under rocks, and near headstones, becoming instantly luminescent if you shine a black light on them. Snakes often infiltrate the cemetery's chain link perimeter, gliding casually among the stone markers, following the scent trails of frenetic kangaroo rats that are also looking for food.

With its tragic history of displaced indigenous culture, not to mention a semi-clandestine military presence, Skull Valley really is a weird place. Watch for the lights that hover over Dugway at night, shooting like spastic stars across the Stansbury Mountains and into Rush Valley to the east, then dashing back, only to disappear over the Cedar Mountains to the west. Human technology or alien? You decide.

Then there's the luminescent beam that shoots straight up from the ground, projecting a perfect column of shimmering light into the night sky. Cue the red lights that hover a few feet above the desert floor like taillights on an invisible car, meandering aimlessly across the nocturnal landscape like big techno-fireflies.

But those aren't the weirdest things I've experienced in Skull Valley.

While I've always been intrigued by the concept of alien life and seen my share of supernatural phenomena, it's not those things that cause me the greatest concern when I'm alone. I recall, as a boy, telling my grandpa that I was afraid of cemeteries. "My boy," he said, "dead people can't hurt us. It's the live ones you have to watch out for." It's true. The world is full of living wackos and you need to learn to spot them before they spot you.

As a young man in my late teens or early 20s, I found myself in Skull Valley on an August day hotter than the hinges on the gates of Hell. I don't recall what pulled me there other than the need for some solitude and soul-searching — a spirit quest if you will — an ephemeral escape from the daily grind of work and school and the claustrophobia of civilized life.

Hiking up a narrow canyon (more of a ravine, really) just east of Horseshoe Knoll, I stripped off my shirt and stuffed it in my pack. Wearing only shorts, socks, shoes, hat, and a deeply burnished tan on my legs and torso, I trudged up the ravine, past the rotting corpse of an old car (a Packard, perhaps?), its weathered skeleton rusted and decayed after decades in this inhospitable

31

place. Looking like a gangster car from a 1940s movie, its bulbous hood and bloated fenders were hot as skillets under a scalding August sun. Where paint still remained, a patina of faded layers made it impossible to tell what color it had been in its heyday.

How did it get here, I wondered? Did someone drive it into this ravine with the intention of leaving it here, or did the desert claim it after it sunk helplessly in the sand? Perhaps someone drove it up the hill from the north, pushed it over the edge and watched as it tumbled ass over axels down the slope to its final resting place. Did someone hate this car that much?

Further on, a scrawny stick of a sapling had foolishly chosen this dry and hellish gulch in which to sink its thirsty roots. I watered it with every drop I had in me. Then, sitting cross-legged on the chalky ground, I pulled an orange from my pack and began to peel it.

Without warning, a small mushroom cloud of dirt exploded a couple of feet to my right, followed by the crack and echo of a high-powered ammo round.

Leaping to my feet, my adrenaline surged upward like mercury in a hot thermometer. A moment later, another puff of dirt exploded to my left, followed by the reverberation of another rifle shot. My heart slammed against my ribcage like it was trying to escape. "What the *&#@!" I yelled, realizing that some idiot was shooting at me! Shading my eyes with my hands, I surveyed the ridge above me. As I did so, another round hit the dirt in front of my feet. There, on the ridge, I could make out the dusky silhouette of a camo-clad man with a rifle and scope.

Thinking maybe he hadn't seen me, I jumped up and down, waving my arms. "Hey!" I yelled up at him, "Hey, I'm down here! What the hell are you doing?" He raised the rifle to his shoulder and fired again. This time the bullet went over my head and exploded in the hard-packed berm behind me. This was followed by yet another report that split the quiet air and ricocheted up the ravine, quickly reverberating into silence. I was completely exposed with nowhere to hide.

I had a .22 pistol in my pack, but my assailant was at least a hundred yards away. My gun was useless at that distance. Besides, shooting at someone who is armed, even in self-defense, is a sure way to die. Especially when that someone holds the high ground and has a bigger gun. This nut job had a large caliber rifle with a scope. Rambo wasn't shooting blindly into the canyon or at some random target. He saw me long before I saw him. With that scope he could probably see the stitching on my cap. He could kill me anytime he wanted just by flexing his index finger and there wasn't a damn thing I could do about it.

Dropping my half-peeled orange and shoving my arms through my pack straps, I scrambled up the shale-covered slope on all fours. Never before had I been so scared, angry, or intent on confrontation. I wasn't about to flee and get shot in the back. If he was going to kill me, he had better have the balls to do it point-blank.

Making upward progress on the flat and crumbly shards of shale that led to the ridge was like climbing a mountain of hot poker chips. I was in the best shape of my life, yet it was exhausting. For every two steps forward, I slid a step back. Still, if it had been an Olympic event, I would have taken the gold.

After a lung-busting crab crawl up the sharp-edged debris of the talus slope, I reached the ridge, sweating and swearing and panting and pissed off. I looked around, not expecting this cowardly predator to still be there. I don't know what I expected. A truck maybe? A license plate number disappearing in the distance? At the very least I expected to see a dirt plume behind a truck, its driver racing away, laughing maniacally after scaring the hell out of some poor kid. But there was nothing. No vehicle, no dust cloud, no bullet casings. He had erased every trace that he was ever there, including his boot prints.

If he had left in a vehicle, there was no way he could be invisible. This meant that he was parked some distance away like I was and could conceivably be lying in the sagebrush just yards from me, watching me, his camo fatigues concealing him in the dusty green and brown desert vegetation. That thought was even scarier than being shot at. It would be an ambush. He could drop me where I stood before I'd even hear the shot and there'd be no way to trace the bullet. He'd get away scot-free. Then again, if he'd been some psycho-sadist who wanted to kill me, he would have shot me in the ravine. He was probably just some weekend warrior getting his kicks at my expense.

Grandpa was right. It's the live ones you have to watch out for.

I've made hundreds of trips to Skull Valley over many years, first with my dad and brother, occasionally with scouts, sometimes alone, but mostly with friends, cruising for snakes on sagebrush-scented summer nights punctuated with stars and stellar conversation, lit only by headlights and a lonely fingernail moon.

If you ever find yourself in Skull Valley after dark, and you see a car with its flashers on, and two or three guys, phones in hand, lying on their stomachs in the middle of the narrow road, try not to run us over. We're just grown men playing in the street at night, probably photographing a snake or some unusual insect.

A huge THANKS to my snakin' friends, past and present, who definitely know the best way to spend a summer night in a weird yet strangely compelling place. I can honestly say that I've never felt alone or bored in Skull Valley.

CHAPTER 3

What the Heck is Herping?

"When one tugs at a single thing in nature, he finds it attached to the rest of the world" – John Muir

Only a handful of people can relate to the life of a true snake addict. Symptoms include: swerving your car to avoid hitting a snake on the road, then pulling over and moving it to safety; photographing snakes on long stretches of barren asphalt in the middle of the night; flipping boards, rocks and logs in the hope of finding your "lifer" species; carrying a stick with a hook on it everywhere you go; hoarding rodents in your freezer; taking vacations to "snake-infested" places; and best of all, having people tell you they're never coming to your house as long as you have "those horrible snakes" there. (This is hardly a threat considering that they are the last people I would ever want to darken my doorstep anyway.) It's just one of the innumerable benefits of keeping snakes as pets. (Thanks, snakes!)

In my younger years, my friends and I considered ourselves herpetologists, if only by the most basic definition. The word herpetology derives from the Greek word *herpeton*, meaning *'creeping thing.'* 'Herps' (short for herpetofauna) is slang for all reptiles and amphibians, while herpetologists are the scientists who study them. It's also the root word for the insidious viral condition known as herpes, and for the same reason. As a kid, this made it extremely embarrassing to tell people what I wanted to be when I grew up.

"What do you want to be when you're older, Dave?"

"I want to be a herpetologist."

"Herpes! What?"

At least that's how it used to be. When I was young, the term 'herping' hadn't yet entered anyone's vocabulary, nor had 'herp' become a verb in the English vernacular. We simply called it road cruising, looking for snakes, or snake hunting. Snake hunting, of course, was often misconstrued by people who thought we were killing them, so I tried to use that term only with my herp-loving friends. Today, 'herping,' or 'to herp' means to go looking for herps, and field herping has become a popular pastime for people of all ages. For those who love snakes, finding and identifying as many species as possible can become an obsession.

Those of you born after 1990 may find it hard to believe, but in those pre-internet days, there was no way to network with others who may have shared your herping interests. Once you left the house, there was no way to communicate with anyone who wasn't actually there with you. There were no social media platforms, no cell phones, and consequently, no texting, no instant photography, no apps and no live streaming. You were lucky if you knew one or two other folks who enjoyed spending an evening cruising slowly through the desert looking for snakes with you, and you had to call them from your home phone to invite them along *before* you left the house. Or, you could put a quarter in a payphone somewhere.

There was no way to rendezvous unless you planned it beforehand. Not only that, but it wasn't possible to share your finds with anyone who wasn't physically there with you. Before the advent of digital photography, it was necessary to have your film developed by a lab, then show your paper photos to your friends the next time you saw them in person. Yes, it may seem primitive by today's standards, and I'm not exactly ancient, but it was a different world and a different way of doing things. But it was all we knew.

Nowadays we are expected to be constantly available. Sure they're convenient, but cell phones have become technological tethers to which we attach ourselves like willing slaves to an electronic master. I'm no Luddite, but I liked it better when I could spend time in nature without the ever-present disruption of a cell phone in my pocket. But I digress.

A little background for newbies is needed here. There are three basic ways to find snakes.

Method One is to walk around looking for snakes on the crawl. This can be a time-consuming endeavor, depending on habitat and terrain, and is typically the least efficient way of finding a snake unless you happen to be in an area with an especially high concentration of snakes or there is a den site nearby. Depending on the time of year, snakes in the northern latitudes congregate at hibernacula in the fall and disperse in the spring to feed and mate. This is when you're most likely to see multiple snakes.

Finding snakes on the crawl is mostly a daytime pursuit. You're unlikely to find nocturnal snakes during daylight hours, meaning that the species you're looking for needs to be diurnal and terrestrial. Knowing the habits, terrain, and general range of your target species is imperative, as is devoting a reasonable amount of time to the quest. But even the most knowledgeable herper on the most ideal day can still come away empty handed.

Method Two is called flipping. As its name implies, this method involves turning over rocks, logs, or human debris such as tin or cardboard in the hope of finding a snake underneath. At least that's what the books say. In a perfect world, there would be a snake under every rock, which is certainly not the case. This is not a perfect world, and snakes don't read the same books we do.

While there is something of interest under almost every rock, finding the snake you're looking for can test even the mellowest herper's patience and resolve. As a masochistic enterprise, it might actually be character building. Then again, standing on a hot hillside for hours, tipping back 20- to 50-pound rocks and peering underneath in the hope of finding a fossorial snake and not succeeding can be an exercise in futility that Sisyphus himself would balk at. Fossorial snakes are those that spend most of their lives underground or concealed under rocks, leaf litter, etc.

As rock flipping goes, the snake gods seem to favor certain herpers over others, which is nothing more than blatant cosmic favoritism. Whatever the reason, there are some who make it look easy. My friend Ethan is one of them, and I'll get him for it if it's the last thing I ever do.

Some elements of flipping are an acquired skill. Knowing when and where to look for your target species is paramount, along with an understanding of its traits and habits. Season, time of day, ambient air temperature, ground temperature, barometric pressure, humidity, type of substrate, moon phase, wind, and the price of duck eggs in China are all factors to some degree. But when all is said and done, 99 percent of successful flipping comes down to plain old dumb luck and the amount of effort you're willing to put forth.

While luck still plays a huge part, Ethan isn't luckier than other flippers. His success comes from studying the snakes he seeks, knowing their ranges, habits, and preferred habitats. Pairing that knowledge with the right environmental conditions maximizes his chances for success. These factors, combined with a balanced investment of time and physical effort, along with a willingness to come up empty handed now and then, have allowed him to find snakes that no amount of luck alone could deliver.

Because the underside of every rock is its own mini-biome, it's important when flipping that rocks be returned as close as possible to their original position and that the moisture barrier is re-sealed if at all possible, especially in a desert climate.

Method Three is the easiest and most popular way to find snakes which is to cruise them in your car. This is the preferred method for less able-bodied herpers, lazy herpers, older herpers, or those who no longer find joy in flipping rocks. Because it's done mostly at night, cruising limits the herper to finding snakes that are nocturnal, or those that resort to nocturnal behavior to avoid excessive daytime temps.

Many people believe that because snakes are cold-blooded, meaning they can't self-regulate their body temperature, that they like it hot. But for the same reason that snakes can't warm themselves internally, relying instead on ambient sources of heat, they also can't cool themselves by sweating or panting if they overheat. All any reptile can do to maintain an optimal body temperature suitable for normal metabolic activity is to alternate between warm and cool places.

Most snakes find temps around 85° Fahrenheit (30° Celsius) to be ideal. A snake that warms itself by basking on a rock in the morning sun risks becoming too warm after a while and must eventually move to a shady spot or rodent burrow to cool down again. A snake may have to repeat this process many times per day in order to maintain a body temperature range suitable for digestion and other essential functions. This process is called thermoregulation. It's not easy being a reptile.

3 | *What the Heck is Herping?*

If you're an active road-cruising herper, you have probably met other herpers on the same road you're herping on, including families with young children. If you've ever been looking for snakes on a particular stretch of road on a balmy summer night, chances are good that you've seen other cars stopped; their head-lamp-wearing occupants huddled over something on the road, phones glowing eerily in the darkness, excitedly taking pictures of a snake or some other critter of interest.

In the event of a seldom seen species of snake or a uniquely aberrant individual, even a DOR (dead on road) specimen may sometimes be photographed for documentation or kept and frozen for further study. Both live and dead snakes are removed from the roadway — the live ones for their safety and the dead ones for the safety of birds and animals looking for an easy meal — preventing them from becoming roadkill as well.

Cruising for snakes can trigger all sorts of false alarms. For instance, I have literally stopped my car to catch fan belt snakes and banana peel lizards. Also, chrome trim, radiator hoses, ropes, bungee cords, weather stripping, exhaust pipe brackets, sticks, cow pies, pieces of tires, cracks in the pavement, and lots of other unusual species that are not supposed to be indigenous to this area.

Field herping — looking for and photographing animals in their natural habitats (known as *in situ* photography) — has blossomed into a worldwide phenomenon since the archaic days before cell phones and social media. Sharing finds with friends and family is now instantaneous, and online forums where herpers can share their adventures have proliferated exponentially over the past decade or two. For newbies, there are apps that will identify a snake or any other animal or plant species, as well as tracking sites that allow herpers to pinpoint their finds for the benefit of others.

This technology, however, while it may be well intentioned, is nothing more than an insidious way to map the locations of species' hotspots, providing poachers and other unscrupulous individuals with a literal roadmap to animals that are highly prized and subsequently sought after by scumbag individuals and organizations for selfish and illegal reasons. There is an entire black market underworld devoted exclusively to the criminal exploitation of the world's animals for profit, and honest herpers shouldn't sacrifice their integrity by using apps that enable this pernicious enterprise to flourish.

Call me old-fashioned, but much of the fun of finding the snake you're looking for, as in the case of a lifer species (one that you've never seen and may only see once in your life), comes from gathering information, learning about the animal's range, preferences and behaviors, then putting in the requisite time to find it yourself. After all, this isn't Pokémon we're talking about; this is the real world.

One aspect that may have changed field herping for the better is the modern awareness of humanity's responsibility to be better stewards of the planet. The death of Steve Irwin in 2006 was a wakeup call, reminding us that we're on our own as far as environmental advocacy goes, and that we had better step up to the plate and take our roles as caretakers of this great garden seriously or risk losing the natural world forever. Governments and corporations will not save us. They are the biggest culprits.

There is, of course, a natural tendency to want to keep an especially rare or beautiful animal. I'm not disputing that. In fact, it's an urge I've had to fight most of my life. But scrupulous field herpers — those with integrity who understand the need to respect nature and the precarious balance she tries so hard to maintain — should strive to achieve a reverence for these animals they love, having enough respect to leave them where they belong. How else can they expect to find another one next year, or their children after them?

Too many ignorant people don't recognize the warning signs of mankind's insatiable greed. For every acre of nature humanity destroys, and for every species we lose to extinction, we cheat ourselves and our posterity out of a treasure more valuable than diamonds and gold.

I told one individual that the rare snake he removed from the wild as a trophy for his collection was the same as killing it.

"I didn't kill it!" he yelled. "It's right here! I take good care of it! I would never kill a snake!" His raging indignation was on full display.

3 | *What the Heck is Herping?*

"I didn't accuse you of killing it," I explained calmly, "but the result is the same. You have a rare animal in your possession to satisfy your ego. It's not where it belongs, which means it can't do the job nature intended and it can't reproduce. You removed an animal with valuable genetic material from a population that's already struggling. It's no different than if you had killed it. If every collector did that, the population would have been wiped out long ago, never to return, and that's not fair to anyone."

He paused long enough to let the message marinate for a moment, but I doubt he has the integrity to put the snake back where he found it.

With very few exceptions, taking snakes out of the wild is an outdated and irresponsible concept in the 21st century. Virtually any species you desire can be purchased at a reasonable price from a reputable breeder, ensuring animals that are free from diseases, parasites, and scars.

As mentioned in previous chapters, I have taken snakes from the wild to keep as pets. It's hard to justify now, but I was young and the snakes were free; they weren't rare, endangered or protected, and most of them were subsequently released where they were found. The rest of them lived long and comfortable lives as education animals. While I have never kept more than a reasonable number of snakes at any one time (I think the most may have been a couple of dozen), the vast majority of them were purchased from breeders.

I pride myself on keeping healthy, happy snakes that live to ridiculous ages. Until recently, I had five snakes, and the two youngest were nine years old. The others were roughly 16, 18, and 23 respectively.

Under the right conditions, they almost never get sick, so I was a little surprised when the 16-year-old corn snake, Cinnamon, showed symptoms of a respiratory infection. I had to take her to the vet every three days for six weeks for antibiotic injections, and I built her a respiratory chamber for inhaled antibiotics using a nebulizer. Initial vet bill: $279. Nebulizer: $75. Twice-weekly injections: $60 each, plus time and travel. A wise person once said, "Teach your children to keep snakes and they'll never have money for drugs." Snakes are a much safer addiction.

The Only Good Snake . . .

People often contact me to ask what's wrong with their snake/lizard/tortoise/frog, or whatever. These animals have very specific needs and not everyone is qualified to keep them, and even less qualified to treat them when they're ill. You need to know a good exotic pet vet or be prepared to give the animal to a qualified rescuer or rehabber if you can't treat it yourself.

My answer to these inquiries is almost always to take it to the vet, and I'm often told they can't afford it. I told one woman that if she can't afford the vet, she can't afford the pet, because now the animal is going to eventually die, but only after a prolonged period of suffering.

She told me I was a jerk. That's right. You have no idea what kind of a jerk I can be when an animal's welfare is at stake.

I'm not a confrontational man. I avoid contention and I detest violence. But on an August morning in 2017, I got in someone's face after he plowed through a flock of pigeons with his car, killing at least one of them. He did not attempt to swerve or even slow down.

I followed him until he pulled into a parking lot. I drove up next to him with our driver windows opposite one another. My adrenaline surged as I told him what I thought of him.

Thank God he didn't get out of his car, but he didn't know if I was armed or just how crazy I might be. On the other hand, he could just as easily have shot me.

Don't ever tell me that a pigeon is just a pigeon. You might as well tell me that a dog is just a dog, a cat is just a cat, or a snake is just a snake. Guess what buddy? You're just a psychopath.

I don't know if I scared him or not, but I scared the hell out of me.

On March 16, 1989, I purchased a pair of juvenile Pueblan milk snakes (*Lampropeltis triangulum campbelli*) from a professional herpetologist at a business called ZooHerp in Sandy, Utah. I was just shy of my 30th birthday and the snakes were about a month old.

I named them Pebbles and Bam Bam. They were among the first individuals of this species sold in Utah, coming from the first breeding colony established in this country from wild-caught specimens brought here from Zapotitlán, a municipality of Puebla, Mexico.

Once they reached maturity, I bred them and sold their offspring. Pebbles produced a clutch of six eggs each year for eight years, and died of unspecified causes about 12 years later, but Bam Bam just kept truckin' for the next 18 years.

Like most milk snakes, Pueblans are a tri-colored species, adorned with red, black, and yellow bands. Over three decades, Bam Bam served as a handsome ambassador, impressing people with his bright colors and gentle demeanor. For many people, he was the first snake they ever met, and he changed many minds about snakes.

Bam Bam succumbed to old age in February 2019, making him 30 years old — an amazing lifespan for any snake, and a palpable loss for me after having this snake for half my life at that point. So long, old friend.

Average captive longevity for this species is 15 to 20 years. I haven't been able to locate recorded longevity statistics, but 30 has to be pushing the limits. Shortly after announcing Bam Bam's passing on Facebook, his obituary found its way to a Russian Facebook page called Snakes Without Borders, and they were kind enough to send a reply. These were their comments, in Russian, along with the English translation:

Змеи без границ - Snakes Without borders — feeling sad.

February 3, 2019 at 10:14 AM

Помните 29-летнего королевского змЕя по имени Bam Bam?

Сегодня его не стало. 30 лет без одного месяца. RIP.

Запомним этого красавца, а так же то, сколько лет может прожить королевская змея в хороших руках.

Translation: "Remember a 29-year-old royal snake named Bam Bam? He's gone today. Thirty years without one month. RIP.

"Remember this handsome man, as well as how many years the royal snake can live in good hands."

I actually got misty-eyed. The reptile community is filled with great people, regardless of where they are in the world, and I thank the people at Snakes Without Borders for their kindness.

The Only Good Snake . . .

A female Grey-banded king snake named Bonita lived for 18 years under my care. With her dynamic grey, white, black, and orange coloration, she also was a great ambassador, and I miss her as well.

I presently have a female Western hognose snake named Harley who entered her 30th year in 2026. This is most certainly a record. I have spoken with hognose breeders who assure me that Harley is not only the oldest living hognose they've ever heard of, but quite possibly the oldest hoggie that has ever lived. Hang in there, Harley!

At six-and-a-half-feet-long, my bull snake, Durango, is just a big scaly bundle of cuddly joy! He is one of very few wild snakes I have kept in many years. My brother and I found him on a dirt road just outside Penrose, Colorado in the fall of 2012. He was a recent hatching, about a foot long with the girth of a pencil. Initially, I regretted taking him out of the wild, but bull snakes are abundant and make impressive and handsome pets. Durango has proven to be a docile and gregarious ambassador at educational presentations and expos. As a complete gentleman, he tolerated the constant parade of humans who wanted to pet, poke and pick him up, never once losing his cool.

Cruising back and forth on two eight-foot tables all day gave him plenty of exercise. As one of the few free-roaming snakes at the expo, he got a lot of attention. The most frequently asked questions were, "What kind of snake is that?" "Does it bite?" "Is it poisonous?" More often than not, the same person would ask the same three questions as though they were reading from some invisible script.

Why in the hell would I put an uncaged venomous snake on public display and let people touch it? Furthermore, why would I let my 10-year-old nephew wrangle it? I answered each of their questions patiently and diplomatically, sometimes biting my tongue to keep the snark from flying out.

A few years ago at the Wasatch Reptile Expo, my display booth was at the end of a long aisle lined with other exhibitors, providing a straight shot to my booth from the far side of the arena. I happened to glance down this lane, largely filled with expo-goers, just in time to see a little boy about seven years old at the opposite end of the large room. His youthful, eager eyes had just spotted Durango cruising on my table from 50 yards away.

With a twist of his hand, the boy broke free from his father's grip and bolted toward my booth at full speed, deftly dodging some bodies and bouncing off others in his zeal to reach his destination. His surprised father, having no idea what his son was running from or toward, began desperately chasing after him, but not nearly as efficiently.

When the kid reached my table, he was grinning so big that the corners of his mouth met behind his head. He placed his hands on Durango's long, muscular form as though he had just discovered the Holy Grail. I waited until his father arrived a few moments later, panting and out of breath. He looked at me and said, almost apologetically, "He really, really likes snakes."

There is no need to apologize, sir. You've done a great job with him. In fact, this is how our children *should* react to snakes if we raise them right!

As a large predatory carnivore, Durango has a prodigious appetite and a fast metabolism. When you keep snakes of any kind, you need a reliable supply of rodents, preferably the frozen variety. Feeding day at my house means that several rodents are about to fulfill their mortal destiny.

I used to have a monthly Sunday morning rat rendezvous with my rodent dealer. We'd meet at a gas station near his house, where he'd hand me a nondescript brown paper bag with the top rolled down and I'd hand him a wad of cash. We met behind the gas station for obvious reasons. I always hoped that the NSA was watching from a surveillance drone. Can you imagine the DEA swooping in to make a drug bust, only to find that the 'contraband' was a bag of frozen rats?

These days, I buy my rodents at one of three annual reptile expos that take place here, or I order them online.

Arriving home one evening, at least four snakes had pooped. Ah, the smells of summer! When I asked who did it by a show of hands, not one of them confessed. I thought I raised them better.

Keeping snakes as pets is a topic all its own, and there are already many great books out there on the subject. Besides, this chapter is about finding and identifying wild snakes.

The Only Good Snake . . .

Of the more than 3,400 snake species throughout the world, Utah claims just 32 of them — not an extraordinary number compared to other places, but a respectable amount. Of those, only eight are venomous and they're all rattlesnakes.

Utah's 24 harmless species include *Charina bottae,* the rubber boa (a true boa similar to the boa constrictor of South America, only smaller), three species of garter snakes, two king snakes, one milk snake, the ubiquitous Great Basin gopher snake, and more than a dozen other innocuous, reclusive, nocturnal or otherwise seldom-seen serpents that inhabit the state from border to border and mountain top to desert valley.

Any snake in Utah that isn't a rattlesnake is harmless to humans. Almost nowhere else in the world does identification get any simpler than that. And because rattlesnakes are extraordinarily easy to differentiate from most other snakes, there is virtually zero excuse for mistaking a garter snake for a rattler or vice-versa. This fact eliminates the need to memorize colors or patterns, head shapes, pupil shape, or any other allegedly or potentially erroneous method of snake identification.

I've been preaching this doctrine most of my adult life, yet word spreads slowly if it spreads at all. The average person wants every snake they see to be a rattler (it makes for a more impressive story to tell their friends and family), and every actual rattler is automatically a diamondback, even though diamondbacks do not occur in Utah. For some reason, this is a hard sell.

Case in point: Once, after giving a presentation at a local state park, I was confronted by a man who argued with me about the eight-foot diamondback rattlesnakes he'd seen. I explained to him that there are no diamondback rattlesnakes in Utah, and no eight-foot snakes, period.

"There ARE diamondbacks in Utah," he insisted. "I saw some when I was 12. They were eight feet long."

"How do you know they were diamondbacks?" I asked him. (I bit my tongue and didn't force the size issue.)

"My uncle told me," he replied indignantly.

"Was your uncle a herpetologist?" I inquired.

"He was an entomologist," he retorted, as though that made his uncle an expert on snakes.

3 | *What the Heck is Herping?*

Well, there you go. I always consult an entomologist when I want to know about snakes. Don't you?

Have you ever wondered why it is that when you tell someone there are one billion stars in the universe, they believe you, but if you tell them there's wet paint, they have to touch it to make sure you're not lying to them? Well, after a lifetime of keeping snakes and nearly 15 years of relocating them, the thing that bothers me most is when I tell someone that the snake in their yard isn't a rattlesnake, and they ask, "Are you sure?"

I want to respond with, "No ma'am, I'm full of crap and have no idea what I'm talking about, but thanks for asking."

Then I want to ask them, "How could you possibly think it's a rattlesnake when it has absolutely none of the characteristics of a rattlesnake, specifically, NO RATTLE?"

My biggest pet peeve is when someone texts me and asks if the snake in the picture is a rattlesnake. More often than not, it's a garter snake (usually bludgeoned and beheaded) or some other harmless species that met its demise at the hands of someone so obtuse I have to wonder how they remember to breathe. Sorry if that sounds insensitive, but you don't call the snake relocator AF-TER you kill a snake! I suppose they want reassurance that it's harmless in case they find more.

Most people never think about snakes until they're confronted with one. For that reason, I don't expect most people to correctly ID every snake they may encounter in those rare instances when one crosses their path. But am I being unreasonable to expect the average adult to recognize a garter snake when they see one? After all, garter snakes are found in virtually every field, vacant lot, city park, creek, stream, pond, and canal in North America, and every adult who ever played outside as a kid most certainly saw one whether they wanted to or not. But for some weird reason, far too many people don't know a garter snake from a garden hose.

The scientific name *Thamnophis sirtalis sirtalis* is a combination of Ancient Greek and New Latin that means, "bush snake that looks like a garter strap." The generic name *Thamnophis* is derived from the Greek *thamnos* (bush) and *ophis* (snake) and the specific name *sirtalis* is derived from the New Latin *siratalis* (like a garter), a reference to the snake's color pattern resembling a woman's striped garter strap.

In most species, three predominantly yellow stripes run longitudinally down the length of the snake's body, differentiating them from virtually every other snake in North America. Any confusion equating these snakes with rattlesnakes is absurd, even for those with no understanding of snake physiology or behavior, because unless you find some extremely bizarre mutation, there are no striped rattlesnakes.

This phenomenon prompted me to write this tongue-in-cheek reference guide. It's sad, but it's true.

A Utahn's guide to snake identification:

Water snake, grass snake, garden snake and gardener snake = garter snake. ("What do you mean it's pronounced GARTER snake? It's still 'poisonous,' right?")

Blow snake = a Great Basin gopher snake.

Bull snake = a Great Basin gopher snake.

Puff adder = a Great Basin gopher snake.

"A big, mean snake that hissed at me" = a Great Basin gopher snake.

Great Basin gopher snake = a Great Basin gopher snake.

Western diamondback rattler = any species of rattlesnake or any harmless snake that shakes its tail or doesn't shake its tail. (Again, there are no diamondbacks in Utah.)

A "poisonous" snake = any venomous and/or harmless snake.

"I seent a snake an' it were all black." No, you didn't. There are no all-black snakes in Utah. No water snakes either. Try again.

I apologize if my snarkasm is showing, but I really don't think I'm being unreasonable by expecting my fellow humans to confidently identify a garter snake when they see one, and certainly before they kill it for no reason.

Early one spring, a lovely lady wanted to know if I would remove several garter snakes from her yard. I told her that I don't typically remove harmless snakes because of the good they do, that they are no threat to anyone, and that she should be flattered that out of all the yards in the neighborhood, they chose her yard to hang out in. (Also, that with a canal nearby, she was always going to have garter snakes.)

I explained that they were just coming out of hibernation (probably next to her foundation), they would soon begin to mate, and once the weather warmed up they would more than likely disperse to surrounding yards in her neighborhood looking for food.

Her question to me was, "What can I do to make me like them?" I suggested that she spend quality time with them. She laughed, and I think she's okay with the situation.

The most common methods people use to identify venomous snakes are head shape, eye shape, and coloration. These methods can be indicators, of course, but they can also be completely wrong because there are no definite rules depending on where in the world you are. Head shape and eye shape vary by species, and as far as coloration goes, there are harmless species whose coloration mimics venomous ones.

Worldwide, many harmless snakes have triangular heads, or can make their heads appear triangular when threatened. Similarly, many venomous snakes have heads that aren't triangular.

Eye shape is also not a reliable factor. Many harmless snakes, including boas, have elliptical pupils, whereas many venomous snakes have round pupils. To complicate matters further, elliptical pupils can appear round in lowlight conditions when a snake's eyes are fully dilated.

Trying to identify a snake by head shape or pupil shape is like trying to identify a car by looking only at the headlights or the grille. Maybe you're right, but maybe you're not.

In North America, all of our pit vipers — rattlesnakes, cottonmouths, and copperheads — have heads that are essentially triangular, along with elliptical pupils, so the rules apply. These three types of snakes, along with coral snakes, are the only venomous snakes on the continent. If a snake has a triangular head but round pupils, it's a harmless snake. Water snakes, garter snakes, and gopher snakes fall into this category.

Coral snakes have neither triangular heads nor elliptical pupils, but rather, round pupils and bright bands of red, black, and yellow, which serve as a warning to predators. This is known as aposematic coloration. On the other hand, some harmless king snakes and milk snakes have coloration that imitates the appearance of the venomous coral snake as a way to deter predators. This phenomenon is known as Batesian mimicry.

Predators that know to avoid the brightly colored coral snake may have a hard time determining if the milk snake is also venomous, which gives it a fighting chance. To many snake enthusiasts, the difference is obvious. For the general public, the difference may be as clear as mud.

Coral snakes have limited ranges and are nocturnal, so most people will never see one. It doesn't stop people from trying to remember the old mnemonic rhyme, "Red touch yellow . . ." etc., which is only applicable in places where both coral snakes and tricolor mimics occur, and even then, only in North America.

Simply put, on the coral snake, the red and yellow bands touch. On king snakes, milk snakes, scarlet snakes, etc., black bands separate the red and yellow bands. I would encourage people not to rely on the rhyme for several reasons.

First, most people forget how the rhyme goes, doing them no good at all when they actually see any of these snakes. Second, the rhyme doesn't apply outside of the United States, and relying on it may lead to a dangerous mistake. Third, I saw a video of a young boy who got the rhyme correct and still managed to think that the coral snake he picked up was safe. Miraculously, it didn't bite him.

The moral of the story is this: if you have to rely on a rhyme to remember the difference, you should leave the snake alone. In fact, leaving snakes alone is better for everyone, especially the snakes. You don't have to memorize every type of snake in order to know if one is venomous or not. By learning to identify the venomous snakes in your area (there may only be one or two), you can safely assume that all the others are harmless.

Still, knowing how to identify snakes can be as fun for laypersons as it is for herpers. The easiest way is to photograph a snake with your phone and let an app like SnakeSnap or SnakeCheck tell you what kind it is. That way, you don't have to remember all the rules. Otherwise, it only matters if you plan to pick a snake up, which is not advisable because even a harmless snake may bite you. Since most people have an aversion to being bitten by anything, especially a snake, the most common sense rule of all, and the easiest one to remember, is to appreciate it from a distance. That way, it doesn't matter whether it's venomous or not. Easy, right?

The easiest way to know if a snake is dangerous is to ask yourself two questions: "Am I leaving it alone?" "Does it have an escape route?" If you can answer yes to both questions, it's not a dangerous snake no matter what kind of snake it is.

Many years ago, in a burst of entrepreneurial inspiration, my friend Dax and I decided to make our own snake sticks and sell them. The local reptile expo would provide us with a ready customer base for our product, or so we thought.

Most snake sticks are nothing more than repurposed golf club shafts retrofitted with a metal hook where the head used to be. Tiring of the heavy steel hooks that were available from most makers, we chose aluminum for ours. Dax, who worked in the aluminum fabrication industry at the time, had access to aircraft-grade aluminum rod.

Bent and broken golf club shafts were free for the taking at nearly every pro shop in town, which had dumpsters full of them. (They were free until the shops found out we needed them, then they were $2 each. Supply means nothing without demand.)

I'll spare you the details of the manufacturing process because that's not the point here, except to say that we made the highest-quality, lightest-weight snake hooks to be found anywhere. They came in various lengths, were reasonably priced, and each stick came with a free lifetime replacement guarantee if the customer broke it. We called them *Snake Snatchers* because of the catchy alliteration, and rented a booth at an upcoming expo, expecting to make a decent return on our investments of time and material.

Our assumption that every snake owner was also at least a part-time field herper couldn't have been more wrong. It seems that most people who keep snakes as pets have never even caught a wild snake and had almost no use for our product.

So where were all those field herpers? Either they don't go to reptile expos or they don't catch the snakes they find, merely documenting them instead. That's a good thing. Harmless snakes, of course, can be caught by hand, and it's illegal to pick up or harass a rattler without permission from the state, making a snake stick totally unnecessary for the average person. The exception would involve moving a rattler off a roadway, and I'm never going to throw someone under the bus for saving a snake, license or no license.

If some field herpers choose not to use snake sticks, that's great. After all, minimizing interaction with, and inflicting as little stress as possible on wild animals is the true essence of field herping, along with respecting the environment and leaving nature as you found it.

A good snake stick, however, has a-thousand-and-one uses, and everyone should own one. They are especially handy for reaching under the bed, on high shelves, or untangling the cords behind your computer desk or entertainment center. They also make great backscratchers!

Hmmm ... a warm spring night, a waning moon, and a recent eclipse. Sounds like a good night to drive to the desert and look for critters. Want to hear my critter call? "Here critter, critter, critter! Here critter, critter, critter!"

CHAPTER 4

Snake Stuff

"Have you ever studied a snake's face? How optimistic they look. They have an eternal smile." –Tasha Tudor

I said in the introduction that I wouldn't overwhelm readers with an undue amount of snake info or jargon, but a brief background in basic physiology, anatomy and behavior is essential, especially for those who are still learning and want to know more.

As one of the most misunderstood animals on the planet, snakes have been alternately revered and reviled by various cultures throughout history, and imbued with mystical powers both good and bad. Unfortunately, in the western world, snakes have been portrayed as harbingers of evil. Despite the metaphorical basis of the Garden of Eden story, the damage is done, and the reputation of the poor, maligned serpent may never fully recover. Adding insult to injury, snakes have become convenient victims of a plethora of superstition and myth, urban legends, old wives' tales, and Hollywood movies.

As with all animals, snakes aren't subject to an abstract social construct of moral behavior imposed on them by humans. Animal behavior isn't based on the concepts of good or bad, right or wrong. It is based on instinct — primarily on the instincts to survive and reproduce — both of which are imperative traits for any creature and every species, including ours.

An absence of limbs makes it hard for humans to relate to snakes in the same way that having eight legs makes it difficult to relate to spiders, so we unsympathetically distance ourselves from them, casting them in a different light than the animals we view with unbridled anthropomorphism and affection.

Far from being emissaries of evil, snakes are merely animals like any other. What most people interpret as aggression is usually nothing more than a snake defending itself, which is the right of every living creature. If someone pokes me with a stick or comes after me with a shovel, I'm going to defend myself, and so are you!

Snakes don't typically eat humans (it has happened but is extraordinarily rare) — and contrary to popular folklore, they don't want to bite us either. On the infrequent occasion that a bite does happen (which, as Steve Irwin wisely noted, is *always* the human's fault), chances are overwhelmingly in your favor that it's not a venomous species. People increase their odds of being bitten when they try to catch, corner, provoke, or kill a snake. If you do spot a venomous snake in your yard, don't reach for the shovel. Call a professional. A trained relocator will safely return it to the wild where it belongs. As for the rest? Give them space. Let them be. They're not trespassers — they're part of the landscape. They were here long before we were, and they'll likely be here long after we have annihilated ourselves.

Snakes live, eat, reproduce and do their best to survive in a hostile world controlled by humans and yet we could not live without them. As voracious predators, snakes are the barrier between human agriculture and the vermin and insects that would devour our food crops, preventing rampant disease and destruction in the process.

As highly efficient predators, snakes make an enormous contribution toward maintaining the balance of nature. Snakes are a gardener's best friend. A harmless snake in your yard is doing you a huge favor by eating the kinds of destructive pests that want to destroy your garden and invade your home. Once a snake has gotten rid of the pests in your yard, it will leave and perform its services somewhere else.

Snakes have turned the apparent disadvantage of being limbless into an evolutionary triumph. They slip through rock crevices like water, climb trees with grace, and can vanish quicker than a magician's assistant. They are streamlined survival experts. Many are stunningly beautiful, adorned in colors so vivid and scales so iridescent they rival anything on nature's color wheel.

For many people, the 'ick factor' makes it hard to bridge the gap between snakes and animals that are more cuddly and affectionate. True, pet snakes won't come when you call them, nor will they display affection or play the way some mammals do, but they are as individually unique in their personalities as any other animal. But because I like my pets to like me back, I also have a cat.

4 | Snake Stuff

Mechanomorphism is the belief that lower animals such as reptiles and other ectotherms rely on nothing but instinct and only require food, water, and heat to survive in captivity.

It is the opposite of anthropomorphism, which is the humanizing of animals by applying human attributes and emotions to them, as in, "My snake loves me," etc.

Studies show that snakes and other reptiles actually can recognize their keepers by scent, and that enrichment in the form of regular handling and diversified caging creates happier, healthier animals, so the truth lies somewhere in the middle.

I once knew a man who insisted that his iguanas loved him, running to meet him whenever he entered the room. It didn't occur to him that it was mealtime and he was carrying a tray full of fresh fruits and veggies.

The cognition, psychology, emotional range, and socialization of ectothermic animals is an area of intense interest to scientists. Research into human interactions with reptiles reveals that they are immensely more complex than previously thought. For example, some zoos engage snakes and lizards in "target training" — a method of eliciting a response to stimuli, resulting in a reward.

Target training is a method by which animals learn to identify and respond to an inanimate object such as a stick, ball, or any object that elicits an interaction in a specific way, usually by rewarding the behavior with food. Most reptiles and other so-called 'lower animals' can be trained this way. This is proof that they are not merely responding to biological imperatives, but are actually sentient beings that are capable of conscious thought and intentional action.

Liza, a woman with years of reptile experience, explains it this way: "The old 'your snake doesn't love you' assumption still survives because no professional person working with reptiles wants to be seen as approaching them in an inaccurate or overly romanticized manner."

"But can we attribute the emotion of love to a snake?" I asked. This was her response:

> I would argue that we are grossly underestimating their sentience. It has been proven that reptiles

can learn and carry out intentional behaviors as well as working with humans in this manner. Of course, they can identify familiar and trusted human caregivers and relate them to safety, provision of food, and other positive and necessary functions. How is this so different from the relationship with a dog or cat or even a young human child?

We call those bonds 'love,' but a bond is a bond. We just insist on using different language depending on whether we're talking about a bond between a human and another endotherm or an ectotherm. My savannah monitor and my royal python actively seek and insist on physical contact with me. Indeed all of my animals moved from initial fearfulness or at least reservation to trust and inquisitiveness quite quickly, based on beneficial interaction and positive reinforcement. That these are complex, thinking, feeling organisms is overwhelmingly clear to me.

This makes perfect sense, of course, the bottom line being that we don't know how reptiles 'feel.' That's the single biggest variable. The best we can do is to empathize with their situation based on their inability to vocalize or show facial expression.

Liza continued:

I don't see animals as lesser beings. I just love them for being who and what they are and doing what they do according to nature's laws. We all need nature to live. How could I look at any living being as anything other than important? Snakes are feeling beings. 'I feel threatened, I feel scared, I feel safe, I feel hungry.' I have held snakes that struck at their owners but in my hands were calm and happy. They felt safe and understood. Everything is feelings with snakes. How could it be otherwise? Their actions tell their story. We don't know if they love, but to assume they do not is a big mistake, too. I don't know if my snakes love me, but I do know I love them.

4 | Snake Stuff

Virtually any reptile keeper with even a moderate level of awareness will tell you that his or her animals sometimes respond very differently to them than to strangers. I can't disagree. I've held both pet snakes and wild snakes that would relax completely in my hands, but would thrash and squirm if anyone else tried to handle them, including other snake people.

Even though I don't handle them as often as I probably should, I like to think my snakes 'know me' better than they know other humans. Maybe it's because I'm familiar to them, or maybe they're just attuned to the discomfort that oozes from people unfamiliar with handling snakes. Either way, there's clearly some level of cognition at play.

More than 2,500 studies have resulted in a verdict: sentience is not a privilege of the human species; it is a biological inheritance shared across the animal kingdom. It's time to retire the dusty dogmas that paint animals — even lower animals — as unfeeling and unintelligent. To write them off as lesser creatures simply because they lack fur and limbs is human arrogance personified.

In March of 2012, I left the lid askew on a cage, and my four-foot Honduran milk snake, Froot Loop, escaped. I spent three weeks treading lightly and keeping a vigilant eye open, hoping to find him as soon as possible. I had a hunch that Nemo knew exactly where he was the whole time, but he wasn't talking. As a devout pacifist, Nemo the Wonder Cat would never harm another creature, so I didn't have to worry about that.

I left the lid open as a reminder of my negligence. One night I glanced up from the TV to look in Froot Loop's cage — and there he was! It is as astounding to me today as it was then. After spending three weeks as a fugitive, he found his way back to his cage, on a countertop, crawling inside as nonchalantly as if he was coming home from vacation. After failing to find food on his own, did he associate his enclosure with food? Some people may chalk it up to coincidence, but I don't think we give these animals nearly enough credit.

The venerable David Attenborough understands this. "Reptiles and amphibians are sometimes thought of as primitive, dull and dimwitted," he said. "In fact . . . they can be lethally fast, spectacularly beautiful, surprisingly affectionate, and very sophisticated."

I can't prove it, but in the case of wild rattlesnakes, I firmly believe there is a sixth sense at play wherein a snake understands that my intention to treat it with compassion and respect is perceived differently from the intent of the person who was harassing it with a garden implement just moments before. Is it trust, intuition, or something else?

People who work extensively with rattlesnakes find them to be extremely intelligent and seemingly able to interpret our intentions, which may be why I get along so well with them. I truly believe they understand, at some level, that I mean them no harm. They mean us no harm either if we would only leave them alone.

Not all Great Basin rattlers are teddy bear docile. For those that aren't, or may have had good reason to be cranky, I can't count the number of times I have seen agitated snakes that seemed to submit to me. Snakes that were previously rattling or even striking changed their behavior, even ceasing to rattle as I placed them in a bucket, took them on a hike, and subjected them to a photo session, all without displaying the least bit of defensiveness. Although I don't recommend it for others, I've even free-handled a few exceptionally calm individuals. It's one of the reasons I was bestowed the moniker "Snake Whisperer." It's not because I claim some special psychic snake ability, because quite honestly, anyone could do it if they were willing to invest the time it takes to truly understand these animals.

In addition to a sense of cognition, the evolutionary adaptations of snakes have equipped them with the tools necessary to survive and thrive in diverse habitats. From their limbless bodies and specialized locomotion to their advanced sensory systems and venom in some species, snakes were endowed by nature to thrive as specialized predators, filling an essential niche in a variety of habitats and ecosystems.

While most people can't identify a particular species of snake, including the ones in their own vicinity, there is probably no one on earth who doesn't know what a snake looks like when they see one. What follows are some of the most common characteristics of snakes:

4 | Snake Stuff

The most distinctive adaptation of snakes is their elongated, limbless bodies. This modification allows them to move efficiently through a variety of environments, including limited burrowing, swimming in water, and climbing trees. The absence of limbs reduces friction and enables snakes to navigate through narrow spaces that would be inaccessible to most other animals.

There are lizards that lack legs, and at first glance, they resemble snakes. Lizards, however, have eyelids and external ear openings. Aside from legs, these are the most obvious differences between lizards and snakes.

To compensate for the lack of limbs, snakes have developed several unique methods of locomotion. These include lateral undulation, whereby the snake moves in a wave-like motion; rectilinear movement, which involves muscles contracting sequentially to move the snake forward in a straight line; and sidewinding, which is a technique used by some desert snakes to move across loose, sandy surfaces.

Someone asked me why some snakes are slender while others are stout. Physiology pertains to the functions and mechanisms of an organism, including musculature. Rattlesnakes and other terrestrial pit vipers lack the muscles required for climbing and constricting since they don't need to do those things . . . but they're still chunky. Because they're venomous, they don't need to rely as much on locomotion for escape. Constricting snakes have muscles that allow them to climb, constrict prey, and hang on to tree branches, with some even having prehensile tails. But not all arboreal snakes are slender, e.g., boa constrictors; and some climbing snakes are both slender and venomous, e.g., mambas, kraits, etc., Physiology can be fickle — its logic often hidden from plain view. But Mother Nature, mysterious as she is, has reasons for everything she does.

Due to natural buoyancy combined with the fluidity of serpentine locomotion, all snakes can swim, including desert snakes that may never see a body of water.

Thigmotaxis, or movement toward a solid object (also known as wall hugging) is a common behavior in snakes. Because their bellies are always in contact with the earth, snakes may feel more comfortable if their sides and even their backs are in contact with something as well. This may explain why snakes crawl next to solid objects and seek out crevices. Crawling next to a wall is safer than being in an open space where they are more vulnerable to predation and provides better leverage and traction than crawling on flat ground.

This need for touch might even explain snakes' tendency to aggregate in large numbers during brumation. (Brumation is the term for reptilian hibernation, although the two words are often used interchangeably.) Rodents also use thigmotactic behavior as a response to fear or stress. Walking close to walls is a tactic used by some humans with agoraphobia (fear of open spaces) because it makes them feel safer outside.

Snakes have evolved a variety of sensory adaptations to detect prey and navigate their environments. They possess highly developed chemosensory abilities, using their forked tongues to collect scent particles from the air and transfer them to the Jacobson's organ, which is the vomeronasal or olfactory organ in the roof of the mouth. Additionally, some species, such as pit vipers, some boas and most pythons, have infrared-sensitive organs that allow them to detect the heat signatures of warm-blooded prey. Often appearing as holes in the snakes' face, these are known as loreal pits.

By yawning, snakes can increase sensory input by exposing the Jacobson's organ to the air, but it is common for snakes to yawn after a meal to return all those ligaments and muscles in the skull back to their proper positions. Rattlesnakes and other pit vipers often perform prolonged yawns after eating, stretching their jaws and waggling their fangs side-to-side. Who doesn't enjoy a good stretch after a meal?

A snake's upper jaw (maxillary) connects to the lower jaw via the quadrate bone, which moves outward, allowing the opening of the mouth to be larger. The lower mandible (also known as the dentary/compound bone) is not fused in the front — what humans call a chin. Instead, a stretchy ligament allows the lower jaw to expand outward from the center with great flexibility. This bone, in combination with the ligament on the lower jaw, allows a snake to expand its mouth and consume an animal several times larger in diameter than its own head.

4 | Snake Stuff

One reason why people fear snakes is the misnomer that all snakes are venomous. In truth, the vast majority of the world's snakes are completely harmless to humans. Out of more than 3,400 total species, only about 15 percent (500 or so) are venomous enough to warrant extreme caution, while only 150 of those have bites that can be potentially fatal without immediate treatment. In most places, there may be only one or two truly dangerous snakes, with Australia being the obvious exception. Supposedly, everything in Australia wants to kill us, not just the snakes. It is safe to assume that this little factoid, true or not, isn't featured prominently in ads from the Australian tourist board.

Snakes evolved venom as a means of subduing prey and defending against predators. Venom composition varies greatly among species, but it typically contains a mixture of proteins, peptides, enzymes, and amino acids that can cause paralysis, tissue damage, or blood clotting. There are hemotoxic, hemolytic, cardiotoxic, neurotoxic, cytotoxic, and myotoxic venoms, each with specific characteristics and symptomologies.

Delivery systems include specialized fangs that can be either fixed or retractable depending on the species and some snakes' fangs are in the back of their mouths, making it necessary to partially swallow their prey before they can envenomate it. Due to their small size and a tendency not to bite, most are completely harmless, although some rear-fanged snakes, such as the Boomslang, can deliver a fatal bite to humans.

Known as opisthoglyphous fangs, these teeth are not hollow and do not inject venom like true fangs, but may have surface grooves that direct venom into the wound as the snake swallows its prey. The venom is produced by two Duvernoy's glands located beneath the upper labial (lip) scales on either side of the snake's head. This is most common in snakes that eat toads as the toxins are derived from the toads' parotid glands — the glands in the toad's skin that help repel predators.

Garter snakes, ring-neck snakes, and several other colubrid (common) species have these teeth as well. Despite those histrionic individuals who use this knowledge to proclaim that garter snakes are venomous, in reality, their venom is only effective for subduing small animals and their bites are not dangerous to humans.

I captured and relocated hundreds of rattlesnakes in my brief career, and although I often took risks for the sake of my customers' peace of mind, I managed to avoid getting tagged.

My closest brush with envenomation happened while walking with my female hognose snake, Harley. I was holding her in my left hand as I walked briskly through my neighborhood in the dark. Showing more interest than normal, she began nosing and nudging my left pinky finger with her upturned, pig-like snout. 'Isn't that cute?' I thought. 'She's never done that before!'

I looked away for only a moment when I felt about 50 needles penetrate the pad of my little finger! I felt her large back fangs sink deep into the flesh of my finger pad and strike bone. This sweet little snake who had never bitten me in 16 years (she's 30 now) suddenly thought I was a snack!

A loud expletive escaped my lips and I hope the people in the houses around me didn't hear my profane cry of pain and alarm. Harley was devouring my finger like I consume a combination pizza, and it hurt!

A nearby house had its sprinklers on. I stuck Harley directly in a cold jet of water and she let go immediately. With my finger dripping blood, we finished the remaining two miles of our walk. I kept a close eye on my little reptilian friend to see if she still had the munchies.

Due to the anticoagulant properties of snake saliva, my finger dripped blood the whole way home. It turned out that Harley had a thing for a particular brand of hand soap. I assume she liked the smell or she wouldn't have tried to eat it. Whatever the reason, I had to quit using that soap. Chalk up another win for reptilian awareness!

I'm happy to say that I survived the seven teeth that remained behind and a slightly diminished blood supply. But it was just a love bite. It's nice to know Harley still loves me after all these years!

Between Harley, her offspring, and several recalcitrant garter snakes, I've been bitten dozens of times with nothing worse than some mild, temporary swelling and itching to show for it.

Pygmy rattlesnakes, like all rattlesnakes, are venomous, however, there's not a single recorded fatality attributed to this species. Their venom was used to develop Eptifibatide, a drug used in the prevention of blood clots and the treatment of heart attacks, saving many human lives. In fact, the venoms of many snakes, Gila monsters, and other venomous animals have led to the development of drugs to treat a wide range of human diseases. Ironically, the treatment for snakebite is processed snake venom.

Snakes have evolved an impressive array of camouflage strategies — collectively known as cryptic coloration — as well as mimicry to both avoid predators and stalk prey. Their patterns and hues often echo the textures and tones of their environment so precisely that they often disappear seamlessly into leaf litter, rock, or sand. In some species, these natural disguises are so effective that you may not notice the silent serpent just feet away.

Great Basin rattlers are not the most attractive members of their genus. Looking more like the scruffy cousins at the rattlesnake family reunion, they have no crisp diamonds, no bold "coontail" like some other rattlers, and they couldn't care less about making a fashion statement. Their earth-tone blotches look like they were daubed on by a distracted painter using an old sponge instead of a fine brush. But that unpredictable asymmetry allows them to disappear more easily into sagebrush shadows and talus slope rubble.

I have undoubtedly walked right past rattlesnakes that blended seamlessly into a background of scattered sunlight, dappled shade, and juniper berries. Most of them may have remained virtually invisible if they hadn't serenaded me with their tail as I walked by.

Many snake species have mastered the art of invisibility, using camouflage not just to evade predators, but to become nearly undetectable to their prey. But their colors do more than hide them; they help power them. As ectotherms — animals that rely on external heat to regulate body temperature — snakes also benefit from pigment-based thermoregulation. Darker snakes warm up more quickly in the sun but must retreat to shade sooner, while lighter ones may bask longer without overheating. Known as poikilothermic regulation, it's all part of a finely tuned system that allows these creatures to function in wildly fluctuating environments.

Snakes exhibit a range of reproductive strategies that contribute to their success. While most snakes are oviparous (egg-laying), some species are viviparous, giving birth to live young. This adaptation allows them to reproduce in environments where laying eggs would be disadvantageous, such as colder climates, watery environments, or places with a high concentration of scavenging predators.

Whenever I gave a snake presentation, someone (almost always a woman) would seek me out afterward and discreetly ask, with a hint of mischievous hesitation, "How do snakes, you know, 'do it?'" There it was — my favorite moment— the chance to explain snake sex.

There is an almost civilized rivalry of ritualized combat when two male snakes encounter each other in pursuit of the same receptive female. It isn't a battle of fangs or violence — it's more of a grappling contest of strength and stature — an elegant vertical sparring match. With heads raised high, each male tries to out-leverage the other, to press his rival downward in a display of serpentine prowess. There's no biting, no blood, just a dance of silent dominance expressed with tension and balance. The victor earns the right to court the female, while the loser slinks away, humbled but uninjured. It is a remarkable sight to behold.

Mating, by contrast, is patient and intricate. A male approaches a female cautiously, as his flickering tongue decodes her pheromone trail. If she is receptive, he aligns alongside her, cloaking her with his body in a serpentine embrace that can last for hours.

Male snakes are uniquely equipped with not one, but two penises. The woman asking the question received that revelation with either prurient fascination or abject embarrassment. There was usually a moment of silence followed by wide-eyed wonder and/or nervous laughter. "Wait . . . two?" she'd ask, making sure she had heard me correctly. That's when I'd nod solemnly, feeling like a reptilian Dr. Ruth.

A hemipenis is one of two male copulatory organs found in male snakes and other squamates (the largest order of reptiles, comprising lizards, snakes, and worm lizards). As a pair, they are known as hemipenes. These organs remain inverted, tucked internally under the tail, either side-by-side or bottom-and-top until they are everted for reproduction. Like the penises of most other animals, including humans, they are comprised of erectile tissue.

Using one of his paired hemipenes, the male connects with the cloacal opening on the underside of the female's tail, also known as the vent. It's a surprisingly tender sequence for such primitive creatures.

Each hemipene is attached to a single testis, allowing a male snake to transfer a fresh batch of sperm even if he has recently mated. Sperm is transported through an outer groove called the sulcus spermaticus, unlike the human penis, in which sperm travels inside the organ via the urethra.

I never went into this much detail, of course, as it was already more of a biology lesson than anyone bargained for. Most of them would thank me, then walk away, looking overwhelmed by this new bit of trivia.

In the same way that young humans outgrow their clothes, snakes outgrow their skin. Because the outer skin layer of snakes does not grow with the animal, it needs to be periodically discarded. This process, called ecdysis, is more commonly known as shedding, sloughing or molting. Ecdysis is a normal phenomenon in reptiles, some amphibians, and all arthropods.

Young snakes will shed up to 12 times per year during their rapid growth phase and will continue to shed throughout their lives, but with less frequency.

While humans shed millions of dead microscopic skin cells every day, healthy snakes shed their old skin in a continuous piece, revealing a fresh, vibrant dermis underneath, which also helps rid the snake of external parasites. Like human fingernails, a snake's skin is made of keratin, and although a shed skin may have a faint pattern, it does not contain the pigment that gives the snake its coloration.

Several days prior to shedding, a snake will appear bluish due to a lymph fluid that helps separate the old skin from the new skin underneath. Even the snake's eyes become opaque during this time, hindering its vision. This can cause some snakes to become cranky or abnormally defensive. Pet snakes should not be handled during this phase due to the potential for damaging the developing skin or the ocular scales that cover the eyes. Abnormal shedding is called dysecdysis.

After several days, the snake will rub its snout on a rough surface, breaking the bond around the mouth and crawling out of the old skin, similar to a human rolling a sock off inside out. The resulting shed is a perfect replica of the snake scale by scale, even though, due to stretching, the shed skin is always longer than the snake that wore it.

A common misconception is that snakes are completely deaf, only able to sense and 'hear', or more accurately, 'feel' vibrations through the ground. This was presumed to be a scientific fact for decades, with even the most hardcore scientists believing it to be true. Recent research, however, suggests that snakes can actually hear some airborne sounds.

You may be familiar with the three bones in the middle ear of mammals that allows us to hear: the malleus, incus, and stapes. Snakes don't have those. Instead, they have just one middle ear bone called the columella. The columella is connected to their lower quadrate bone, which ostensibly allows snakes to hear, although they don't hear airborne sounds the same way we do.

Vibrations transmitted through the air hit the snake and are transferred into its body for the snake to process. It can't hear everything though, only processing sounds between 80 and 1000 Hz. In contrast, humans can hear sounds between 20 and 20,000 Hz. While a snake may be able to hear a person talking at close range, it can't necessarily hear a canary singing in the same room, as the typical songbird only transmits at 2,500 Hz and above. Snakes use their low-frequency hearing to detect predators and prey.

Humans burden snakes with all kinds of ridiculous assumptions. As a result, snake behavior is often misunderstood. For instance, gopher snakes and all members of the bull snake family are consummate bluffers — hissing, striking, and scaring the socks off anyone who provokes them, intentionally or otherwise. It is a response to fear. Snakes are infinitely more afraid of humans than the other way around; although I've had several people try to convince me that's not true. It isn't a guarantee that a snake won't bite as a justified means of self-protection, but like the gopher snake in chapter one, it is often just a form of intimidation that can be easily defused by simply stepping back and walking away, or by demonstrating that you mean no harm.

A thorough understanding of snakes isn't necessary in order to appreciate them. A simple awareness of these hypnotic creatures is all it takes to ignite a lifetime's worth of passionate wonder. This is why snake encounters feel oddly sacred. Each one is an intimate interruption of the ordinary. You're no longer just a passerby — you're an audience to something so primordial and perfect that even the most seasoned herpetologist finds themselves humbled. Even nonprofessionals like me have dedicated years to decoding their quiet mysteries only to discover that the more we learn, the more the horizon expands. Each revelation unzips another layer of biological brilliance — almost like a masterclass in elegant adaptation.

Because they're such incredible creatures, snake encounters are always a welcome experience. Every approach with such a secretive creature feels extraordinary — almost intimate. After settling in, some serpents even respond inquisitively to gentle touches like a tickle under the chin, although initiating physical contact with a wild one is a bit like greeting a stranger with a kiss on the cheek. You may remember it later, but for all the wrong reasons.

CHAPTER 5

Gearing Up

"Catching rattlesnakes is far easier than most people think. You've got a bitey end and a rattley end, and as long as you can tell the difference, you'll be fine." –Some snake guy

Urban snake removal is a straightforward, low overhead business. Equipment consists of a few high-quality plastic buckets with ventilation and screw-on lids, smaller containers for tiny snakes, an assortment of snake sticks of varying lengths, a set of snake tongs or two, and a plethora of assorted hardware that grew larger each year I was in business. These included items you wouldn't normally associate with snake relocation.

Beyond the standard gear like sturdy hiking shoes and extra socks, I accumulated a backpack, hard hat, face masks, gloves (both fingered and fingerless), rubber gloves, reflective vest, knee pads, garbage bags, sandwich bags, coveralls, flashlight, headlamp, baby wipes, hand sanitizer, knife, multi-tool, scissors, hand mirror, pry-bar, first aid kit, bottled water, and enough other paraphernalia to fill the back of a medium-sized SUV.

Rescuing snakes is hard on footwear. Every summer saw the sacrifice of several pairs of socks and at least one pair of shoes, mostly due to the prevalence of Russian thistle, foxtail, cheat grass, goat head burrs, and a variety of other sadistic weeds. Releasing snakes meant going off trail where hosts of insidious and invasive desert plants infiltrate shoes and socks with belligerent impunity, turning every step into a form of podiatric punishment.

These botanical torments have invaded western rangelands, replacing native grasses with plants so repugnant even cows won't eat them. In the interest of karmic justice, I hope the person who transported these vegetative vermin from the motherland is forced to stuff them in his socks while hiking through Hell for eternity and that demons use his guts as guitar strings.

My decision to start my own business was based largely on the desire to provide an essential service, not only to the citizens of Salt Lake City, but mostly to its resident snake population.

5 | Gearing Up

Teaching people about snakes and being a snake ambassador have always been second nature to me, and I knew early on that saving snakes was a cause I believed in.

With a full-time job and far too little space at my disposal, I had no desire to run an animal rescue. Starting my own snake relocation business, on the other hand, would be the culmination of a commitment to educate the public about these animals, providing a responsible, reliable way to protect snakes from the wanton destruction that so often befalls them when people are suddenly confronted with a snake in their yard and don't know what to do about it.

The Division of Wildlife Resources had no problem issuing me a Certificate of Registration (COR) based on my prior snake removal experience. This certification is a requirement for dealing with native rattlesnakes for any reason, and each one is tailored to a specific purpose. For instance, my COR allowed me to capture, transport and release urban rattlesnakes, limiting their time in my possession to a few hours. This differed significantly from the COR of Scales and Tails Utah — a local reptile education and entertainment venue whose COR allows them to house rattlesnakes in a commercial building and display them at offsite venues for the educational benefit of the general public.

The second step was to register a business name with the Department of Commerce. I considered several names, finally settling on Wasatch Snake Removal. Wasatch refers to the Wasatch Mountain Range that forms the eastern boundary of the Ogden, Salt Lake, and Utah Valleys, home to nearly 3 million people, and the extent of my jurisdiction at that time. I would come to regret the name years later when the business expanded to include St. George, 300 miles to the south.

Known as "Utah's Dixie," St. George is a desert paradise that sits at the junction of three unique geographical regions: The Great Basin, the Colorado Plateau, and the Mojave Desert, making it a cornucopia of reptilian diversity. Five of Utah's eight rattlesnake species call the area home, and a snake relocator could certainly do well there using a locally appropriate business name.

I only received a handful of calls from the area, certainly not enough to keep my two relocators there, Chris and Aspen, happy.

The Only Good Snake . . .

The single biggest deterrent to running a 24-hour snake relocation service would be the restrictions placed on it by my full-time job in a local government office. Therefore, the first thing I did was to approach my employer with the idea. There would undoubtedly be times when I would need to leave work to move a snake. After all, if someone called at 10 am with a rattlesnake in their yard, I couldn't very well tell them I'd be there by 5:30. Knowing that this would be the biggest hurdle to starting my business, I approached my immediate supervisor, Susan.

"You have to do it off the clock," she told me. "That means using your vacation time."

I assured her that I understood completely. This was going to be easier than I thought.

"If you want to waste your vacation time chasing snakes, it's okay by me," she reiterated. "Just make sure you clock out before you leave and clock back in when you return. And make sure the work gets done."

I assured her that I did indeed want to "waste" my vacation time chasing snakes.

It was a huge concession for a government office to make, but at the same time, my accrued vacation hours were mine to use as I pleased whether it was for two weeks or two hours at a time. Susan's willingness to grant me this privilege was the single biggest reason why Wasatch Snake Removal became a reality.

It was slow going at first, but my website gradually gained favor with the web crawlers, quickly propelling my page to the top of the search engines. It helped that I was the only game in town, and my phone began to ring. Between my previous duties as a volunteer rescuer and the several years I operated my business, I moved, housed, rehabilitated and rehomed hundreds of snakes and met all kinds of people.

One of my first calls came when a man tried to sneak two ball pythons through security in his carry-on luggage at Salt Lake City International Airport. An alert TSA agent noticed the snakes in a plastic shoebox as it passed through an X-ray machine. One python was approximately 30 inches long and the other was about 18 inches long.

70

5 | *Gearing Up*

The man was detained and the snakes were confiscated. The man, who was from San Juan, Puerto Rico, had just flown in from LAX where the snakes passed through security undetected.

According to an airport official, the man cried when the snakes were taken from him. He kissed the smaller snake, saying it was a gift from his girlfriend. They were cold and stressed but otherwise healthy.

My customers ran the gamut from those who hated snakes but were too afraid to kill them, to those who thought having a rattlesnake in their yard for a little while was an interesting novelty but didn't want it to overstay its welcome. That was completely understandable. After all, no one is expected to host a rattlesnake in their yard unless they choose to or until the novelty wears off.

A woman named Martha told me she had a rattlesnake living in her yard. It had been there for a month, which is unusual unless there's a perpetual food source. Sure enough, she fed wild birds. Birdseed attracts rodents and rodents attract snakes. It's a no-brainer. She admitted that she hadn't seen a rodent since the snake showed up.

She named the snake Rigoberto (it sounds cooler if you roll the Rs). Her dog didn't bother Rigoberto, and neither did she, but after a month she began to feel like Rigoberto was taking advantage of the situation. He liked to bask in a particular spot each day around 4 pm and she was going to call me the next time she saw him. I never did meet Rigoberto. After eating all the mice in Martha's yard, he must have finally moved along on his own.

Most homeowners with a rattlesnake in their yard wanted it removed ASAP. These were my favorite people, because although they may not like snakes, they didn't want to see one harmed. Statistically, there was no way to know how many homeowners killed the snake in their yard as opposed to how many of them called me, but the tide has been slowly turning toward a more 'live and let live' approach to conservation.

I was on call 24/7 during the summer months to move rattlesnakes that found their way into suburban yards and homes. Snakes live in close proximity to suburbia, not because they invaded our territory, but because we encroached on theirs. The secret to getting along lies in understanding these amazing creatures.

More than once, I was asked, "Why move rattlesnakes? Are you crazy?"

Well, the wheel did fall off my barrow (that's not some weird metaphor, it really did). I've been called a "weird but lovable snake fanatic," and while I would have preferred eccentric over weird, I'll take it! Merriam-Webster defines weird as "Of strange or extraordinary character: odd, fantastic." Regardless of how it was meant, I chose to take it as a compliment.

The state of Utah, like many other states, ostensibly protects its native herpetofauna (reptiles and amphibians) from wanton or indiscriminate killing, and the state granted me a license to remove what it refers to as "nuisance rattlesnakes." I detest the term 'nuisance', because it implies they don't belong there. In truth, these snakes are simply occupying ancestral habitat that has been invaded by humans. There aren't more snakes now than before as urban legends suggest. In fact, as we destroy more habitats, quite the opposite is true. But as we encroach further into snake territory, encounters become more frequent.

While there will always be people who try to justify killing every snake they see, more people are beginning to understand that we have a responsibility to nature and all her creatures, and that we can learn to co-exist, even with rattlesnakes. Calling a relocation specialist is the best way to do this.

For safety's sake, I transported snakes in plastic buckets. They were yellow with red screw-on lids. On opposite sides of each bucket in black letters was the word CAUTION, and below that in red, VENOMOUS SNAKE. They were real conversation starters on public hiking trails, opening doors to discussions about rattlesnakes and giving folks a close-up look at an animal they may have never seen.

One man and his five-year-old son were enthralled by the opportunity to look at the rattlesnake in my bucket. As we parted ways, I heard the man say to the boy, "That was pretty cool, huh? You got to see a real rattlesnake today!"

Another man was indignant. "You can't put rattlesnakes on this mountain!" he shouted. "My kids hike here!" I suppose it hadn't occurred to him that rattlesnakes had occupied this land for millennia. When I asked him how many snakes his kids had seen while hiking, he sheepishly admitted that they hadn't seen any. And that's when he lost his own argument.

Snakes were captured using a variety of tools, primarily a snake hook or tongs. However, I have had to grab snakes by the tail with my hand in order to prevent them from escaping into holes or under immovable objects. In one instance, I had to carefully pull a large Great Basin rattlesnake by its tail from beneath a kiddie pool filled with water. He was not a happy snake, but it was a better alternative than the fate that awaited him otherwise, or of having a child bitten.

I had only one chance to capture the snake on someone's property. If I was unsuccessful and the snake escaped, I had to make a second trip. This wasn't convenient for me or for the homeowner who still had a venomous snake in their yard and couldn't let the kids or the dog out to play.

When I captured an urban rattlesnake, state law required its release into the nearest suitable wild habitat. Contrary to popular belief, I wasn't hauling backyard snakes miles away — an act that would almost certainly doom them. Rattlesnakes know their terrain. They have social groups and ancestral dens. Uprooting them can cause lethal stress and disorientation. Keeping snakes within their home range gives them a fighting chance, especially when winter comes. If taken too far away, most will perish in an attempt to return to familiar territory, whereas keeping them close helps ensure the highest likelihood for survival.

The pattern on top of each rattlesnake's head is as unique as a human fingerprint. Known as a head stamp, this identifier was always photographed for future identification of each individual snake, along with the date and location of capture. Repeat offenders were given a 'three strikes and you're out' sentence by the state, after which a snake that had violated this arbitrary injunction was to be dispatched. This was tantamount to telling a bird not to land on the same tree branch three times in a row, and there was no way in hell I was ever going to kill a snake for exercising its eons-old right to exist and traverse its rightful domain.

In addition to dispatching three-time offenders, the state also thought it was a good idea to paint the rattle of every snake, thereby identifying it as a parole violator if it was seen again. Why would I flag a snake with brightly colored paint only to make it more visible to predators and snake killers? These were the only two rules I clandestinely refused to follow. Everything else was done by the book.

It was always gratifying to put these animals back into wild habitat where they're not necessarily safer than they are in suburbia, but is where we relegate them for our own comfort and safety. The most popular option for the ignorant and ill-informed is to kill them.

Most states make it illegal to wantonly or indiscriminately kill snakes of any kind, including venomous snakes. This is because of their vital importance in the biotic community. By removing urban rattlesnakes that crawled into yards in Salt Lake City, I tried to educate people about the virtues of these cryptic creatures.

It sometimes felt like the world was poking me with a stick. I had to set a radio commentator straight one morning over some ridiculous assertion about rattlesnakes, and a short time later on the news, a state wildlife employee gave every snake-hating yahoo in Utah permission to kill any snake anytime, anywhere, in direct violation of state wildlife laws.

Wildlife officer (let's call him Bubba), said you can kill any snake that poses a threat to you. That's not true, Bubba. Native snakes are protected from wanton killing in Utah. All snakes. Statewide. The only exception is that you are allowed to kill a Great Basin rattlesnake in your yard in the rare event that you might be in imminent danger, of which there is a high improbability due to this species' docile disposition. All you have to do is take three steps back. But Bubba said it was okay to kill a snake, any snake, just because you're afraid of it.

This declaration was a death sentence for all 32 snake species in the state because there is a ridiculous number of people who can't differentiate between a rattlesnake and a harmless snake, or who think all snakes are dangerous. Silly me. All this time I thought the DWR's mission was to protect wildlife.

5 | Gearing Up

I worked too hard to have my efforts subverted by the very agency that made the laws and issued me a license to save snakes and provide an option for the safety and benefit of the snake-fearing public.

Killing snakes goes against everything I stand for. This is true whether someone else does the deed or it falls on my shoulders. When road cruising, we often find snakes that were hit by cars but are still alive. Some of them have suffered for hours. With no chance for survival, I feel a responsibility to euthanize them as humanely as possible. This detestable task puts me in a foul and vulgar mood.

I am patient with most people most of the time, doing my best to understand that fear, no matter how irrational it may appear, usually has a solid footing based on indoctrination or trauma. On the other hand, some people have no justification for their actions other than sheer ignorance, cowardice, or an insecure need to look tough.

One of the worst calls I ever got from a homeowner happened a few years in. It came from an affluent neighborhood on Salt Lake's east bench where most of my customer base was located. It was a typical summer day and a normal removal call, or so I thought.

Arriving at the house, I was greeted in the front yard by a small group of people consisting of the homeowners and a few neighbors. On the front porch next to the front door was a bucket, and next to that, a seemingly out-of-place shovel leaned conspicuously against the wall.

"The snake's in there," one guy said, callously pointing at the bucket.

As I walked toward the porch, the head of a very attractive young rattlesnake, not quite three feet long, appeared over the bucket's rim, eyes alert and focused, her curious tongue tasting the morning air as though nothing was the matter. She looked perfectly normal other than the fact that she wasn't trying to escape from the bucket, nor did she retreat into it at my approach. Upon looking into the bucket, the awful truth became apparent.

This gentle, sweet snake, which had done nothing to anyone, had been lacerated down the upper third of her body on the left side. Her entrails were exposed, still moist and glistening from her recent assault. Below that, about half way down, her spine was not only broken and bent at a 30-degree angle, it was also twisted 180 degrees so that her ventral surface was facing upward in a grotesque and unnatural distortion. I was livid but tried to suppress my rage.

Surveying the group, I asked in a demanding tone, "Who did this?" They just stood there, most of them looking sheepishly at their shoes. Then a woman, presumably the homeowner, spoke. "One of our neighbors did," she said quietly.

"Was it one of these guys?" I asked, gesturing toward the four men in the group. No one said a word. Most of them tried to avoid my gaze, but one guy glanced up at me with a stare so full of malicious contempt there was no doubt he wanted to dispatch me with the shovel.

The culprit had revealed himself.

I'm normally a very composed and diplomatic person — the proverbial nice guy. Too nice for my own good most of the time, even to people who don't deserve it. But this was no time for niceties. I was dealing with a sadistic coward — one that didn't have the guts to admit what he'd done. I glared back at him.

"So, the big, strong man can't even kill a little snake with a shovel, is that right?" I tried to contain my anger. "That's kind of pathetic, don't you think? Don't you know that civilized people don't kill animals with shovels? But you started the job so you should have had the balls to finish it. Now you're going to make me do your dirty work for you, am I right?" I told him with anatomical accuracy where he could ram his shovel.

Silence was the only sound. I gently transferred the snake to my bucket, her unblinking eyes unable to convey the agonizing pain she was feeling. I didn't want things to escalate to physical violence and I most certainly didn't want their money. Not that anyone offered. I just wanted to be rid of these awful people.

"You could have called me to move this snake," I reminded them as I was leaving, "but it's a little late for that now, isn't it?"

Perhaps the homeowner had called me first, but then this demented dipstick took over. I have no idea. The nice guy side of me tries to give everyone the benefit of the doubt, but by covering for each other, these people were all complicit. Worse still, they waited until they had botched the job before doing the right thing.

"You don't call the snake removal guy AFTER you screw things up on your own," I reminded them. "This snake is the property of the state and I ought to report you. You're also guilty of animal abuse and torture."

It was the type of act I would have reported to the DWR if I thought they'd do anything about it. The wanton killing of snakes is supposed to be illegal, but the state doesn't care because someone might actually have to leave their air-conditioned office to investigate.

Killing a snake or any other animal out of fear or ignorance doesn't make someone a tough guy. It makes him a gutless coward. Trying to kill an animal with a shovel and failing is even worse. I will never understand how any conscientious person can resort to this sort of unprovoked barbarism and consider him or herself to be a rational human being.

Could I have been more diplomatic? Of course. But I had been pushed beyond diplomacy. Sadly, you can't fix stupid. Sometimes all you can do is shame it in front of its peers. This troglodyte may or may not kill the next rattlesnake he sees, but I hope he thinks twice about it.

I have seen far too many instances of toxic masculinity gone wrong. So many big, tough guys kill snakes, because apparently, looking down and seeing something more than two inches long intimidates them. Men with this problem also have a tendency to drive really big pickup trucks. Based on this factor alone, there are hordes of insecure men with major shortcomings. Must be an epidemic.

The group stood there as I drove off, my blood boiling and adrenaline surging. I took the innocent victim of human stupidity home, placed her in a Tupperware container and put it in the chest freezer in my basement. The cold would do the rest. It would be a quick and painless, albeit unnecessary death for an animal that didn't deserve such an awful fate.

It's not unusual for people to fear snakes enough to want to kill them, but it's unnecessary in a time of heightened environmental awareness and unprecedented access to information.

Relocating a snake is always the preferred way to mitigate a snake dilemma as opposed to the antagonistic 'shovel method' of snake removal. Of course, there was no way to know how many snakes met the business end of a shovel for each one I rescued, but there are conservation-minded folks out there who understand and appreciate the interconnectedness of all life and don't want the daunting task of deciding which creatures get to live and which ones should die. Killing any animal is usually an arbitrary, flawed, and misinformed decision.

With the type of apathetic ineptitude I've come to expect from a bloated bureaucracy, the DWR does very little to enforce Utah's non-game wildlife laws.

More recently, under the direction of a new state herpetologist, new rules were implemented that placed already unenforceable wildlife laws in the hands of citizen herpers who are expected to be self-policing. Field herping now requires an annual fee, passing an online quiz, and a mandatory reporting of field data by laypersons. Animals that were previously protected as "species of special concern" had those protections removed, allowing collection with the purchase of an inexpensive permit. This includes out-of-state residents.

I have three major issues: 1. Why would people pay to do what they've always been able to do for free? 2. How can the state "require" people to report field data? 3. Why would Utah sell collection permits to non-residents? What's the benefit in having out-of-staters absconding with Utah's wildlife?

Obviously, it's a way for the state to make money from non-game animals. I'm surprised it took them so long to figure something out. The only animals that have ever been important were the ones they could sell licenses to shoot. These changes won't do anything to protect native herpetofauna or thwart poaching. This comes as no surprise in a world that's doing its best to monetize absolutely everything, including the exploitation of the natural world.

Snakes are unique and vital members of the biotic communities in which they live, and any ecosystem with snakes is a vibrant and healthy habitat. Snakes are mid-level predators, meaning that they eat certain animals, and they in turn, become prey for other animals, making them vital components in the food chain.

When human beings established the first agrarian societies, the greatest threats to our survival were the rodents that would have decimated food crops. Those crops are still at risk from rodents today. Because snakes are just sentient rodent traps with teeth, they're the best defense against hordes of hungry vermin and the diseases they can carry. Everyone should want a harmless snake or two in their yard to control pests.

In addition to rodent control, snakes are invaluable for their contributions to medical science. Snake venoms and their derivatives are used to treat a host of human conditions. Ironically, the same toxins that can kill a mouse or rat can also destroy cancer cells while leaving healthy cells untouched.

According to the Asian Pacific Journal of Tropical Biomedicine, "Snake venom is a complex mixture of enzymes, peptides, carbohydrates, minerals and proteins of low molecular mass with specific chemical and biological activities. Components of snake venoms can be used in the treatment of cancer, arthritis, thrombosis, multiple sclerosis, pain, neuromuscular disorders, blood and cardiovascular disorders, infections and inflammatory diseases."

We'll talk more about venom in the chapter entitled *The Venom Factor*.

In the Western U.S., with the exception of parts of Arizona, New Mexico and Texas, if a snake doesn't have a rattle, it's completely harmless to humans. People who live in cottonmouth and copperhead country, or where coral snakes are found, need to take additional precautions and remain alert when recreating outdoors in snake-conducive conditions. (There are other types of venomous snakes but their venom is too weak to affect anything besides their prey, or they are simply too small or too disinclined to bite a human.)

In addition, many kinds of snakes shake their tails but that doesn't make them rattlesnakes. I have been preaching this doctrine for more than 50 years, yet I'm constantly bombarded with questions about how to identify a rattlesnake.

The Only Good Snake . . .

The most obvious and notable distinction of a rattlesnake is, of course, the rattle for which the snake is named. This structure at the end of the snake's tail is a segmented, hollow appendage that makes a distinctive sound when shaken. Some people say it sounds like a Rain Bird sprinkler. A snake's rattle, along with its scales, are made of keratin, the same substance of which our hair and nails are made. All other snakes are harmless serpents whose tails taper to a point. Sometimes a rattlesnake's rattle will break off, but a rattler will never have a pointed tail. A harmless snake may lose the end of its tail to a predator, leaving it with a blunted rather than a pointed tip, but that doesn't mean it's a rattlesnake.

In case the tail isn't visible, harmless snakes generally have a shiny appearance much like glossy paint. In contrast, rattlers have a dull finish more like flat primer, along with an obvious ridge on each scale known as a keel, giving them a rougher, textured appearance. They also have elliptical pupils and an obvious "pit" on each side of the face between the eye and nostril. These are the infrared heat detection pits that identify them as pit vipers.

Snakes are secretive creatures that rely on camouflage and stealth to avoid predators and catch their prey. As cold-blooded animals, snakes can't control their internal body temperature, putting them at the mercy of their environment. This is why you may see them basking in the sun on rocks or trails throughout the day. Once they reach the optimal temperature for regulating digestion and other metabolic processes (around 85° F), they go back into the shade or underground to avoid overheating. Many species become nocturnal during summer months to avoid extreme daytime temperatures.

August was always a slow month for snake calls because of the heat. When I'd tell some people this, they looked confused. "But," they'd ask, "snakes are cold-blooded, so don't they *like* the heat? Don't they *need* the heat?" These are valid questions. Basically, snakes like the same temps we do, which are 70s and 80s; they can't handle temps in the 90s or 100s, at least not for very long.

Reptiles are completely at the mercy of their ambient environment, generating none of their own body heat. If they get too cold, they cannot function, and many of them will die even before they freeze to death because metabolic processes like digestion and circulation cease.

At the other extreme, reptiles will most certainly die if they can't escape from oppressive heat. This is known as heat-induced rigor. The only way a reptile can warm up or cool down (known as thermoregulation) is to move to a location where the temperature is conducive to optimal metabolic function. During times of oppressive heat, snakes go into rodent burrows or other places where temps are in the moderate range, sometimes becoming nocturnal until things cool down again.

There was almost always a lull in August when my phone would hardly ring for two or three weeks. These snakeless days meant it was just too hot for snakes to go about their normal routines during the hottest part of the summer.

In the Northern Hemisphere, snakes are active from late spring to early fall, depending on the weather, and you can expect to see some species, like garter snakes, in city parks and vacant lots where they manage to survive quite well in suburbia. Depending on where you live, you need to be in specific habitats to see certain species. Anyone who recreates outdoors on a regular basis has certainly seen snakes — even rattlesnakes — in their travels. But what if you're someone who doesn't want to see a snake? What should you do?

Even though snakes can hear more frequencies than previously thought, making noise won't necessarily scare them away. They do feel vibrations through the ground, so if you want to reduce your chances of seeing snakes, walk with heavy steps. You may get tired feet, but the snakes will know you're coming and will have a chance to get out of your way.

If you're hiking, be sure to look on the other side of rocks or logs before stepping over them, and always look before you sit down. Stay away from rocky areas and thick brush, and never reach into a hole or place your hands on a ledge if you can't see what's there.

People who live on the fringes of suburbia adjacent to wild habitat can expect to share their yards with all kinds of wildlife. Like many other animals, snakes come into our yards looking for food, water, and cover. As opportunistic predators, snakes will go where the food is. If they can't get a meal in your yard, they'll move on to the neighbors' yard. Remove outdoor pet food, birdseed, garbage, thick vegetation, and anything else that attracts rodents.

Many of my customers used poisoned bait containers in their yards, yet they wanted me to remove the harmless snake that would rid them of rodents at no charge and without using poison. From a logical perspective, this made no sense, but fear overrides logic most of the time.

I encouraged these folks to consider the consequences. The words "insecticide," "pesticide," "herbicide," or any word that contains the suffix "cide" means to kill, often killing life forms far beyond their intended targets. Wild birds and animals as well as pet dogs and cats often eat poisoned rodents. If you really don't want a snake in your yard, please use live traps and release rodents away from your home where they provide a food source for other wildlife. We don't make the planet a better place by poisoning it. If you have ever watched in anguish, as I have, as a hawk or an owl dies from ingesting a poisoned rodent, you know what I mean.

Glue traps are another insidious form of controlling pests. If your pest control company tries to push these traps on you, tell them to take a hike. These traps yield tragic results by trapping the very animals that would eat many more insects in a few days than one of these traps can kill in a month. It might feel like an effective solution because you can see the results, but a small paper patch isn't an accurate indicator of your overall pest problem. There are far more humane and effective options available.

Whether a snake hangs around for a while or just passes through depends on the available food supply, access to water, places to hide, shed, lay eggs, or give birth. Random encounters are normal, but there are things you can do to mitigate a persistent snake problem.

Every yard inspection included a list of do's and don'ts for a rodent-free, snake-free yard and home. If a yard isn't inviting to rodents, it's not inviting to snakes either, because they typically won't stick around where there's no food. If you went to your favorite restaurant and it was closed, you'd go somewhere else, right?

When you're a snake, everything wants to eat you, so most displays of aggression are an attempt to frighten away a potential predator, and to a snake, you are a potential predator. The snake that rattles or hisses at you from the side of the trail when you're hiking isn't a mean snake, a mad snake, or an aggressive snake, and he's not threatening you. He's just trying to save his own life by letting you know he's there so you don't step on him. This is for your safety as well as his. This makes rattlesnakes the most courteous of all snakes.

Winter snake calls were rare but not unheard of. My first December snake call took me 80 miles south. A restoration company was tearing the sheetrock out of a basement due to mold when they discovered a trio of gopher snakes hibernating in the wall. They also found a mummified bat and a hornet's nest.

Critters were getting inside the house along with unwanted moisture that was causing mold. I inspected the foundation and took pictures of all potential ingress and egress locations.

The three amigos spent the winter at my house until I could release them in the spring. They were three of the homeliest gopher snakes I have ever seen, but just as deserving of being rescued as any other animals. It was the first time I caught snakes in one calendar year and released them in another, but it wouldn't be the last.

For the next decade or so, snake relocation would fill my life with meaning and purpose. These creatures — misunderstood, overly vilified, yet strangely compelling — gave me a reason to lace up my boots, dodging thistle and bramble, to do a job most people would rather watch from a comfortable distance.

Far from being the scary villains of lore and legend, snakes deserve our gratitude. When you find a venomous snake in your yard, eating rodents and keeping us all safe from disease, you can repay it by calling someone like me to escort it back to its rightful home.

Each snake had its own story: residing under a porch, coiled beneath an air conditioning unit, sunning next to a swimming pool, or hopelessly tangled in plastic garden mesh, unaware of the stress it was causing some poor human. And there I was, part mental health counselor, part extraction specialist, part myth-buster, armed with snake tongs and worn-out boots. I served as ambassador for some of nature's least-loved but most vulnerable and vital creatures.

For me, it was like stepping into quiet chaos and nudging it gently back into balance. Each time I saw panic give way to curiosity or watched someone shift from fear to fascination, I knew that what I did mattered to both man and beast.

I had the best part-time, summertime job anywhere. The question now was whether I could make it profitable.

CHAPTER 6

The Money Conundrum

"If you can get paid for doing what you love, every paycheck is a bonus." –Oprah Winfrey

Someone asked how I planned to make money rescuing rattlesnakes. It was a good question. From a profit perspective, rescuing urban rattlesnakes is a poor man's enterprise at best. Or maybe I'm just a lousy businessman.

Before starting Wasatch Snake Removal in the summer of 2014, I spent six years moving snakes for a guy, the owner of an alleged reptile rescue organization, whose methods were less than professional. His interest in reptiles stemmed mostly from his acquisition of them and less so in their welfare. He was an animal hoarder, ill equipped financially to run a rescue, but like so many other members of the herp community at the time, I hooked up with him. After all, he had permits for all the cool stuff: large constrictors, alligators, snapping turtles, and venomous snakes — what herpers call "hots."

Someone once said, "If you're good at something, never do it for free." I earned my stripes by moving snakes as a volunteer for six years to get the experience, but once I made the decision to go into business for myself, I intended to be paid. And I fully intended to raise the bar for urban snake removal from what was currently available. (Libel laws prevent me from going into further detail at this time.)

Utahns are cheap. Ask anyone in the service industries, where 10 to 15 percent gratuities are still the norm. Those same people are only willing to pay a minimal amount of money to save a snake. Any more than that and some of them will go to the garage and grab a shovel. For many, economics is more important than ethics.

There was a period of trial and error before I found the right price point for relocating a snake from a residential yard. There would be a standard flat fee with adjustments based on the difficulty of each scenario. For instance, I would charge more for out-of-county calls, night calls, multiple snakes, and difficult or dangerous captures such as crawling under decks or through dense shrubbery.

My plan, initially, was to charge a flat rate of $50 to remove a snake from a residential yard. This amount covered time, gas, and other overhead costs, but it didn't leave much in the way of a profit margin. To make matters worse, I received pushback from the very start.

"Fifty dollars! Why should I pay 50 dollars for you to move a snake when I can kill it for free?" This oft-repeated mantra got stale in a hurry. As a result, I lowered my price to $35 where it remained for the first two years. It was a ridiculously low sum for so much work and the potential risks involved.

Although the guy who ran the rescue claimed to move snakes free of charge, his ruse was to make small talk with the homeowner while tapping his foot and clearing his throat, making it clear that he expected remuneration. But free means free, so it was both dishonest and disingenuous. I refused to play that game.

I spent the first two years solo. My business model, if there was one, was the ethical conviction that I would move snakes regardless of the profit motive (or the lack of one), because saving snakes, not making money, was my primary goal. If this sounds shamelessly altruistic or hopelessly naive, so be it, but I was already accustomed to not being paid, so what did it matter? Still, it would be nice to make a little money instead of spending hundreds of dollars out of my own pocket, which I did as a volunteer.

Reasonable people, I assumed, would pay a reasonable fee for a valuable service provided by a professionally licensed, state approved company. After all, what other professionals give their work away? It was going to be an interesting venture and a giant learning experience, but it wasn't my first rodeo. I ran my own wedding photography business for many years. That, combined with my job in local government meant I was no stranger to working with the public. Those jobs taught me more about human nature than I ever cared to know.

By my third year in business, I was up to my eyebrows in snake calls, often getting a call while I was already on a call — especially on weekends. It was time to bring someone else onboard.

It was a pleasant surprise to learn that I didn't have to advertise for employees. They always came to me. Every year I was in business, at least one person, and often more, would call and want to work for me. Only a few of them were qualified, whereas the majority had no snake experience whatsoever. That was fine as long as they were willing to learn and presented themselves well. Others were downright scary.

I already knew many of the folks in the local herp community, some by reputation only, but I alienated a few of them by opposing a proposal by the DWR to allow the breeding and subsequent sale of Midget-faded rattlesnakes. Based on my presentation to the state wildlife board, the proposal was withdrawn. It made me a bit of a pariah for a while, even among those who had no intention of breeding. Still, there were good people who wanted to relocate rattlesnakes, at least until the glamor aspect was stripped away and the difficulty factor was revealed. As a result, I burned out a few short-timers in a hurry.

One of my first truly dedicated employees was Jordan, a young, newly married man who was pursuing a degree in invertebrate biology. As a genuine people person, he was working as a presenter for a local reptile education venue, giving reptile shows at parties and public events. Despite being gregarious and enthusiastic, he lacked experience with venomous snakes. Moreover, he lived a county away. That wasn't a bad thing as it allowed me to more easily expand my service area, but it didn't provide me the additional help I needed in the heart of the Salt Lake Valley where 80 percent of my customer base was located.

Jordan learned the ropes quickly and soon became an indispensable cog in my snake-moving machine, taking calls in both counties and providing exceptional service. Customers appreciated his friendly demeanor and his knowledge of the natural world, which extended far beyond snakes.

Of the many compliments I received about Jordan, the best one came from a man who was serving in Iraq. Jordan had moved two amorous gopher snakes for a woman who was leery of them living in the rock garden near her front door, but mostly she was afraid she might accidentally back over them in the driveway.

After capturing the four-foot snakes, Jordan performed a standard short-distance translocation, making sure to move them far enough away that they wouldn't return, while keeping them in familiar territory as mandated by the state.

A few days later, I received the following email from the woman's husband:

> Dave,
>
> Thank you so much for the service you offer and the professional and caring way your staff work with clients and handle snakes.
>
> My wife discovered two snakes at our house and called your service. Within two hours Jordan arrived, captured the snakes, released them unharmed back into their habitat, assured my wife that all was well, and she also received a follow-up call from you within that time period. Amazing, caring customer service!
>
> I'm especially grateful because I am in the military and working away from home, so I couldn't be there, but your team made my wife feel comfortable and safe. She expressed how great Jordan was in finding and capturing the snakes, and especially how careful he was to explain what he was doing and why, and why the snakes were there, and how he was going to release them safely.
>
> You obviously care about wildlife and the environment and train your staff very well.
>
> Sincerely,
> Greg

Thanks for the kind words, Greg, and thank you for your service to our country.

As the team grew, we helped anyone with a snake-related issue within a four-county area and beyond. More than once, one of my team members or I drove 200 miles round-trip to help someone who needed it. We provided a valuable public service and we were damn good at what we did, with excellent response times and nominal fees, which sometimes barely covered our overhead costs. That's why I found it interesting that there were (and still are) individuals in the local animal community who believed we were money-grubbing miscreants for moving rattlesnakes and charging for it. It was nice of them, I thought, to be so generous with our time and resources.

When I started Wasatch Snake Removal, I did it with the understanding that I would sacrifice my summers to save snakes. I couldn't leave town for a weekend or even shut my phone off because I was on call 24/7. My rapidly growing business took a lot of time — so much time in fact that I had to bring even more people on board so I could help everyone who called. This was in addition to my full-time job.

After the third year, business was just too good. I needed more help because I wanted to move snakes in more than just the four counties that had been my initial bailiwick. At a meeting on August 12, 2016, the State Wildlife Board unanimously approved my request for statewide jurisdiction to relocate all of Utah's indigenous snake species. All I needed now were more bodies to help me.

I started by pressing into service one of Utah's most renowned field herpers. Jamison would cover the area from North Salt Lake northward to Weber County. It's a large area, but wasn't a source of frequent calls. Jamison worked from home and couldn't be bothered too often, but he was always Johnny-on-the-spot when I needed him. Once, after he "saved" a woman from a baby garter snake, I texted Jamison to tell him that he was a bold and intrepid snake man.

His reply was, "You misspelled old and inept." He's a funny guy.

I brought others on board as needed, training them as I went, filtering out the ones who weren't sincere, or after a short time decided that snake removal wasn't the glitzy job they had seen on TV. It was inconvenient, sweaty, tiring work.

Casey was my guy in Northern Utah, fielding calls from Weber County and adjacent areas. With a knack for working with snakes and most other wildlife, he later went on to start his own multi-species relocation business.

Jason came pre-trained and ready to rock and roll, assisting Jordan with calls in the southern part of our service area. As the business grew, Aspen and Chris moved snakes 300 miles to the south, near the juncture of Arizona and Nevada.

Averi and Bebe were the only two women who applied and I hired them both. They were enthusiastic if not experienced in the beginning. I loved the fact that I could send a woman to a customer's home to remove a rattlesnake. People expected an ugly, hairy man to show up, so when an attractive woman knocked on their door, snake bucket in hand, the reaction was quite different. I'm guessing that many men were ego-shamed at the sight of a woman capturing a rattlesnake and placing it in a bucket as casually as picking a flower.

Averi and Bebe would prove to be invaluable members of the team, providing the assistance I needed while putting a pretty face on the gritty business of snake removal.

Petite and poised, with curly locks of flaming red hair and a vivacious personality, Averi defied every stereotype of what a snake wrangler should look like. She was the last person anyone would ever suspect of relocating rattlesnakes. A piano teacher by profession, Averi once moved a snake in a prestigious gated community. She called to check in once the snake was safely released and to make a confession.

"I hope you don't mind," she said, "but I signed the people's kid up for piano lessons while I was there."

"Damnit, Averi!" I joked, "No moonlighting on the job!"

My 2017 Certificate of Registration arrived from the DWR. The state approved all of the subordinate individuals (I despise that term) whom I chose to help me relocate rattlesnakes. All eight of them were knowledgeable, enthusiastic, competent, and trustworthy. All we needed at that point were some snakes to move, and that certainly wasn't going to be a problem.

Moving snakes was a huge commitment for those who were up for it. Individuals on my COR couldn't just run around moving snakes on their own. It had to be done under the auspices of Wasatch Snake Removal. No freelancing. I needed to know what hours each of them were available to take calls, dispatching the closest person whenever possible, and there were other caveats involved.

6 | *The Money Conundrum*

I often had to leave family parties, dinners at restaurants, church, work, personal projects, etc., to go on snake calls. I couldn't even go to a movie in the summertime because I couldn't turn my phone off for two hours. I didn't expect the same level of commitment from the members of my team because they had lives, jobs, and families of their own, but they relieved me of a gigantic burden.

Technically, they weren't employees of mine, but rather, contracted agents. I didn't pay them because they got paid directly from the homeowners who called us, and I made it explicitly clear that they were to provide their own equipment and insurance. Except for work on movie sets, I never took a dime of what my people made. If they were willing to subject themselves to the aforementioned conditions, they deserved every penny they got, if they got any at all. Like an old mother hen, I expected them to maintain contact, calling or texting to let me know when a snake had been captured, and again after it had been released and they were safely on their way home.

As a team, we moved dozens of snakes every year, but it wasn't always easy. We usually got paid enough to cover our expenses, but not always. It was definitely an ethical conviction and a labor of love.

My customers ranged from confirmed snake haters who may have actually killed a snake except for the fact that they were too afraid to do so, to those who accepted snakes as a fact of life and didn't want to see one harmed. Many of these folks acknowledged that the snake wasn't in their yard, but it was they who were the real interlopers. This valley and its surrounding foothills belonged to the wildlife long before white settlers arrived in 1847. It has been a slow but steady series of battles against nature ever since, and nature is losing the war.

Whereas rattlesnakes were extirpated from the valley decades ago, the western foothills of the Wasatch Mountain Range, with its many canyons and riparian ecology, remains prime snake habitat. Bordering the Salt Lake Valley on the east, it is also a prime area for real estate development and the building of luxury homes, making it rife for snake/human conflict. Each call gave me an opportunity to educate my customers about the fact that it was a violation of state wildlife law to kill a snake.

By the third year, we were a known quantity and it was time to raise our prices. Jamison reminded me that $35 was no longer a reasonable fee because, as he put it, he was in a deficit situation even before he left the house. He was right, of course, so I raised our fee to $50 with surprisingly little pushback.

Even our customers knew we were worth more than that. One man told me he would have paid 10 times the amount I charged him to remove a rattler from his yard, but he said it after he already paid me. How convenient.

Another man said there was "no way in hell that he could ever put THAT snake in THAT bucket with THAT stick. Not for a million dollars. Not for 10 million."

A few (potential) customers didn't want to pay for professional rattlesnake removal at all, so they opted to do it themselves. This is illegal because a certificate is required from the state to interact with a rattler, but I'm never going to lower the boom on someone who wants to do the right thing by saving a snake.

On the other hand, if someone killed a snake without cause, we'd be having a long talk about conservation, ecological balance, peaceful coexistence, and responsible anthropogenic dominion.

The risks of do-it-yourself venomous snake relocation are not something most people want to deal with, and for good reason. Even though no one dies from snakebite in Utah (and the odds are astronomically low everywhere in the U.S.), a bite from a rattlesnake, even a species as benign as a Great Basin, can be crazy expensive due the exorbitantly high cost of antivenin, also known as antivenom.

A bill for a rattlesnake bite can easily reach $100,000 or more, but the risk can be eliminated entirely by calling a professional to do the job safely and efficiently for everyone's benefit, snakes and humans alike. Surely this was a service that rational people should willingly pay for, and that professionals deserved to be paid for.

So, for my critics, I had a few questions:

It's acceptable to own a pet store and make a living at it, right? In fact, it's expected. It's okay to run a groomery, or be a dog walker or a pet sitter and charge a fee. It's also expected that if you run an animal education or entertainment enterprise that you charge for your expertise and your overhead costs. It's normal to make a full or partial living as a reptile breeder or an animal importer/exporter. It's okay to run a non-profit rescue or be a rehabber who can solicit donations, claim tax exempt status, yet still draw a salary, am I right?

No logical person would argue these facts. Yet for some reason, if I understood it correctly, I was supposed to relocate rattlesnakes at my own expense. Okay, if I only moved a few snakes here and there, I'd do it for free, no problem. But with volume comes costs, and it would cost me several thousand dollars per season to move snakes at my own expense. I know this because I did it for six years, so I already paid my dues. Not only that, but I couldn't expect to retain a team of professionals unless they were being fairly compensated for their time and skill.

In Arizona, businesses like mine charge between $150 and $250 for snake removal and no one bats an eyelash, and I was quickly tiring of those who said I should do it as an altruistic endeavor — a free public service. I didn't see them stepping up to move snakes, free or otherwise. They wouldn't have lasted a week during my busy season.

Homeowners expect to pay for a professional service. After all, have you ever heard of a plumber or painter who gives their skills away? (If so, I'd like their numbers.) I've had homeowners tell me how much they appreciated our quick arrival times, how we provided answers to their questions about snakes, and how they enjoyed the peace of mind that came from not being afraid to use their yard because there was no longer a venomous snake in it.

These were the people who paid me without hesitation. They loved our educational website with its snake ID page, knowing that they could call or text and have their snake questions answered quickly 24-hours a day. Oddly, I even fielded snake questions in the frigid months of winter.

We often moved snakes at no charge because I didn't ever want someone to not call me because they couldn't afford the service, or to kill a snake because they didn't have the money to save it. I never refused service to anyone over money.

We didn't get paid by police departments because it wasn't worth the hassle of setting up billing accounts with so many municipal agencies, so police calls were always free. The same was true of animal control agencies and humane associations. This was my public service — my way of giving back to the community.

There have been times when we didn't get paid by homeowners because they assumed we were paid by the state (in actuality, I had to pay the state for the privilege), or simply because they were too cheap.

The average snake relocation took two to three hours from the time the phone rang until we got back home. We may have driven five miles or 50 miles. We got stuck in rush hour traffic. We had to crawl through thick shrubbery, under decks, porches or crawlspaces, into window wells and basements, fish a snake from a nasty toilet or scale a 20-foot-high retaining wall. We had to enter scary neighborhoods after dark and deal with hostile or hysterical people.

Sometimes the snake got away from us, and sometimes it was long gone before we got there. Most of the time, however, we caught the snake. Then we had to take a hike to release it. This usually meant an uphill hike on the west-facing slopes of the Wasatch Range during the heat of a summer day.

For their long-term well-being, snakes require releasing within a specified distance from the capture site in suitable habitat, within range of an unidentified hibernaculum, but away from hiking trails and other human activity whenever possible. If these protocols aren't followed, mortality rates increase substantially and there's no point in saving a snake today only to have it die when winter comes.

Doing it right is essential. My predecessor didn't do it right, killing virtually every snake he ever claimed to save, because he was too lazy to follow the rules. But no one, including the DWR who granted his license, ever questioned his methods. This was because he was a convenient dumping ground for every exotic or invasive reptile that popped up or made the local news, thereby taking the burden off the state for having to relocate an alligator to Louisiana or a snapping turtle to Texas. The public, for its part, was made to feel warm and fuzzy, believing that the animals had been 'rescued,' having no idea that it was actually the place where reptiles went to die or be sold.

Under the stipulation of my license, the state, which thought snake removal only happened on weekdays during normal business hours, prohibited a snake from remaining in our possession longer than a few hours. Nevertheless, I discouraged my people from doing night releases due to safety issues. I didn't want them hiking mountain trails alone in the dark, especially after Jordan suspected he was stalked by a mountain lion while releasing a snake by himself after sundown. The rule was, if they wanted to release a snake after dark, it was up to them to be careful. If not, they were to take it home, leave it in the bucket, and release it the next day. The state didn't need to know.

Snake calls were almost never convenient, usually coming at the worst possible times and often overlapping. Conversely, days would go by without the phone ringing, especially during the hottest part of the summer when snakes avoided the heat by aestivating in rodent burrows. August was the peak month for these reptilian doldrums.

With nothing else to do, I sometimes found myself bored out of my mind and begging the universe for a snake call. But I found the solution! All I had to do was watch a movie, sit down to a meal, call a friend, drive more than 10 miles from home, jump in the tub or take a nap, and voilà! Snake call! It never failed. Sadly, it also worked with telemarketers.

One Fourth of July during the pandemic, I was called away from the finest barbequed feast I ever had the privilege to salivate over. After driving 20 miles to the house, the owner informed me that a rattlesnake had slithered across his pool deck and into a retaining wall that was almost completely hidden by an impenetrable barricade of rose bushes. The roses were on a narrow ledge where the yard dropped off into a steep, rocky ravine. Wonderful.

Wearing only shorts and a t-shirt, I had no intention of pursuing that snake. Not without a suit of armor. All I could do was spray the area with a hose and hope to dowse the snake enough to make it come out on its own. After spraying every crevice and saturating the area thoroughly there was no sign of a snake. It was a waste of my time and all I wanted was to get back to my patriotic meal.

After 45 minutes, I told the owner that the snake was probably deep enough in the wall that it wasn't getting wet. I also told him about the perfectly cooked steak and all the fixings I abandoned in response to his call in which he had failed to mention anything about rose bushes. He was unfazed.

I never felt right about charging a fee when I hadn't produced a result, but this was a national holiday and he had sabotaged it with his faux snake call. I'm not saying there wasn't a snake; I'm sure there was, but it wasn't necessarily a rattler. It could just as easily have been a gopher snake. But I had made a time commitment and a 40-mile round trip only to get stiffed by Chippy McCheapskate. He probably wouldn't have paid me even if I had caught the snake.

With a second part-time job writing and editing for a local magazine, I hemorrhaged a ton of money in taxes each year. It's a travesty that the government works so hard to disincentivize (and even penalize) small business initiative and entrepreneurship. It took one of my part-time jobs to pay the taxes for both of them. I didn't make much money at either one, but I either wrote and edited for free, or I saved snakes for free. Writing and editing is too much work not to get paid, so it's a good thing that saving snakes was a labor of love, because thanks to Uncle Sam, that's almost what it became.

I bought team shirts for my people, fancy engraved pens for my customers, and spent $40 each for fancy lids for $7 snake buckets. Even snake bucket lids have gone high-tech, and I just had to have some! Reinvestment in the business would lower my tax liability.

Before long, Wasatch Snake Removal had business cards, a bank account, debit card, website, a growing customer base, and was even turning a modest profit. It's like I've always said, "Be nice to snakes and they'll be nice to you!" I made a corporate donation to a local non-profit group and was listed in their fall newsletter which helped with advertising. Most important, my people were making money.

6 | *The Money Conundrum*

Adding to the frustrating cost of running a small business was the fact that many of my customers were extremely wealthy. Filthy, stinking rich as the saying goes. I've been to homes that looked more like palaces, resplendent with the types of fine, hand-made, imported furnishings, art, and knick-knacks that could just as easily have been displayed in a castle or museum.

Tucked back in the green recesses of our local canyons — one in particular — these "estates" as they are known, make the average suburban home look like a hovel. Sitting on lots that encompass acres of land, doing a yard inspection at one of these homes could take hours. For that reason, yard inspections were billed at an hourly rate.

It took me a while to realize how many homes had video doorbells. Many times I stood on the front porch of some grotesquely oversized McMansion, making snarky, out loud comments to myself such as, "Got enough money?" or "I feel so bad for these poor rich people." I don't know how many of them heard me, but it could explain why I didn't get better tips.

One of these palatial yards belonged to a couple, both of whom were doctors. After purchasing an expensive pure-breed puppy, they wanted reassurance that there were no snakes in the yard. The "yard" consisted of five acres of mountainside that included an alpine meadow, aspen grove, pine forest, small wetland, large rock outcrop, and a thirty-foot-tall retaining wall to keep the mountainside at bay, complete with a manmade waterfall and wading pool.

I hobbled over every square foot of that yard on a knee that was long overdue for a good scoping to remove bits and shreds of torn cartilage. After prodding every crevice and flipping every reasonable rock, I explained to them that just because I didn't find a snake was not a guarantee that there weren't any, or that one wouldn't crawl into the yard at any moment. They understood, signed the disclaimer, paid me handsomely, and referred me to their neighbors. I needed more gigs like that.

But every coin has a flip side. I busted my butt getting to a home in an elite gated community where a rattlesnake was patiently hanging out in a rock garden. I prided myself on a fast response time for every call, and some of these truly affluent customers were willing to tip extra well for speedy service. Not this guy.

The home was a three-million-dollar fortress (I looked it up) on top of a mountain where it had no business being. It had garrets, turrets, and a 270-degree view of the Great Salt Lake and most of the Salt Lake Valley. In the driveway, a Lamborghini and a Range Rover sat side-by-side.

The owner, a short, loud, braggadocious man, pointed at the snake under a shrub in the front yard. "It's been there for a couple days," he said, "so I finally decided to call you."

"I appreciate it," I told him, as I hooked the snake, lowered it into a bucket, and screwed on the lid. Then I walked around the house and yard as a courtesy, just to make sure there weren't any more. It was standard procedure. Part of the service.

He probably thought I was done at that point, but in reality, my work hadn't even begun. I still had to hike this snake a safe distance away from the neighborhood while staying within required parameters from the capture site. This meant trudging up a hot, barren hillside with almost no shade, finding suitable habitat for the snake, photographing it, releasing it, then climbing back down and driving home for a much-needed shower.

"What do I owe you?" he asked, yanking his wallet from his back pocket.

"It's $35," I told him. (This was in the early days when people still balked at the thought of paying for snake removal. I cursed my predecessor for that.)

He rifled through his fat wallet where I could see a healthy wad of bills.

"Will you take $25?" he asked. Was he serious? Did this multimillionaire really intend to screw the snake guy out of 10 bucks?

"Is that the best you can do?" I asked

"Take it or leave it," he said. So I took it and left. And that dear reader is the difference in people.

The first rattlesnake call of 2015 came on May 24 at around 9 pm. I was on my (almost) nightly jog and completely out of breath when the call came. A guy near the zoo texted me a pic of a small buzzer butt in a crevice in his retaining wall. I hurried home, sweaty and panting, and called him back. I was ready to head out until he asked what I did with the snakes I moved. When I told him I was required by the state to release them, he said that didn't sound very exciting. He thought I should take them to schools and teach kids about them. I told him that I did a lot of public education but that my license didn't allow me to keep or display rattlesnakes, and even if it did, I couldn't possibly keep every snake I caught. Then, when he learned that I charged a whopping $35 to relocate a rattlesnake, he said he'd do it himself. Seriously? Hell, I'm worth $35 for the entertainment value alone!

For those who still think I should have relocated rattlesnakes at no charge, please feel free to elaborate. I'd love to hear your logic.

CHAPTER 7

The Museum

"Study nature, love nature, stay close to nature. It will never fail you." –Frank Lloyd Wright

The July sun rose reluctantly, like a giant bloodshot eyeball, spilling a hazy light onto the weary world below. Its soft rays crept around the edges of the curtains, filling my room with a surreal glow and prying my eyelids open with gentle fingers. Behind me, nestled in the small of my back, Nemo's quiet purr sputtered and rumbled like a Harley Davidson at low idle.

As a morning denier, I firmly believe that mornings shouldn't begin before noon. Still, I rubbed my weary eyes and peered out the window where Sunday morning was strutting its finery like a peacock in full regalia. It would be a shame to miss it.

I didn't get up this early to go to my day job, so no one was more surprised than me to find myself sitting on the front porch at 6 am wearing nothing but a bathrobe and ruminating about the cosmos with Nemo the Wonder Cat. He was a very philosophical feline.

Together we pondered the profundities of the universe, namely, why my navel, which used to be an innie, was working so hard to become an outie in my mid-life crisis years, but the revelation didn't come.

Just after seven, I waited patiently in the McDonald's drive-thru for the crackling, disembodied voice to take my order. The cheerful-sounding girl on the other end must have been a morning person. Bless her heart.

With a freshly brewed cup of motivation in my hand, I walked around the Utah Museum of Natural History, visible only to the jabbering magpies that patrol the skies and the security guards who watched me from the bowels of the building on glowing LCD screens. I acknowledged the cameras that monitored my every move, giving them a nod and a wave. I knew the guards, and they knew me. I was looking for rattlesnakes, but wouldn't you know it? The day I got up early was the day they slept late.

7 | *The Museum*

I met Ryder, the museum's newest security guard, who said he saw a snake a half hour after I left on Thursday evening. Apparently, the snakes don't come out when I'm there. That means I'm the best snake repellent the museum ever had. I should charge them more.

After starting Wasatch Snake Removal in the summer of 2014, the museum became my first commercial client. The Director of Facilities was a congenial, dignified man named Mike, who hired me at our first meeting. As he showed me around the grounds, Mike pointed out the various architectural features of the building, ruminating on its evolution and construction from conception to completion.

The Utah Museum of Natural History is a behemoth structure — a cavernous five-story concrete bunker festooned with copper cladding — a nod to the Rio Tinto Group, owner of the biggest open-pit copper mine in the U.S., and the corporate mining conglomerate that helped fund its construction. This was in addition to government funding and philanthropic support from many organizations and private citizens. But Rio Tinto claims most of the credit.

Rio Tinto (formerly Kennecott Copper Corporation) uses the museum as a public relations tool to boost its less-than-stellar corporate image as one of the Salt Lake Valley's biggest polluters, and before the technology boom, its largest employer as well. Their slogan, as it pertains to the museum, should be, "Promoting nature as we destroy it."

(In the interest of full disclosure, I should mention that my father spent 40 years of his life as a machinist at Kennecott's refinery. My sibs and I were housed, clothed, fed, and educated with Kennecott Copper money.)

Sitting on 17 acres in the foothills of the Wasatch Mountains, adjacent to the University of Utah, the museum is an imposing, southwest-facing structure visible from many parts of the valley, especially in the evening when the setting sun glances off the building's slowly oxidizing copper facade, making it glint like a giant, faded penny.

As an institution devoted to the teaching of natural history, anthropology, and all things wild, the museum's overarching goal is the identification and protection of the natural world, especially the flora and fauna within its own purview. This includes snakes.

I couldn't believe it! I had spent my life up to this point attempting to eradicate the systemic social stupidity of human beings toward snakes with no expectation of a reward, yet Mike was going to pay me to catch and relocate the museum's snakes. Not just for the safety of visitors, mind you, but primarily for the well-being of the snakes. The museum is very protective of its snakes. Poke me with a stick! I had died and gone to rattlesnake heaven!

The obvious dichotomy is that the museum's construction required that a huge chunk of mountainside be chiseled out, creating a ledge for the cavernous structure to sit on and lean into. The cut-away mountain fully encases five stories of the rear of the gigantic edifice in a reluctant embrace. You enter the front doors at ground level (the former level of ancient Lake Bonneville), but there is a rear exit from the fifth floor onto a mezzanine at another ground level five stories up, along with several terraces at various levels on the south side. In typical Rio Tinto fashion, a lot of nature was destroyed to commemorate nature.

Mike was especially proud of the grounds. With the state arboretum right next door, the landscaping is a mix of native and non-native vegetation — an invasion of native shrubs and grasses combined with a touch of human intervention for the sake of aesthetics and biodiversity. Native vegetation consists mainly of sagebrush and assorted grasses. Cacti and other drought-tolerant plants dot the area, and small trees are being encouraged to grow, but the prospect of any real shade is a distant dream.

Underneath it all is an elaborate network of pipes and sprinkler heads that water the thirsty plants during Utah's hot and mostly rainless summers. Once upon a time, a host of volunteer gardeners kept the myrtle spurge and other undesirable plants at bay, but during Covid, maintenance of the grounds was halted. This allowed the noxious and invasive plants to proliferate, causing the grounds to fall into weed-infested, fecund disarray, looking more like an abandoned lot than a curated desert garden.

Five large swales encircle the back and sides of the building. These are basically just large trenches filled with boulders of varying sizes, designed to divert spring runoff around the structure and into a large underground drainage system.

If you wanted to create rattlesnake-conducive habitat, you couldn't do better than to dig large trenches and fill them with rocks, especially on a mountainside where rattlesnakes already thrive. To a snake, these swales are like giant flashing neon signs that say, "Free Buffet and Lodging: Rattlesnakes Welcome Here!"

I didn't know it yet, but I would walk around this building hundreds of times over the next 10 years or so, moving rattlesnakes and hiking them back up the mountain. Under my agreement with Mike, I would walk the grounds twice a week at my convenience, moving any snakes I happened to find. In addition, I would respond to calls 24/7 from the security staff to relocate snakes that were discovered on the grounds by employees or visitors. I would track my time and submit a monthly invoice for payment.

The obvious disconnect to removing snakes from this place is that the snakes have every right to be here. This land was theirs millennia before humans arrived on the scene. In a court of law, the snakes could claim eminent domain but they wouldn't win. Not anymore. Public opinion is stacked against them and the best they can do is try to survive in a world filled with too many hostile humans.

Interpretive signage warned visitors about rattlesnakes without resorting to the pejorative language that only makes people more afraid. In essence, the message was, 'there are snakes here, they belong here, deal with it.

One evening, I was looking for an elusive buzzer butt that had no intention of being found when my phone rang. Saved by the bell! It was a homeowner in a gated community only ten minutes away.

After punching the security code into the keypad, the heavy steel gate rolled open with a groan. After driving through the gate and up the winding road, the house was easy to find. The place was lit up like a Christmas tree in July. Several neighbors had shown up and one guy had parked his jeep sideways in the driveway, its headlights illuminating the retaining wall of stacked rocks that paralleled the drive. This is where my buzzer butt was allegedly hiding.

It was an easy snatch and grab. I hooked the little cutie and gently pulled her out on the first try. After everyone took pictures of her in the bucket, they all entered my number into their phones. They were the nicest people, and they were going to tell their friends and neighbors about me. I always appreciated the folks who took the time and effort to do the right thing by saving a snake.

The following afternoon I got another call from museum security. A new security guard met me on the steps to the children's patio area — one of three patios on the south side and the one most favored by snakes, either for basking or to escape a cold drenching when the sprinklers popped up to water the xeriscaping. Here, kids could play in a large sandbox while pretending to dig up dinosaur bones. It was one of the first places I looked for snakes when doing a walk-around.

The snake was a young female with an attitude problem. She was hotter than a two-dollar pistol and had a chip on her proverbial shoulder. I'm not saying she wasn't a nice snake, but she definitely woke up on the wrong side of the rock pile that morning. She lay coiled next to the concrete stairwell about two steps down from the top, rattling and striking randomly, undoubtedly terrified. A crowd of about 30 people had gathered to get a good look at a real rattlesnake, and I suppose, to see how I was going to deal with her.

I unscrewed the lid from my bucket and was about to tong this little firecracker when a man's voice erupted from the group: "Why don't you just kill it?" he yelled. A low murmur rippled through the crowd.

I stopped what I was doing and turned to face my audience. My first inclination was to reply with, "Why don't we just kill you instead?" But realizing the opportunity to influence so many people at once, diplomacy overtook me and I blurted out something like, "Snakes are smackdab in the middle of the food chain. They eat a lot of things and a lot of things eat them. Every time you kill a snake, you deprive an eagle, hawk, owl, fox, or some other critter of a meal. Snakes are extremely important members of the biotic systems in which they live, and we need them, just like we need every other animal."

I don't know if it made any sense to the knucklehead, but another voice, this time a woman, piped up and said excitedly, "I never thought about it like that!"

I placed the snake in my bucket to the applause of the group. Perhaps I had reached at least one of them, maybe more, who knows? And that, my friends is about the most anyone in this business can ever hope for.

As I was about to leave, the young security guard, glancing at my attire, which consisted of short pants, t-shirt, socks, and sneakers, asked me, "Do you always catch rattlesnakes in shorts?" I looked the young lad straight in the eye and said with all seriousness, "Rattlesnakes don't wear shorts. They don't have the hips for it."

He must not have appreciated my smart-assery because he didn't even crack a smile. He stared at me as if I were the biggest dork on the planet. It didn't matter. I had persuaded at least one soul to think about snakes in a more positive light, and as they say in baseball, "You can't win 'em all."

In July 2020, someone spotted a rattlesnake tail disappear under a three-tiered metal water fountain in front of the building. I naturally assumed the snake would have gone below the concrete where the pipe comes out of the ground. I tried flushing it out with water through a narrow gap between the fountain's base and the sidewalk. When that didn't work, security called a team of plumbers who unbolted the fountain from its concrete mooring on the sidewalk and cut the pipe.

Rattlesnakes are not great climbers, but this sneaky serpent had actually shinnied up the PVC pipe and into the fountain itself. We tipped the fountain over, removed an access plate, and voilà! The snake was resting comfortably in the middle fountain compartment. It was the first and only time I ever needed two security guards, two grounds persons and three plumbers to help me retrieve a snake.

On a Monday morning in August 2018, Wasatch Snake Removal relocated three rattlesnakes before 9 am. Parker, my newest relocator, found two snakes at the museum while making the area safe for kid's camp, and I got a call at 8:30 to move a snake from a yard on Shakespeare Place.

The only "trail" out of the neighborhood was a barely navigable talus slope up a steep ravine and I had to cross through private property to access it (with the homeowner's permission, of course). I only fell once, but I landed squarely on my padded backside, thereby avoiding any permanent damage. Bloody and bruised and sweating like a stevedore, it wasn't an easy release. But that little cutie was worth it.

The summer of 2018 was an abnormally bad fire season. California was burning, sending us its exported smoke, while local fires filled the valley with our own choking smoke and cinders, strangling the populace in a literal chokehold. It was like living on a strange planet with a dense atmosphere and a big orange moon that was visible all day long. Hiking the Ferguson Canyon trail to release a snake was like walking through the nine circles of Hell in Dante's *Inferno*. On the upside, as unhealthy and unpleasant as it was, it created some incredible sunsets.

One midsummer night during snake patrol at the museum, a family with three girls got excited when they saw my snake bucket. "We love snakes," the oldest one said, brimming with enthusiasm. "I wrote a report about snakes," said the youngest, who was maybe eight or nine. "Snakes are an important part of biodiversity," she exclaimed.

I was beyond impressed. "That's exactly right," I told her. She prattled off some other insightful information for one so young. "You rock!" I told her as she scampered to keep up with her family. She hollered back, "You rock, too!"

A few minutes later I had a great conversation with a nice lady about bats. It was good to be the snake man!

One particularly memorable evening during snake patrol, the usual summer ambiance rose to new heights. As I probed the ground's familiar crevices and shrubbery, the transcendent guitar riffs of Carlos Santana wafted, wailed, sung and soared across the side of the mountain, flooding the warm night air and the nearby canyons like a musical tsunami.

This was the music of my generation — classic rock! It wasn't someone's stereo blasting. It was the real deal! Carlos Santana himself was playing live at the amphitheater north of the arboretum. The acoustics bouncing off the mountainside were better than any concert hall. I began timing my snake sweeps to coincide with the summer concert schedule, catching the bands I wanted to hear while avoiding whatever it is people call music these days.

It wasn't long until I knew the grounds at the Natural History Museum like the back of my hand. I came to know every step, patio, bush, tree, rock, swale, sprinkler head, and valve box on the premises, and I knew all the security guards on a first-name basis (Amy, George, Joe, Ryder, and the new kid, Chance). I had permission to walk through the rock gardens and revegetation areas where the signs say no one is supposed to go. I even found a snake now and then.

When museum security spotted a tiny rattlesnake on a patio after dark, I arrived within 20 minutes. No one kept an eye on it, prompting an intensive search by flashlight. It was nowhere near the spot where it was last seen, but I found it. I also caught a gopher snake. Hey, they don't call me the Snake Whisperer for nothing!

The landscaping crew (Katy and Christophe) called me one afternoon about a rattlesnake in one of the swales. Katy wanted to see one last year but it didn't happen. That day, however, she got her wish! It was a large male, more than three feet long, and docile as a puppy. Katy took pictures before I hiked him up the hill. On the way, we had a long talk about staying off the trail and away from people.

(Yes, I talk to snakes. If people can talk to houseplants, I can talk to snakes. In the case of both snakes and plants, you're not crazy unless you hear them talking back. I would now like to plead the fifth before I incriminate myself.)

One summer evening just before dusk, Amy, my favorite security guard, managed to sneak up behind me, causing me to jump and pivot in midair. She laughed as I attempted to restart my heart, then made me an offer I couldn't refuse.

"Would you like a tour of the museum?" she asked. "It's kinda scary when the lights are out and no one's here."

I had seen the movie, *Night at the Museum*, where exhibits come alive at night, and I wasn't about to miss my own personal version of it. Amy guided me through the museum, holding a flashlight and pointing out exhibits that may have appeared benign in the daytime but took on an eerie dimension at night. One of these was a taxidermied white wolf in a glass case.

Shining her light on the wolf, Amy said, "We have to walk through the whole building a few times a night, and every time I walk past this wolf, I swear he looks like he's breathing."

Looking closer at *Canis lupus*, it really did seem to be alive, watching us, trying not to fog the glass display case with its hot, carnivorous breath. I could almost envision it springing into action, posthumously howling and growling in defense of its territory, perhaps even gnawing on our tasty bones.

Amy showed me how the massive dinosaur skeletons sway on steel cables suspended from the ceiling, their bony, elevated tails wagging slowly like giant prehistoric puppies when the HVAC system came on.

Until now, I had been in every part of this massive building *except* the public areas. I had seen the basement more than once, the subbasement, furnace room, even the server room, each time looking for errant racers and gopher snakes that had somehow breached the exterior concrete walls, although I could never figure out how. I had seen the areas where the off-display exhibits are stored, and the paleontology room where dedicated student scientists painstakingly chip away at ancient sediments, trying to liberate the fossils inside.

But perhaps the most interesting room in the museum isn't a room at all. The architect of this edifice left a four-foot gap between the rear wall and the mountain, presumably as an expansion space. Known as "The Mote," this space has been visited by only a handful of people, mostly employees. Mike showed me the mote one day as we tried to figure out how snakes occasionally entered the building.

Accessible only from the subbasement level, the mote has evolved from a mere foundation trench into a living, breathing cave. Hundreds of feet long, five stories high and just wide enough to walk through, this cavern creates its own subterranean biosphere, dripping water from its manmade ceiling like any natural cave. No light enters here, making headlamps a must. The floor was littered with the carcasses of unfortunate snakes, kangaroo rats, mice, voles, and beetles that somehow fell in but couldn't escape. Being locked in this dungeon-like room at any time of the day or night would make for a terrifying and perpetual night at the museum, casting doubt on what's actually natural about the history of this place.

Being the snake man has granted me access to a number of places that are off-limits to the public. For instance, I gave a snake presentation to the employees at the Mormon Church's granite vaults where millions of microfilmed genealogical records are stored in a bombproof and heavily guarded underground repository. I spent an enjoyable two hours talking to the employees about snakes, spiders, scorpions, and other cuddly critters.

The vaults are an amazing feat of engineering that very few people get to see. You don't just walk into the vaults because security clearance is required. The church called me a couple of weeks beforehand to get my permission to run a background check.

Vault employees have an issue with rattlers crawling down from the hillside and onto their parking lot in the summertime, sometimes seeking shade behind the tires of their cars, which accounted for most of my calls there.

I was once escorted inside a cancer institute's radiation generator room to remove a "baby rattlesnake," which, much to my delight turned out to be a reclusive night snake. University Police escorted me into several labs and clinics, the Department of Psychiatry, and places on campus I didn't know existed, all because a determined snake had managed to find its way inside.

It was truly gratifying to receive so many calls to save snakes that could have been dispatched in other ways with far less effort. Of course, when state law prohibits the killing of native snakes, you would expect law enforcement to be the first to comply. But not always.

After receiving a call from campus police to pick up a small rattler from a cafeteria courtyard at the U of U, I prepared to leave work and get the snake. I called the dispatcher to verify the address and tell her I was on my way. Within minutes, she called back to say that the situation had been resolved. One of the officers had deemed the situation to be too dangerous, drew his sidearm and shot the snake.

Really? It sounds like Barney Fife is alive and well and working at the U of U. It's pathetic that he thought it was safer to discharge a firearm on a crowded college campus than to let me relocate the snake.

I could have been there within 30 minutes or less, captured the snake, put it in a bucket and released it in the foothills with no one getting hurt. Was it really safer for an officer to fire a gun in a crowd of bystanders at a small, scared animal that didn't want to hurt anybody and only wanted to escape? It was a knee-jerk reaction to a non-event.

The sad result is that most of the people who witnessed the event probably think the acceptable solution to removing a snake is to kill it.

A rattlesnake appeared next to the front doors of a nearby medical center, causing several people to be late for their appointments. Any closer and it would have been in the lobby. Later that night, at the request of campus police, I spent four hours looking for a rattlesnake in the parking lot during a concert at the amphitheater. Peering under hundreds of cars to make sure no one received a love bite as they were leaving, I never did find that snake. In fact, I highly doubt there was a snake at all, just someone's idea of a bad joke.

Working with various police agencies became almost routine, mostly because some people, upon finding a snake in their yard, call the police to deal with it. This makes no sense of course. Police officers have no training in snake removal and lack the necessary equipment to capture and contain them. Most animal control agencies don't respond to calls involving wild animals, and they definitely don't deal with venomous snakes. Therefore, homeowners would call the police and the police would call me.

Whereas the Salt Lake Valley once had only a handful of police departments, there are now dozens. Over time, a single unified police agency was fractured as numerous cities and townships voted to incorporate, establishing their own departments. For me, this made billing a nightmare, so I didn't bother. Police calls were always free. This was my gift to the community.

7 | *The Museum*

The most disturbing police call was the one that never happened. One night in 2018, police dispatch called to say that a man in the area had a gopher snake in his yard and was threatening to shoot it. He was completely freaked out and noncompliant, convinced that the snake "was going to attack his wife." Police at the scene warned the man that he needed to put his shotgun down or risk having every cop in the valley in his yard. Or worse.

Shortly thereafter, the officer called back to say the guy had already killed the snake with a shovel, convinced that it had indeed attacked his wife. That kind of hyper-phobic ignorance benefits no one, but it's so deeply ingrained in some people that it's almost impossible to cure with reason and logic alone. Any attempt to set him straight would have been pointless.

I told a DWR officer that I fully expected the state to follow through with charges and fines. He said they would investigate, but I doubt they followed through.

It's a disturbing commentary that people can be so afraid of a harmless animal that they put themselves and those around them, including the police, in extreme danger, or that the police are allowed to put the public in danger, but there's no acquaintance between ignorance and logic.

County Animal Control called to say there was a gopher snake inside the state prison. Jordan was on it like a duck on a June bug until the prison told us they put it in a sack and released it themselves. If everyone had done that, I'd have been out of business!

A call came from campus police on a Sunday evening because a large tortoise was roaming the grounds at the Museum. I told them I had no place to keep a hundred-pound Sulcata tortoise, but that I knew people and would make some calls.

My friend Cary saved the day. He picked up the tortoise and took it home to join his own large menagerie, if only temporarily. We hoped the tortoise hadn't been abandoned, but that someone was missing him and would report it.

Sure enough, the very next day, University PD got a call from the VA Hospital. They were frantically missing Frankie, their mascot tortoise, and were beside themselves with worry. Cary returned the wayward reptile to a group of concerned veterans who were delighted to have him back home.

According to Cary, Frankie was happy as well, and the hospital had already made the necessary repairs to prevent another escape.

We have no idea how Frankie crossed at least one major thoroughfare without being hit or reported, but this tortoise tale had a happy ending.

One of the most fortuitous events that took place at the Museum happened on a serene August evening in 2017. Long shadows stretched, reaching toward the east. Across the valley, the sun in the western sky, tired after a long day, was sinking sleepily behind the horizon.

I was probing the thirsty vegetation at the museum next to the Shoreline Trail when curiosity caused a dignified older couple named Mary and Glen to ask what I was doing. I knew Mary by reputation as the executive editor of *Salt Lake Magazine*, and her husband Glen was a renowned local journalist known for speaking truth to power. For me, it was an opportunity to meet two journalistic legends and we enjoyed a lively conversation.

They asked more questions than normal people do, even taking notes. And I, ever willing to talk about snakes, regaled them with tales of snake lore and translocation methodology. Mary said she'd like to feature me in the magazine.

A photo shoot for the piece took place the following February, resulting in a photo and blurb on the contents page in the April 2018 issue. It was the best free advertising I could have hoped for.

Being the snake man granted me access to people I would never have met otherwise and opened doors to off-limits places where only serpents can enter, silent and unseen, providing privileged glimpses into their furtive, secret world.

CHAPTER 8

In Defense of Rattlesnakes

"The last word in ignorance is the man who says of an animal or plant, 'What good is it?'" –Aldo Leopold

Tales of the Old West with its legendary outlaws and larger-than-life characters are part of the western mystique. So too are the stories of the creatures that live here.

Rattlesnakes have always played an iconic role in the mythology of western lore and are featured in virtually every Western movie ever made — always as the villain. But those depictions are based on misplaced fear and condemnation, not on fact and understanding.

The most common depiction of rattlers in the movies shows them rattling and ready to strike. That's because some joker is just off camera provoking an otherwise passive snake into a state of defensive frenzy just to convince moviegoers that the protagonist is in peril. The snake isn't mean. It isn't dangerous. It's terrified and confused. We watch the movies and we swallow the hyperbole, convinced that rattlesnakes are aggressive, sadistic creatures when nothing could be further from the truth.

In fact, rattlesnakes are just like every other creature; they have an important role to play in nature's grand plan. They are not malevolent, evil, or scheming. Those are human traits. And they most certainly are not "out to get us" as many people falsely believe. Rattlesnake behavior is much more predictable than human behavior, and I trust them more. People lie, cheat and steal, but rattlesnakes will always be 100 percent completely honest with you.

Rattlesnakes want nothing to do with humans and if they weren't venomous we might not give them a second thought. As for that whole Garden of Eden debacle, if it had been a squirrel that tempted Eve, today's gullible humans would probably be smacking squirrels with shovels. How ridiculous would that be?

Rattlesnakes are shy and elusive creatures that don't want to be seen or bothered, and they rely on cryptic coloration, also known as camouflage, to help conceal them. That's their first line of defense. Their second line of defense is to lie perfectly still and let the threat pass by without giving their location away. Third, if they don't have a quick escape route, they may rattle as a warning. And finally, as a last resort, they may bite. This is not something they want to do, but everything bigger than them usually wants to eat them and they are entitled to defend themselves.

Utah has seven documented rattlesnake species and one that has yet to be recognized by the state. But only one, the Great Basin rattler, lives within the densely populated regions of Northern Utah. It is one of the most docile and least toxic of all rattlesnakes, posing very little threat to humans. Almost no one believes that of course, because they're rattlesnakes, and a bad reputation is a hard thing to shake (pun intended), even if it is undeserved.

The Great Basin rattlesnake is Utah's most common rattler and the one with the largest range, occupying the entire western half of the state, frequenting a variety of habitats from desert valleys to timberline elevations as high as 8,000 feet above sea level.

Great Basin rattlesnakes are surprisingly benign in both temperament and toxicity. Like most snakes, these gentle serpents are reclusive and will usually retreat if given the chance. They are reluctant to strike unless provoked and human fatalities are extremely rare, with only a single documented case dating back to the late 1800s, before the advent of antivenin. Modern snakebite treatment has reduced mortality and morbidity rates significantly, ensuring that most victims experience a quick and complete recovery.

Seldom exceeding five feet in length, this is the only venomous species found near the population centers of Northern Utah. From the Wasatch Front westward, these snakes inhabit much of the Great Basin region, often finding their way into hillside neighborhoods that have encroached into their domain. Like all of Utah's snakes, state law protects them from wanton killing.

Snakes don't need people, but people need snakes. Snakes made it possible for us to advance from nomadic tribes to established agrarian societies by preventing the destruction of food crops by vermin, thereby enabling the stabilization and progression of human civilization.

Modern farmers have learned to appreciate snakes as a form of free rodent control, compliments of Mother Nature. If snakes were to disappear tomorrow, it would be a short matter of time before our crops, grain silos, and even our storerooms and food pantries would be ravaged by rodents.

As prolific vectors for disease, rodents are carriers of numerous pathogens including tularemia, Hantavirus, tick-borne encephalitis, Lyme disease, Rocky Mountain spotted fever, plague, and a host of other serious and potentially debilitating and fatal conditions. If you have never suffered from any of these maladies, you should probably thank a snake. Yes, even a rattlesnake.

By staking my claim as a rattlesnake relocation expert, in no way do I mean to imply that what I did was extraordinary or life threatening. Of the 36 species of rattlesnakes found in the Continental U.S., Mexico, and parts of South America, *C. o. lutosus* (lutes for short) are considered the cuddly cousins of the *Crotalus* genus. Other relocators, such as Rattlesnake Solutions in Arizona, deal with multiple species of rattlers, all of which rate higher on the venom spectrum than the snakes I routinely dealt with. Most of them are also more easily provoked. Arizona claims 15 rattlesnake species, the most of any state, with the Western diamondback being the most common.

I have often wondered how different my approach would have been if I'd had to deal with larger, more toxic, and potentially more defensive snakes. For one thing, I probably wouldn't have shown up to move a Western diamondback wearing sneakers or low-cut hikers — a common habit of mine when catching local buzzer butts.

My preferred method of capture is to use a procedure known as "tailing." This involves supporting the anterior or forward part of a snake's body with a snake hook in my right hand and holding its tail with my left hand. In this manner, I'm behind the snake and not confronting it head-on, giving it very little reason to be defensive while allowing me full control of its actions. The fact that all these gentle snakes want to do is get away from a human makes tailing them easy. It is not advisable to use this technique on other, more volatile species, however. For those snakes, tongs are the preferred tool of choice.

The snake that rattles at you when you're hiking isn't being aggressive, threatening or mean; he's just letting you know he's there. This makes locating one easier than trying to find a snake that doesn't announce itself. My job would have been much harder and more dangerous if I was looking for a silent venomous snake, which is why I have so much respect for relocators in other parts of the world.

A harmless snake in your yard is an invaluable source of natural pest control. Once he eliminates the pests in your yard, he'll move on with no prompting from you. Best of all, he won't send you a bill.

A rattlesnake in your yard needs relocating to prevent an accidental encounter. A good snake relocator will return a snake to a suitable place within its home range where it can do the job nature intended without presenting a risk to people.

The state mandated that any snake I relocated could not be moved further than .62 of a mile from the capture site. Known as a short-distance translocation, this protocol ensures that snakes remain within the home range where they were born and where they actually 'know' their relatives and are able to locate their hibernacula come wintertime.

Snakes that are relocated outside of their home ranges will attempt to return, often traveling in concentric circles to do so. This is based on studies in which PIT tags (Passive Integrated Transponders) similar to those used to microchip your dog or cat are implanted in the snakes' bodies, allowing their movements to be monitored and mapped.

This attempt to return to familiar territory is called site fidelity, and is a powerful intuitive homing mechanism similar to that utilized by migrating birds. Unlike birds, however, the inherent dangers of human habitation make it unlikely that a snake could traverse any significant distance in suburbia and survive.

Most North American rattlesnake habitat has been invaded by humans. Since neither of our species is going anywhere, snake encounters are inevitable and we need to learn to get along peaceably.

8 | *In Defense of Rattlesnakes*

When I was relocating snakes, homeowners often asked me where I was going to release the snake that had made its way into their yard. I learned early on that telling them I was only going to take it a little more than half-a-mile away was not what they wanted to hear. I had to convince them that the snake hadn't sought them out and was only there by happenstance. I assured them that the snake did not know their address and was unlikely to return.

Each snake's head stamp was photographed, allowing us to identify what the state referred to as a "repeat offender" in the unlikely event that we saw the snake again. However, after relocating hundreds of snakes, I don't believe I ever removed the same snake from the same yard twice, or the same snake twice, period. At least not in the same season.

One woman (we'll call her Karen) was so upset by the idea of a short-distance translocation that she accused me of being lazy. Karen was as unpleasant as she was unattractive. I'm not saying she was ugly, but homely would have been an upgrade. Her makeup looked like it was glopped on with a serving spoon and smeared with a stucco trowel, and her hair had been combed with an eggbeater. This frumpy hausfrau insisted that I drive the snakes "at least five miles away." When I explained to her that I was only following state law, she told all her neighbors in the gated community not to call me anymore.

Fortunately, most people aren't Karens, and many of my customers found this information interesting. After all, if they weren't concerned about the long-term welfare of these transient guests, they wouldn't have called me in the first place.

The laws in many states make it illegal to kill a snake or any native herpetofauna, which includes all reptile and amphibian species. Why? Because these animals are important members of the biotic communities in which they live, and because dead snakes can't protect us from vermin and the threat of multiple diseases.

Even before I became a snake relocator, I enjoyed teaching people about the intrinsic value of snakes in the environment and their direct benefit to humans as a free source of rodent control. Rodents are prolific little buggers. While it's true that hawks, eagles and owls eat mice and rats, they only eat the adult animals, whereas snakes go into nests and burrows to consume the babies, effectively eliminating hundreds of thousands of future rodents.

Someone calculated that 200 captive snakes eating one mouse every five days would consume 14,600 mice over the course of a year. If we subtract 10 weeks for brumation, that number is reduced by 2,800, leaving 11,800. If you extrapolate that, removing 200 snakes from the wild allows those 11,800 mice to survive and reproduce. In the end, killing 200 rattlesnakes results in more than 100,000 mice, rats, and other rodents proliferating and adding to the vermin population over the course of a year.

I'll never know how many snakes were killed each year by homeowners versus how many called me to remove one, but this is why humans need snakes, even venomous ones, and is the main reason why killing snakes is illegal in most jurisdictions. It's unethical and immoral everywhere.

My highest-profile and most controversial relocation occurred on July 9, 2017 when I responded to a call from the opulent Federal Heights neighborhood. The homeowner had a rattlesnake that had become trapped in deer netting on his patio.

Deer netting is an insidious and largely unnecessary deterrent intended to keep deer from munching on rich people's ornamental shrubbery. (If you live in the foothills and don't want deer in your yard, consider moving or getting a better fence. In all fairness, the deer were there first.) Made of green monofilament nylon line woven into a mesh pattern resembling a large fishing net, its effectiveness is questionable, while its tendency to ensnare smaller animals is notorious and often fatal.

Turf and sod netting is a heavier nylon matrix used to prevent erosion on slopes and as an underlay for sod. It too, entraps many small animals, including birds. Like the cruel and insidious glue trap, this mesh should be outlawed. At the very least, it needs redesigning to eliminate its lethal impact on benign wildlife. I have had to cut snakes free from many kinds of mesh over the years and none of it seemed to be performing a truly necessary task.

Arriving at the home, I discovered an almost three-foot rattlesnake hopelessly ensnared in mesh that was draped over bushes and shrubs but hadn't been trimmed along the bottom, leaving the excess to flop on the ground. Whoever installed this netting didn't know what they were doing.

I had removed snakes from mesh before, cutting the netting around the snake, and then taking the still-entangled snake to one of my team members who would carefully snip each strand of the netting from the snake's body while I held its head.

Another method involves 'tubing' a snake by placing the snake's head and upper body in a transparent plastic tube made for this purpose, although a piece of regular PVC pipe of the right diameter works just fine. This makes it a one-man job. In this case, however, I needed access to the anterior portion of the snake that would have been in the tube. Lacking an assistant and not wanting to drive across town and back again, I decided to go it alone. The homeowner wasn't about to help out and I couldn't jeopardize his safety by asking him to.

Using a pair of small scissors, I began to extricate the snake as the homeowner filmed the ordeal with his iPhone. As a chance to prove the truly docile nature of these snakes, a video of me cutting one out of deer netting barehanded would be worth at least a thousand words. On the other hand, there would be no escaping the vitriolic accusations of dumbassery that would forever follow me if a video of me getting bit while essentially free handling a buzzer butt was to find its way to the herp forums — even if I was trying to save its life.

Holding the snake with my left hand, I used my right hand to snip the tangled netting from her slowly writhing body, one strand at a time, keeping my eyes on her head while staying alert for any signs of agitation. The only hint of possible annoyance was a gentle, infrequent, and involuntary *cha-cha-cha* from her lazy rattle. Near her middle, the netting was more tightly knotted, cutting into the tender flesh between and under her dorsal scales. I wondered how long she had been struggling to free herself only to make the situation worse. Using just the tips of the scissors, I worked my way toward where the netting ended a few inches behind her head.

As mentioned previously, most Great Basin rattlers are amazingly docile. This snake didn't understand the predicament she was in, wanting nothing more than to escape from this large, bipedal creature that was pestering her.

The netting didn't restrain her enough to stop her from turning around and tagging me, but as with tailing, as long as I stayed behind her she didn't seem to feel threatened. It also helped that she was probably tired from her struggle.

While it may sound far-fetched to some, she may have even understood at a subliminal level that I was there to help her. Most animals possess a highly developed sixth sense, making them far more cognizant than we give them credit for, and pit vipers like rattlesnakes are known to be quite sentient. The biggest misconception people have about snakes, especially rattlesnakes, is that they want to bite us. Nothing could be further from the truth.

Although this snake could have easily bitten me almost any time she wanted, I successfully freed her from a most cruel and certain death. In doing so, I never felt threatened for a moment. Lifting her by the lower third of her body with my right hand, I placed her gently in a bucket, screwed on the lid, and smiled for the camera.

That snake was fortunate. As with glue traps, most wildlife that get caught in bird netting doesn't survive long enough to be rescued, sometimes suffering for weeks before dying of starvation or dehydration. Homeowners need to know that there are alternatives to netting such as Agribond and frost cloth.

The owner said something about it being the most amazing thing he'd ever seen, then emailed me the video. I took a short hike, returning this very lucky snake to suitable habitat on the mountain behind the neighborhood where she eagerly vanished into the relative security of scraggly underbrush.

I would probably not have attempted this maneuver with another species of rattlesnake. Great Basin rattlers are considered to be the least defensive, most tolerant members of the rattlesnake world for their almost genteel dispositions. That doesn't mean you'll never meet a cranky one (I've met plenty) or that they don't have bad days or legitimate reasons to be defensive. They do. The fact is, I may not have been able to do this with a different snake in the same predicament, or even with the same snake on a different day, depending on her level of comfort, trust, and tolerance at the time.

The video is out there. It floats around in the virtual realm, popping up on Facebook occasionally, accompanied by mixed reviews from people who think I'm the biggest moron they've ever seen, or alternately, commending me for my willingness to help an animal in need. I'm not about to argue with either opinion, but I hope it changes some wrong-headed thinking about rattlesnakes.

Regardless, some people will never understand the rationale behind snake relocation or the mentality of those who do it. Perhaps they consider us to be a few notches below normal or not smart enough to be afraid.

After picking up a snake one morning from a home on Plateau Drive, I was hiking it up the mountain above the Shoreline Trail. Another hiker saw my bucket and asked what I was doing, so of course I told him. He said I had more balls than him. I don't know how many balls he has, but I only have two. But mine are bigger.

In another unusual rescue, a realtor called to say that a rattlesnake had scared a radon remediation crew from the crawlspace of a $1.5 million dollar home for sale. They exited the space like a bullet from a rifle barrel, refusing to return until the snake was gone. In fact, they refused to return until all the insulation was gone, because that's where the snake was hiding. The sale of the home and the commissions for two realtors were on the line if I couldn't find the snake.

It was a frigid night in early December. Snake season had been over since October, but I've had calls in every month of the year. Over time I've moved snakes, even wild ones, from November through March, often from crawlspaces, basements, garages, and behind sheetrock where they were contentedly sleeping away the winter. Snakes are extremely opportunistic animals, instinctively seeking respite from the cold in places that should have been inaccessible to them. I've learned to never underestimate these incredibly adaptive and clever creatures.

Working in the cramped, dusty confines of the crawlspace, wearing masks to prevent the inhalation of fiberglass splinters and Hantavirus spores, I found a tiny surprised buzzer butt hiding behind a slab of pink insulation. Jordan and I removed all the insulation and Visqueen and were reimbursed handsomely by the home's wealthy owner.

I couldn't have run Wasatch Snake Removal without my outstanding team.

Jason and Jordan removed a rattlesnake from a turkey farm. Turkeys will attack snakes, and this snake had a flesh wound from an alleged encounter with at least one aggressive fowl (although the bird had a swollen leg, so the snake presumably got even).

What did my guys do? They pulled out a can of spray-on hydrogen peroxide to clean and disinfect the snake's wound before releasing it. Rattlesnake first-aid!

Speaking of snakes and poultry, some people say snakes taste like chicken, but they have no drumsticks, thighs, or breasts. It's more like eating a big rubber band. How about a juicy, golden brown turkey with all the trimmings instead?

A woman approached me after a presentation to tell me about her personal rattlesnake encounter. She works in one of the larger canyons east of the city and on summer days she enjoys spending her lunch breaks at a shady spot near the stream that playfully frolics and tumbles its way to the valley below.

One particularly fine day when her lunchtime was nearly up, she put her book down and began to gather the cruft of her lunch and put things away. Glancing down from the large rock that doubled as both table and chair, she froze at the sight of a rattlesnake, coiled and content, a couple of feet to her right.

"It must have been there the entire time," she said, "but I didn't notice it till then. It was looking at me so it knew I was there. Are they always so mellow?"

"As long as we don't bother them they have no reason to bother us," I told her. "He was probably waiting for you to share your lunch with him." She laughed.

"I always wondered what I would do if I saw a rattlesnake, but after that experience I'm not as afraid. Everything you told us about them is true."

I can preach the virtues of these animals until the cows come home, but sometimes it takes a firsthand experience for someone to lower their defenses and drop a lifetime of superstitious baggage. In so doing, these individuals can finally free themselves from the dungeon of their fears, stepping into the light of truth for the first time. I loved being able to facilitate that freedom.

I wish more people could see rattlesnakes the away I see them in their day-to-day existence — tranquil, passive and completely non-threatening until they're forced to defend themselves.

Despite some deeply ingrained wives' tales and urban legends, snakes are completely antisocial creatures. They have to be, because everything wants to devour them, especially when they're young. They can't possibly defend against predators many times their size; therefore, if they can't make a hasty retreat, they often try to bluff their way out of an encounter. Aggression usually stems from provocation or from being unable to escape from a threatening situation. Cornering a snake is always the most dangerous thing you can do.

If you find yourself face-to-face with a snake, you can mitigate the threat to both yourself and the snake by taking three steps back and allowing it to retreat safely. If you're hiking and there's a snake on the trail, just walk around it, maintaining the same safe distance. If you're lucky enough to encounter a rattlesnake, give it space and leave it alone. It has an important job to do!

In true human fashion, absurd notions abound. The list of fallacies involving snakes could fill this book (which is why I wrote this book). Perhaps the most prevalent and often repeated fallacy concerns baby rattlesnakes and their alleged inability to "control" their venom. Also, that they are more venomous than bigger snakes. People rarely ask me if this is true. Instead, they tell me it's true as if it's the one snake fact they're absolutely sure of. We'll get back to that topic in the chapter on venom.

One little-known truth is that rattlesnakes, while often misunderstood and feared, are critically important to human health, playing an important role in the food web as both predator and prey. Not only do rattlesnakes help control pest populations, but all types of snakes are a food source that other animals like birds of prey, wading birds, carnivorous mammals, and even other snakes depend on for survival.

Rattlesnakes offer other ecological benefits as well. One team of researchers from the University of California at Berkeley found that rattlesnakes, by eating rodents, thereby become seed dispersers, saving and distributing seeds that might otherwise be lost. This is great news — not just for pollinators like birds, bats, bees, and butterflies — but also for the small mammals and rodents that depend on the microhabitats that dispersed seeds help create.

Additionally, rattlesnakes remove disease vectors and rodent-borne illnesses from their environment by means of their natural predation on rodents. One study from the University of Maryland found that a single timber rattlesnake could remove up to 4,500 ticks annually. That may not sound like a lot until you realize that it also prevents those 4,500 ticks from reproducing.

Even though a rattlesnake encounter can be frightening, most people would rather be rattled at than risk getting too close to a snake they didn't see or hear.

Rattlesnakes have been called "the most polite of all snakes" because of their tendency to warn us of their presence. This is for our benefit as well as theirs, and the notion that rattlesnakes are losing their rattles is just another fallacy in a litany of snake-related myths and misconceptions.

There is a theory that in areas of high human/snake confrontation, the more aggressive snakes are the ones that are most likely to be killed by humans, leaving the more docile individuals to propagate and produce offspring that are also docile until the entire population of snakes becomes super mellow and less inclined to rattle defensively.

Another bit of conjecture being promoted at one time stated that rattlesnakes are slowly evolving to not have rattles any longer. The theory claimed that a mutation to remove or diminish the rattle has allowed quieter snakes to live longer around humans and to produce quieter offspring than 'normal' snakes.

It is possible, I suppose, but there are too many variables involved — the biggest being whether or not the tendency to rattle is a dominant or a recessive genetic trait (many snakes without rattles shake their tails, perhaps as a physiological response to stress or as a warning to predators). Even if it is true, it only means that docile rattlesnakes would be less inclined to rattle, not that they are physically losing their rattles.

There is no known mutation in any population of rattlesnakes that physically causes the rattle to disappear. The only rattle-less rattlesnake is the critically endangered Santa Catalina Island rattlesnake (*Crotalus catalinensis*), and it took eons for that anomaly to occur, possibly due to the absence of large ungulate animals like bison on the island, which may be one reason why rattlesnakes evolved rattles in the first place. While it ostensibly evolved as a warning mechanism to prevent being stepped on, the rattle serves other purposes as well. It would require additional eons for a physical feature like a rattle to disappear through the process of evolution, and it would have to benefit the snakes in some practical way. Evolution is not a random or speedy process.

There are some who don't accept the overwhelming evidence for evolution and that's their prerogative. It depends on whether you believe God is a scientist or a magician. Regardless, the theory of evolution is backed by an overwhelming abundance of proof, with fossil records and genetic studies reinforcing the fact that species — all species — evolve over excruciatingly long periods of time.

Evolution has been observed in many short-lived organisms. You can literally watch it happen. All of us at one time during our embryological development had gills and a tail. That in itself is a form of evolution. It's not something one chooses to 'believe in' or not believe in. It's not astrology.

Another common question is, "Do rattlesnakes always rattle to let us know they're there?" No. A rattler may be sleeping, its rattle may have broken off, or a young snake may not have a fully developed rattle.

Physical factors aside, each snake, just like each person, is a unique individual. Some are even-tempered, bordering on complacent. These snakes may not rattle simply because they're not easily bothered. If you don't hear them, you generally won't see them either. This keeps them invisible and safe. Granted, a rattlesnake that doesn't rattle is potentially more dangerous than one that warns you of its presence; although a snake docile enough not to shake its tail when confronted may be just as unlikely to strike in self-defense. This may partially mitigate the danger of being bit. I met rattlesnakes so calm I could have slung them over my shoulders and hiked them up the hill.

Some snakes are tolerant until you piss them off. These snakes don't want a confrontation, only engaging if you cross their boundaries. Remember, you are an unknown threat. The best response is to back away and allow the snake its space.

A few snakes are jerks all the time, or they at least have jerk potential. (We all have jerk potential, right?) These are the snakes people call "aggressive." In reality, these high-intensity individuals' heightened responses may stem from genetic traits or individual dispositions. Unfortunately, these highly reactive snakes are often killed due to human intolerance of assertive behavior.

It is important to remember that terms like "mellow" or "aggressive" are human interpretations. Snakes act according to instinct, not attitude. Defensive displays are survival mechanisms, not evidence of hostility.

Snakes don't typically bite unless they're provoked or you invade their space. If a snake has to go into defensive posture, you're too close.

Most rattlesnake bites are not accidental, but are instigated by humans trying to harass or kill it. Because rattlesnakes are naturally shy and reclusive, most bites could be eliminated entirely if people would simply leave them alone.

No one knows how legends like rattle-less rattlesnakes get started, but ignorant people need a reason to be afraid, and rattlesnakes have always been convenient scapegoats for urban folklore and other spurious and superstitious claims.

Often reviled, sometimes revered, and too often mischaracterized, rattlesnakes are majestic creatures that maintain nature's balance and add beauty and diversity to our world. They have as much right to exist as any other creature, including you and me. The only good rattlesnake is a live rattlesnake.

Please, if you see a rattlesnake, enjoy the experience and leave it alone. It really doesn't want to bite you. Uneducated people and scaremongers will always try to vilify these animals so it's imperative that those of us who know and understand rattlesnakes remain vigilant in their defense.

CHAPTER 9

Heads and Tails

"No paradise is complete without a serpent or two." –My personal opinion

The pristine country surrounding Moab, Utah is a geologic wonderland of sandstone arches, castles, monoliths, and petrified sand dunes locked in timeless splendor.

Driving along the Colorado River corridor in October 1991, an obscure road appeared between the trees on my right, practically begging to be explored. After exiting the asphalt, my two-wheel-drive pickup slogged and slipped in loose, dry sand the color of freshly ground paprika.

My friend Darrel was with me, and surprisingly, we weren't looking for snakes. Darrel isn't a snake guy. We came to this slick-rock Mecca to ride mountain bikes and immerse ourselves in the primordial landscape. As participants in Moab's annual mountain bike festival, we were going to be there for the next five days and we needed a place to camp. As my tires tried desperately to grab whatever traction they could on the sloppy incline, we were on the lookout — not for snakes — but for a patch of bare ground big enough for two tents and a campfire ring among the waving tamarisk and cottonwood trees that stood between us and the river.

In a rare moment, an unexpected gift appeared on the road before me. The snake gods can be fickle, but they had favored me before. On that day, they were especially generous.

There, in the rapidly warming orange sand lay a slender snake about 26 inches long — except that it wasn't slender at all. As it tried to slither out of the path of my truck, it struggled and strained to drag itself along, so encumbered by a recent meal it could barely move. The snake was ponderously impaired, looking like a long, skinny nylon stocking stuffed with a large potato. Without this impediment, I may not have caught it or even seen it. It would have been long gone. I could tell from its physiology — primarily its large eyes, scalation, and build — that it was a rat snake of some sort, although this particular morphology wasn't listed in any field guide.

A short time later, due to the stress of capture, the rotund serpent disgorged a long-legged wading bird. It wasn't a large bird from a human perspective, but for this little snake it was the equivalent of a massive python swallowing an ostrich.

The snake was a female, silvery gray with bronze saddles. I don't remember how I contained her for the rest of the trip, but I kept her shaded and cool over the next several days as Darrel and I pedaled, pushed and grunted our way over and between Moab's sandstone fins and mesas. It would have been far more convenient to have found the snake on our last day there, but the snake gods don't always consider the timing of their gifts.

At that time, the only other documented rat snake anywhere in the region was the Great Plains rat snake, also known as Emory's rat snake (*Elaphe guttata emoryi*) [Stebbins 1985] which occurs east of the Manti LaSal Mountains and eastward into Colorado and the Great Plains, but this individual did not resemble that species.

Word of my find spread quickly and in November of 1991, I received a letter from Dr. James MacMahon, Dean of the College of Science at a local University, requesting custody of the animal. Dr. MacMahon's research would reveal it to be a specimen of the Moab rat snake (*Elaphe laeta intermontanus*) as documented by Woodbury in 1942. [Woodbury, Angus M.; Woodbury, Dixson M., 1942, Title: "Studies of the rat snake, *Elaphe laeta*, with description of a new subspecies." Source: Proceedings of the Biological Society of Washington 55: 133-142]

It was a species whose existence near Moab had not been verified since the 1940s, and of which only a single preserved (road-killed) specimen existed. Apparently, I was the first person to see one in nearly 50 years, or at least the first person to recognize its significance. It caused quite a commotion within scientific circles due to its potential as a little-known subspecies, or perhaps even as a new species altogether, undergoing serious taxonomic scrutiny and DNA sequencing.

The excitement over a potential new species lasted for several years; however, *intermontanus* was eventually downgraded. According to Wikipedia, "This species has undergone extensive re-classification since it was first described by Spencer Fullerton Baird and Charles Frédéric Girard in 1853 as *Scotophis emoryi*. It has often been placed in the genus *Elaphe*, but recent phylogenetic analyses have resulted in its transfer to *Pantherophis*. *Pantherophis emoryi* has been elevated to full species status and downgraded to a subspecies of *Pantherophis guttatus* multiple times."

Unfortunately, although this animal looked very different from *Pantherophis emoryi*, the Moab population has since been determined to be an intergrade species located in a disjunct area and "does not appear to be a distinct lineage. It has since been synonymized with *emoryi* [Burbrink 2002]." Since that time, the genus *elaphe* has been relegated to the dustbin of scientific nomenclature.

Disappointing as it was, it remains my sole contribution to science as an amateur herper, and I still have the letter from Dr. MacMahon requesting custody of my specimen based on its "potential scientific significance."

Since my discovery, others have found specimens as well, and are breeding them, as evidenced by the hatchlings I saw for sale at the local expo a few years back.

That experience made me wonder what else might be lurking out there, just waiting to be discovered. More outliers . . . more mysteries in the underbrush. This forces me to make a confession. Though my reasons for relocating snakes were always deeply rooted in respectful remediation and education, there was one silently selfish motive, too.

I had dreamed — since I was a kid — of finding all the snakes that call Utah home. But most of them live in the redrock deserts and hidden canyons down south, a part of the state I rarely visited. Even less so once my time was monopolized by running a snake relocation business in the northern part. The more time I spent wrangling phone calls and rescuing snakes, the less time I had to chase that lucid dream.

There were local species I hadn't seen despite my earnest efforts to find them, and I surmised that by relocating snakes in a large metropolitan area, I would eventually find the snakes I was looking for. The Utah milk snake had eluded me for 50 years, but a customer was eventually bound to call with a milk snake in his garage or basement, right? In addition, I hoped to find aberrant specimens such as a leucistic or albino buzzer butt, or perhaps even a snake that had no business being in Utah at all. Even if my logic was flawed, I was still optimistic about the outcome.

In April 2020, Covid was still in the beginning stages of throwing our lives into chaos, and wearing masks had just become mandatory. On April 7, a farmer in a town about 135 miles southwest of Salt Lake, texted me a photo of a little pink snake he found while fishing at a small reservoir near his home. He left it where it was. Trying to conceal my excitement, I asked if he could look for it again. Astonishingly, he went back to the reservoir and found the snake a second time! Finding it once was a rarity to be sure. Finding it again was a one-in-a-million longshot. At less than a foot long, he kept it in an uncovered milk bucket until I could pick it up the following weekend.

I made enough of a fuss that I assumed the farmer, whose name was Shawn, would expect payment, so I stopped at my bank and withdrew a wad of cash. I took Jordan with me. When we finally found the house (in an area as remote as the Australian Outback), the three of us chatted about snakes for a while. Then Shawn, gentleman that he was, unceremoniously handed me this unique and possibly one-of-a-kind snake, asking nothing in return.

The snake was a wild-caught, neonate, hypomelanistic Great Basin gopher snake. This genetic misprint may occur more often in nature than we realize, but these animals have a shorter-than-average life span due to their lack of natural camouflage, making them extremely vulnerable to predation. She has other physiological deficits as well; namely, her proportions are stunted and not like those of a normal gopher snake, indicating a form of dwarfism. And I soon discovered that she's blind. That particular genetic defect, at least in captive snakes, is often accompanied by sterility as well.

Hypomelanism refers to a condition in which an organism has less melanin than normal, resulting in reduced pigmentation compared to the wild phenotype. The term is commonly used in the context of describing animals or individuals with lighter or paler coloring than normal due to this melanin deficiency. Melanin is a crucial pigment found in various organisms including humans. It plays vital roles in UV protection, hair and skin pigmentation, and has implications for survival in various environments.

Shawn called her Pinky and the name stuck. She is essentially a pale pink gopher snake with darker, rose-colored saddles and facial markings, and while she's obviously a gopher snake, there is nothing normal about her. Her chances of survival were slim to grim, based on a complete absence of natural camouflage and an inability to see. She did survive her first winter, however, somehow finding a place to brumate, and she had obviously been eating. I'm constantly amazed at how well Mother Nature takes care of her children.

This little cutie has been with me for five years now. She's much bigger, approaching 32 inches in length. She will never reach the size of a fully-grown gopher snake, but she will live out her life safe from predation and exploitation.

My first snake call of 2021 led me to a non-native snake that I had never seen in person. It was a Gray rat snake (*Pantherophis spiloides*) in a basement bathroom. With a dark dorsal surface and a white chin and venter, these handsome snakes occur east of the Mississippi River from Indiana to Florida. I wish I could believe it randomly found his way to a house in Utah, but my guess is that he was a pet, they got tired of him (possibly because he was a tad bitey), and they called the snake guy to take him away. Stranger things have happened.

Like the time I was called to pick up another non-native snake, this time an albino corn snake. The story was that it must have crawled in through the doggie door, but I was skeptical from the start. I carefully extricated it from under the fridge. As I was preparing to leave, the son of the owners, a six-year-old boy, confided in me that it was his dad's pet snake but mommy didn't want him to have it anymore.

These people had gone to elaborate lengths to contrive a lie by letting a pet snake loose in the house and making up a story about how it got there. I would have picked up the snake and rehomed it regardless of the reason, but the most disturbing aspect is the example of dishonesty they had set for their child.

When a homeowner called about a little pinkish-orange snake in his yard, my first thought was 'albino corn snake.' They're common in the pet trade, relatively inexpensive, and they occasionally get loose or are released by people who don't understand the implications of releasing an animal outside its normal range.

I forwarded the texted photo to Jordan, and even though it wasn't a great image, he agreed that the pattern, although faded and ghost-like, was definitely that of a gopher snake. Beyond that, the heavily keeled scales were a dead giveaway. Jordan went to the house to pick it up.

This was no corn snake. No siree! This was a wild-born, free roaming, albino/lavender Great Basin gopher snake that someone found on their suburban farm. An animal like this occurs once in every 20,000 to 100,000 births, and is a true and natural work of art! I named her TLKM (pronounced Tilkum) after an alien in a documentary I saw once.

Some people go looking for cool snakes. I only had to wait for my phone to ring!

I shudder to think what the result would have been if this unique animal had crawled into a different yard — one owned by someone with a fear of snakes. Unable to differentiate between a common snake and one with a unique genetic makeup, a snake hater may have killed this animal for no valid reason other than a visceral ignorance weaponized by fear, resulting in the destruction of something rare and irreplaceable. TLKM is on breeding loan with a friend in Reno, Nevada, and we look forward to one day hatching a clutch of her equally unique and beautiful offspring.

A property management company called. One of their clients needed to rent his house but was afraid to divulge the fact that his prior tenants' six-foot python was loose and he couldn't find it. I told him there was a chance that the tenant would find the snake during the packing and moving process, and if not, that the new tenants likely would. This of course, is what he didn't want. He would have to disclose the fact that there might be a large constricting snake on the premises, which isn't a desirable amenity for most renters.

When the tenant finally moved out in April, the landlord called to say that the place was available for inspection. I searched the house but could not definitively say whether there was a snake there or not, only that there was a low probability that there was a large snake in the house. This satisfied the legal requirements for not having to disclose to new tenants that there may be a large, uncontained snake on the premises and risk not being able to rent it, or for other liabilities it might incur.

If it had died in the house, no one had smelled anything after six months. If it was still there it was probably still alive. A six-foot python shouldn't be able to avoid detection for too long, although they can be pretty stealthy despite their size.

After performing a visual inspection of the home's interior, I checked the garage and an outbuilding, looked behind and inside two refrigerators, behind two washer/dryer sets, two stoves and the furnace. I shone my headlamp into the dark recesses of floor joists, under the stairs, heat registers and ducts. I opened all cabinets, cupboards and drawers, inspected all exterior vents for possible egress, and walked the yard twice. I checked window wells, looked in trees and shrubbery, and even dismantled a woodpile.

Based on my inspection, it was highly unlikely that a live exotic snake remained on the premises. The fact that the tenant noticed no sounds or smells in the home in the six months following the escape were strong indicators that the snake either escaped from the home, was removed from the home, or died in an inaccessible location and was no longer considered a deterrent to new occupants. Furthermore, the likelihood of an exotic snake surviving outdoors over the winter was impossible, and any potential threat to neighbors or pets had been negated by that fact.

Still, something didn't seem right. Common sense and intuition said it had to be there, and I really wanted to find that snake. Starting over, this time in the basement, I began pushing up on the suspended ceiling tiles with a broom handle. After all, my own large snake had escaped into a ceiling when I was a kid, so why not use that as a starting point? After 20 tiles or so, there was resistance above one of them and I felt something shift. Could it be?

Climbing on a footstool, I removed the tile to discover a beautiful but very cold, hungry, and thirsty red-tailed boa constrictor. I named her Lucy because she had been 'loosie' in the house for so long. After several days of warming her up and feeding her, I gave her to my friend Cary to use in his educational animal programs. She'll have a good home, excellent care, and be a goodwill ambassador by teaching kids about snakes.

As coincidence would have it, the new tenants had a snake of their own. They may have been ecstatic, but nonetheless surprised, to have found this one waiting to welcome them to their new abode.

Her "owner" forfeited his right to get her back. In fact, the landlord sent him the bill for my services. After all, someone who doesn't know the difference between a boa and a python doesn't deserve to have either one.

The homeowner was glad he didn't partially demolish the house looking for the snake, and I couldn't have been more tickled if I had swallowed a feather duster. Most important, the snake was safe and well.

A guy two counties away found a large orange and yellow snake in his yard and he was pretty sure it wasn't native. He didn't send a photo. My first thought was that it might be an escaped pet rat snake. Yellow rat snakes are common in the pet trade, are long and slender, can reach six feet in length, and like most snakes, are stealthy enough to escape from an insecure enclosure. I sent Casey to check it out. A short time later, he called me.

"You're not going to believe this," he said. He was right, I didn't.

Incredibly, it was an adult male albino blood python (*Python brongersmai*), a native of the Malay Peninsula, Sumatra, and Thailand. It was a long way from its tropical home and had spent several miserable days outside in cold and rainy weather. As a result, it was extremely hissed off!

The snake was massive! While only about five feet long, its girth in the middle was as big as my thigh and it must have weighed 50 pounds. Having nothing big enough to contain it, Casey handed it over to me. He had managed to confine it to a large plastic tub in the back of his van with a piece of plywood on top, held in place only by a worn-out bungee cord. His four children scrambled to maintain a safe distance during the 20-mile drive, probably wishing they were in a bigger car.

Blood pythons are ambush predators, relying on stealth and power to catch rodents and other small mammals. Shorter and stockier than other pythons, these snakes don't move around much. Historically, blood pythons were considered aggressive, but that reputation mostly came from wild-caught adults. Captive-bred individuals tend to be much calmer and more manageable, especially with regular, respectful handling.

I doubt this one had been handled much, and he didn't give a rat's hind end that we considered him aggressive. He was mostly content to stay in his bin, lunging open-mouthed with intimidating ferocity when someone took the plywood off. With a head the size of a pie spatula, and six rows of large, recurved teeth as an arsenal, a bite from this snake could do serious damage.

Blood pythons are fascinating creatures known for their remarkable coloration, which can range from deep crimson to rusty orange. Those vivid hues are what earned them their name. As an albino bred for the pet trade, this one was yellow in color, making it especially desirable to collectors and breeders.

Highly sedentary by nature and too heavy to pursue their prey, blood pythons lie in wait to ambush an unsuspecting meal that comes within striking range. These lazy, ponderous snakes do not like to move more than necessary, and there is no way this one got outside on its own. My vet gave him an enthusiastic thumbs-up and I was able to find him a good home with a local python breeder.

This was, without a doubt, the most exotic and socially maladapted snake my team and I ever encountered.

When a call came on Halloween night of 2021 about a snake in a toilet, I assumed it was a prank, but the man on the phone assured me it was true. It did seem a bit ironic being Halloween and all, so I pressed him for proof.

"There's a snake in my toilet," he said adamantly, "and it's moving." He was emphatic about the fact that he didn't like snakes. This one, he told me, was black and about four feet long, but he didn't know how to text me a picture of it.

Unable to go myself, and still skeptical, I called Bebe. Not knowing what to expect, I told her to take her boyfriend along. They arrived at the house, and sure enough, there was a snake in the toilet. Not just any snake, and not a native one, but a handsome young Phantom Golden Child Reticulated Python. It belonged to the man's brother who failed to mention he had a pet snake.

Neither the snake nor the brother was welcome in the house any longer, but I found the snake a good home. The brother is on his own.

In the spring of 2024, I spent a weekend in St. George with herper extraordinaire, Ethan the human snake magnet. Our goal was to locate two specific species; the variable ground snake (*Sonora semiannulata*) and Smith's black-headed snake (*Tantilla hobartsmithi*). Ethan had seen ground snakes before, but both species would be firsts for me.

Ethan contacted me in the summer of 2021 to inquire about becoming a relocator. With an obvious passion for snakes, he had the enthusiasm, the drive, and the tenacity to do the job, but there were two major drawbacks: he lacked venomous snake experience and he was only 17.

The state stipulates that no one under the age of 18 can possess or apply to be on a COR, and although his 18th birthday was only a month away, the bureaucratic hassle of adding him to my certificate so late in the season was a drawback, as was the time remaining to train him.

Ethan and I went herping soon after, and despite the difference in our ages, we quickly became friends. With a vast repertoire of snake knowledge and a focus on field herping, Ethan has a large following and a well-deserved reputation as the creator and host of *Snakes on the Brain*, a popular YouTube channel for snake lovers and those wanting to learn more about them. He is also a world-class martial artist, actor, and all-around great guy.

Unbelievably, Ethan struck gold on our very first day in the field, unearthing both of our elusive target species like a seasoned prospector uncovers shiny nuggets. He struck the motherlode on day two with the discovery of 15 more ground snakes and another black-headed snake, all flipped within the sandy, rock-strewn sanctuary of a riparian stream bank.

Ground snakes and black-headed snakes are masters of concealment — small, unassuming, and so secretive they seem to weave themselves into the desert shadows. Ground snakes in particular are little gems, delicate and smooth, typically with vivid black and orange bands wrapping their bodies. However, they may also be striped, solid-colored, or have black crossbars on a base color of brown, tan, gray, blue, green, cream, yellow, orange, pink, or red. Some individuals may have a head that is darker than the body; they may or may not have a neckband, while others may have a vertebral stripe.

Most snake species exhibit a broad range of coloration and patterning, which is why it can sometimes be difficult for laypersons to identify what type of snake they're looking at. This explains why the snake you see when you're hiking may not look exactly like the one in your field guide. Like snowflakes, no two are exactly the same.

These color morphs are highly inconsistent even in the same location, making the ground snake the most variable snake species in North America. Fossorial by nature, they conceal themselves in loose or sandy soil or hide under rocks. Looking like they belong on a charm bracelet, these diminutive snakes are fragile and utterly enchanting. You're lucky to spot one before it melts back into the substrate.

Smith's black-headed snake, while not considered rare, can be a challenge to locate, and many herpers have failed to find one despite tireless efforts. Named in honor of herpetologist Hobart M. Smith, it is also known as the Southwestern black-headed snake. According to the Utah Division of Wildlife Resources, "[This] species is secretive, and although it may not be exceedingly rare in Utah, it is seldom found in the state." Distribution and documented sightings are limited to only three or four remote areas in Washington County, and only a few lucky individuals have ever seen one. Disjunct subspecies can be found in California, Nevada, Arizona, New Mexico, Colorado, and Texas.

Large, grooved teeth in the rear upper jaw deliver mild venom, but as one of the smallest snakes in North America, this snake is not dangerous to humans. *Tantilla* or *Tantillum* is Latin for "so small a thing," and even a large specimen will seldom reach more than a foot in length.

As a nocturnal, terrestrial snake, much of its life is spent in crevices, buried in loose (moist) soil, or hidden under rocks and other debris during the day. It can be found on the surface at night, especially after a rainstorm. If you are lucky enough to find a black-headed snake, take lots and lots of pictures! Then, do the right thing and leave it where you found it.

Later that day, Ethan scored again by flipping a generic looking rock to reveal a juvenile coachwhip snake. After posing for pictures, its slender, spring-loaded body blended back into the desert like a blur.

Yes, this is what snake people do for fun: crawl through dirt, flip stones, and whoop with joy over a glint of shimmering scales. I can't speak for the snakes, but for Ethan and me, it was a field day worth every drop of sweat and every smile that ensued.

One idyllic spring morning in 2024, Ethan, like a magician pulling rabbits from a top hat, conjured a pair of Utah milk snakes from under a single rock. My hands trembled as I held these red, white, and black-banded snakes that looked like hand-painted works of art. They felt almost velvety. I stood speechless, barely able to express my astonishment and joy. Without a doubt, Ethan is the finest flipper I have ever known.

For many years it was believed that Utah had 31 official snake species because that was the number that got tossed around and was generally agreed upon. However, once the dust settled, the actual count should have been 32.

Utah's eighth and completely unacknowledged rattlesnake is *Crotalus lutosus abyssis,* the Grand Canyon rattlesnake. This attractive, pale, and nearly patternless serpent is native to both rims and the floor of the Grand Canyon in Arizona. It makes its way to Utah's Kaiparowits Plateau via the various drainages of the Escalante and Paria Rivers in Kane and Garfield Counties.

The seemingly barren moonscape of the Kaiparowits Plateau belies the fact that some of Utah's most stunning desert hide-a-ways lay concealed within deep canyons carved by tributaries of the Escalante and Colorado rivers. Canyons like Egypt, Davis Gulch, Harris Gulch, Coyote Gulch, Fiftymile Creek and others, are perpetual oases, providing backpackers with ready sources of water from perennial streams that flow through canyons so verdant and lush you'll forget you're in a desert.

Despite being documented many times by reliable individuals, the Grand Canyon rattlesnake lacks the required documentation for inclusion as a Utah species, because the state, with the indifference I've come to expect, can't be bothered to verify it as indigenous.

I saw my first Grand Canyon rattlesnake on a rafting trip through the Grand Canyon when I was 19, and I was fortunate to have found a second specimen several years ago while backpacking in Utah's Grand Staircase-Escalante National Monument. (See back cover photo.)

My most recent non-native acquisition in the summer of 2024 caught me completely off guard. A woman in a nearby city claimed to have a snake in her garage. Nothing unusual about that, right? Except that her description was so atypical that I asked her to repeat it.

"It's a white snake," she explained again, "and it has freckles." Assuming this woman hadn't taken a hallucinogenic detour from reality, her description left me stymied. "Can you text me a picture?" I asked.

The photo she sent was far away and a little blurry. It appeared to be some kind of corn snake or rat snake, but it didn't look like any morph I had ever seen. But she was right. It was a white snake with freckles! I forwarded the photo to Ethan. His reply? "WTF!" This wasn't a snake either of us was familiar with.

We met the woman at her apartment complex. A maintenance man had placed the snake in a bucket with a piece of plywood on top. When he lifted the board, Ethan and I scrambled to make sense of the incredibly beautiful snake that began climbing out of the bucket.

We looked at each other in disbelief. It was a corn snake all right, but what morph? There are hundreds of corn snake morphs in the pet trade, and while I know many of them, I didn't know this one.

Research revealed it to be a Palmetto morph corn snake. Of all the corn snake morphs, this may be the most unusual and attractive.

This unique morphology derived from a single wild-caught specimen from South Carolina in the early 2000's. Popular in the pet trade, and initially selling for about $4,000 each, it is essentially a leucistic (partial loss of pigmentation) variant with an incomplete dominant trait. With their cream-white bodies and orange, red, and gray flecks of color, these snakes are visually stunning.

Now worth about $500, someone is missing a valuable and very handsome pet, but management wasn't aware of any tenant with a pet snake. In accordance with Wasatch Snake Removal policy, I kept it for 10 days, allowing ample time for the owner to call and claim it, but no one did. He now belongs to me.

"Confetti," as I call him, is still with me today. His bulgy eyes, which are also part of the genetic mutation, give him the goofy appearance of a cartoon snake, and even folks who don't like snakes comment on how handsome he is.

These were the primary incidents of locating unusual, aberrant, displaced or exotic snakes, and while I didn't discover a new species, I did meet serpents that challenged the narrative — proof that discovery doesn't always conform to expectation, and that serendipity sometimes slithers in unannounced.

In recent years, reports of non-native reptiles have become commonplace. As the number of exotic reptiles kept as pets continues to increase, some of them escape, while others are deliberately released. Ball pythons are prime examples of this. Over the years, I picked up dozens of ball pythons that had been callously dumped in parks and recreation areas when their owners allegedly got tired of them. Most were sick with upper respiratory viruses, predators had attacked some of them, and others couldn't shed their skin due to the lack of humidity in an arid climate. As tropical snakes, all of them die when winter comes. It's a cruel and undeserved fate for such gentle animals.

9 | Heads and Tails

Large numbers of invasive species have insinuated themselves into environments where they don't belong. This is always the result of human interference and laziness. When abandoned pets turn up in the wrong places, animals and ecosystems pay for these careless human choices. Bullfrogs don't belong here, but we have them. Soft-shelled turtles, red-eared sliders, and even snapping turtles now live in local waterways, and occasionally an alligator makes an appearance on the news. There is even a breeding population of corn snakes near a particular city. Corn snakes are not native to Utah.

Don't take wild animals home as pets, and don't release pet animals into the wild! It's not just irresponsible — it's reckless. Most animals can't survive outside their natural territories. Like pythons in the everglades, those that do often prey on native wildlife or become victims of human stupidity. Pets, no matter how resilient, aren't equipped to become part of the ecosystem they're displaced into. Most will die. The ones that don't will survive at the expense of something else — decimating native species or spreading disease.

A friend of mine told me about a woman whose young grandson caught a horned lizard on a family outing and brought it home. Confronted with the reality that it eats ants, the woman no longer wants the lizard, but it's doubtful that she'll take the time to drive it back to where it was found. It will either die a slow and miserable death from neglect and starvation, or it will be released into an urban environment where it will be killed by a cat, car, lawnmower, stupid person, or some other inescapable hazard of concentrated human habitation.

We've all done it; brought home the lizard, frog or snake we caught at summer camp or the family picnic at the local canyon, pond or park. We were probably just kids, although adults do it too. Our intentions were always good. We'd remove the critter from its rightful environs, take it home, set it up in a bottle or terrarium, try to feed it (even if we had no idea what it ate), and give it a dish of water. It would be a novelty, something unique, a little bit of nature brought indoors to cheer us up. Something to brag about to our friends. Show and tell time!

And then the inevitable happened; we'd lose interest or we couldn't provide its specialized food requirement. Deprived of sunlight, a suitable environment, and proper diet, the creature languished and died. We didn't mean to kill it — but we did — and a helpless animal became the victim of our good but misguided intentions.

Multiply this scenario by the hundreds of thousands of innocent animals that are removed from their natural habitats each year and killed, intentionally or otherwise, and you have exponential carnage on a massive scale, along with environments that are out of balance as a result.

The natural world suffers enough from the relentless onslaught of a human invasion. Animals are having a harder time trying to avoid humans and the carnage inflicted by our roads, cars, reckless expansion, guns, industrial processes, pollution, habitat destruction, climate change, herbicide and pesticide poisoning, and a general disregard for animals and a natural world that too many people just don't understand or care about. Many species are in decline and many more teeter on the brink of extinction due to human stupidity and indifference.

Please, when you find that frog or tadpole, garter snake, baby bird, butterfly or beetle, enjoy it where it is. Teach your children about it. Let them see it in its natural realm. Take its picture. Catch it if you have to, but better yet, try to photograph it "in situ" — in its natural place and pose. Then, leave it there, where it belongs. When you get home, you can look it up on the internet or read about it in a book. If you just can't help yourself, at least be willing to return it back to where you found it after a reasonable period of captive observation.

If you find an injured animal, entrust it to the care of a qualified wildlife rehabilitation specialist. Without the proper skills and knowledge, you can cause an animal greater harm by trying to help it yourself.

Wild animals aren't available for the taking. Animals are the property of the state in which they reside. Laws protect many species and a permit is required to capture or keep them. Some people think it's okay to catch wild reptiles and sell them. If a moose wandered into your backyard, would it be okay to sell it on the internet? Of course not! It's no different with reptiles and amphibians. The illegal taking of an animal for any reason is known as poaching, and that's not something anyone should want to be guilty of.

I'm not saying we shouldn't have pets, because most of us do, but virtually any animal you can think of, especially a reptile or amphibian, is available from a breeder or a pet store that buys from breeders. Captive propagation has produced impeccable animals that are disease and parasite free, and you won't be removing an animal from its natural habitat where it can thrive, reproduce, and live out its life in accordance with nature's laws.

Better yet, adopt a reptile from a rescue or sanctuary. These animals need a good home and you'll be doing everyone a favor!

CHAPTER 10

Friends in Low Places

"I know people freak out at the word 'snake.' But this planet was not made just for humans. Every species on Earth needs a place." –Peter Mallett (former snake-hater)

Long before I had a team to help me move snakes, I had a part-time sidekick named Cooper.

Urban snake removal is, for the most part, a one-person job. At least it was when I first started. Still, it was always nice to have company, especially on the hike to release a snake, which was often the most arduous and time-consuming part of any relocation.

As my neighbor's grandson, Cooper accompanied me on numerous snake calls and releases despite the verbal 'no minors' stipulation of my COR, which I assumed was more of a legal afterthought than an ironclad rule, considering that it didn't appear in the printed document.

For about three years, beginning when he was nine, Cooper spent occasional weekends with his grandma, a lovely woman named Debbie, who was my next-door neighbor for nearly 17 years. Several times each summer, the three of us would cruise the Skull Valley road, followed by waffles and banana splits at a 24-hour diner in the wee hours of the morning. I usually knew when Cooper was coming over and I'd invite him to join me on snake calls.

Cooper was a towhead, blonde as a Viking. He was bright and articulate. His good nature was punctuated with a permanent grin that matched his personality. A loud or rambunctious kid would have been too much of a distraction, even a liability, but Cooper's demeanor was always pleasantly polite and pensive. He carried himself with a quiet confidence and didn't ruffle easily, staying grounded even when things got tense. Best of all, he was just enough of a smart aleck to keep me on my toes and laughing at all the right moments.

Once, on a call to remove a buzzer butt from a garage at an affluent home, Cooper's intuition proved invaluable. He was 11 at the time. The woman of the house (we'll call her Connie), explained how she had entered the garage from her kitchen to get a broom. Upon turning on the light, she saw a snake scoot under a shelf. "It rattled at me," she exclaimed, "and that's when I called you."

Connie's garage looked like most American garages — filled to overflowing with the flotsam of excessive consumption — leaving no room to park a car. Looking at the stacks of boxes and assorted junk that intruded into the space and covered the walls from floor to ceiling, Cooper and I had our work cut out for us.

"Don't worry," I assured Connie, "if there's a snake in here, we'll find it." 'But,' I mumbled to myself, 'it isn't going to be easy.'

I have always appreciated rattlesnakes. Whereas it could be extremely difficult to detect any other snake in a situation like this one, a rattlesnake will usually rattle as a warning if you get too close, thereby revealing its location.

For safety reasons I couldn't include Cooper in the actual search for the snake, but he made an excellent lookout in case I flushed a snake without realizing it or it decided to dash to a different location behind my back.

I lay on my stomach on the concrete floor and began prodding under the shelves where Connie had seen the snake. With a flashlight in one hand and a snake stick in the other, I peered under the shelving with my left eye, trying not to grind the corner of my glasses into the concrete. There was a three-inch gap between the floor and the bottom shelf, and if it was under there I should have been able to pull it out and be done. But that would have been too easy.

Snakes are masters of hide and seek. Going counterclockwise around the garage, I moved everything on wheels first: garbage cans, lawnmower, snow blower, golf carts, etc., placing them in the center of the room. There was no sign of a snake. No motion, no rattle, nothing.

I began by prodding under and behind every stationary object that was too heavy to move, listening intently for the telltale buzz that would reveal the snake's location. It would then be a matter of getting it out. Again, nothing.

Shining my headlamp down behind the furniture, shelving, and heavy boxes, I hoped to spot my worthy opponent crawling along the base of the wall. It is a common behavior in many animals.

When looking for a snake in a house, it's always a good idea to check along the baseboards first. When doing a yard inspection, I always started by walking around the foundation of the home.

"Well Coop, what do you think?" I asked. Cooper had been watching and listening as well, recommending objects to move and look behind. This snake was outsmarting us even though we were in human territory and had the home court advantage.

The only option left at this point would have been to use a garden hose. This technique is effective for flushing snakes from burrows and retaining walls, but it wasn't an option in Connie's garage.

I was ready to concede this round, when Cooper, looking even more introspective than usual, said, "I think I know where it is, Dave."

"You do?" I asked skeptically. "Where?"

We were standing at the entrance to the garage. The bottom edge of the door was directly overhead.

"Up there," Cooper said, pointing to the rubber weather strip that sealed the door to the concrete driveway. It was a hollow rubber tube with an opening at each end.

"You think so?" I asked. "If he's in there, he's a pretty smart snake."

"Where else could he have gone?" Cooper asked the question as if I was a seeker of knowledge and he was the all-knowing guru who lived on top of the mountain. "We looked everywhere else. He must have crawled in there before we got here." Cooper spoke with the veracity of a true pragmatist.

"Let's find out," I said. Starting at one end of the weather strip, I began squeezing it gently, working my way toward the center. About four feet from the right-hand side there was something solid in the tube. And it moved.

"Son of a . . .!" I stopped myself midsentence as Cooper flashed an 'I told you so' grin. "How did you know?" I was incredulous. Perplexed. Dumbfounded.

"It's the only place we haven't looked," he said with sagely wisdom. Was this kid for real? He was probably thinking what a moron I was for not thinking of it too, but he was too polite to say so. He also needed a ride home.

The snake was pointed toward the left side of the door. The far side. I kept palpating the tube as the snake slowly inched its way along this cramped corridor for the remaining 14 feet to the other end. Finally, a head popped out. It was a scaly, inquisitive rattlesnake head, its tongue lolling slowly and deliberately up and down in the warm afternoon air.

I kept pinching the snake's butt inside the tube to keep it moving, and using my snake hook, I tried to guide it toward my bucket. The snake, however, had a different plan.

Wanting to escape from whatever I was, the snake began to wedge itself into the grooved track that guides the wheels and keeps the garage door in place, finally going up and over the curve where the track bends from vertical to horizontal.

"No! Don't go in there!" I shouted at the snake as if it knew English. If it had been any other local snake, like a gopher or racer, I could have simply grabbed it with my bare hands and worked it free. Getting bit wouldn't have been a problem. But this was a rattlesnake and I had no desire to be envenomated. Not that day. Not any day.

The snake's determination to elude me was proof that these animals have zero desire to deal with humans. Unaware that we were there to help, it only wanted to be left alone.

Now fully in the track, the snake climbed up and onto the top of the open garage door which was now a large flat surface parallel to the floor with only a foot or so between the door and ceiling. There was about a foot-wide space between the edges of the door and the walls on either side. If I could determine the snake's location on the door, and as long as it didn't keep moving, it would be a simple matter of slowly closing the door and sliding the snake into my bucket. I needed to know its location on the door, however, because I didn't want the snake falling 10 feet to the ground if I miscalculated. With their many ribs and vertebrae, snakes are fragile creatures and easily injured.

The Only Good Snake . . .

I grabbed a stepladder and poked my head up between the wall and the edge of the door. As I did so, I found myself face-to-face with my reptilian fugitive. He could have been anywhere on that large surface, but there he was, looking at me from mere inches away. He didn't rattle, and thank God he didn't strike.

I slowly ducked down and told Cooper to hit the button until I said to stop. As the motor groaned and the wheels rattled, the snake came into view above me. Holding my bucket up and in front of me, I placed it where the snake could slide right in.

I treated Cooper to a burger and shake before hiking our buzzer butt friend up to a suitable location in the foothills. I really don't think I would have found that snake without Cooper's help, chalking it up as the one that got away, or simply assuming I was off my game that day.

Heughs Canyon became a familiar hike after moving several snakes from the neighborhood that had sprouted uninvited on the moraine below. We had returned many of them back to safety in this steep, narrow cut that provided water to the valley's early settlers. The trail closely followed the route of a rusty old pipe that had embedded itself into the landscape over the past hundred years or more.

I was about to park my carc-ass on a rock in Heughs Canyon when Cooper, casual as could be, politely informed me that I almost sat on a rattlesnake.

"I did not!" I replied indignantly. But yes, I did. Cooper didn't joke about things like that. We had already released the snake we brought with us. This was a different snake. I suppose the snake didn't like my butt in its face because it started to crawl slowly away. Cooper held the calm serpent with a snake stick while I took their picture. This snake hung out under a specific rock and we visited him each time we hiked the canyon. We called him Fred.

Cooper and I came across two Great Basin rattlers while hiking one Saturday morning. Cooper caught both of them. I held one of them, allowing it to glide gently away from me, alternately moving my hands underneath its smooth belly like letting go of a slow, smooth rope. Neither snake had any inclination to be defensive, only wanting to be left alone. For most snakes, this is entirely normal behavior and not an exception. I have spent most of my adult life attempting to dispel the negative publicity that ignorant people choose to spew in their delusion.

Cooper was a heck of a good kid and the best snake assistant I ever had.

Good neighbors like Debbie and Cooper are hard to come by because you don't get to choose your neighbors. You're lucky when you get good ones and you never want to take them for granted.

Snakes make awesome neighbors too, and can best be described as our friends in low places. Humans have more in common with snakes than most people realize. Both species breathe air, drink water, eat food, and defecate. We have red blood, feel pain and fear (including the innate fear of falling), and live in social groups. (They may not use social media, but snakes have social lives, too.)

Most of the time when someone called, there was a snake of one type or another in their yard. This presented homeowners with a dilemma; namely, what kind of snake was it, did it present a danger to their children or pets, and what could they do to prevent other snakes from entering their yard?

Most snake calls were pretty routine: take the call, drive to the house, catch the snake, release the snake within prescribed parameters, go home. Not all calls were that cut and dried of course, and some didn't include live snakes at all.

One day in early March, I was summoned to a home in a wealthy suburb. A woman was having her kitchen floor replaced and the workers had allegedly found a dead rattlesnake and several shed skins in the crawlspace beneath the floor.

In truth, the crawlspace had become the tomb of a dead gopher snake. It was laying in the dirt, straight as a stick, its viscera having turned into gelatinous goo over many months of decomposition in a cool, dry, musty space. Even the smell had dissipated.

There was a shed skin, presumably belonging to the once-living gopher snake, and the shed skin of a Western racer, which had presumably found its way back outside, although I couldn't tell how or where. Turning off my light should have revealed any point of ingress or egress where snakes could come and go, but no daylight penetrated the space. A walk around the exterior foundation wasn't helpful either.

I removed the dead snake and the solitary skin, making sure there were no live snakes brumating in the crawlspace. The construction workers were free to finish the job of replacing the floors.

One call that I'm pretty sure was made under false pretenses had me looking for a snake in a large patch of weedy backyard that had been a flower garden at one time, but ground cover now choked the area and native plants had invaded as well. It was a landscaper's nightmare and a snake's real estate dream come true.

The woman who called me didn't seem concerned about the rattlesnake she claimed she saw. I was skeptical that she had seen a snake at all in the tangled mass of unruly vegetation. I couldn't even see dirt let alone burrows where a snake might be hiding. All I could do was walk alternately back and forth in rows east and west, then repeat the process by walking north and south until I had completed a grid pattern over the entire area. If there was a rattlesnake in there somewhere, it should rattle at me if I got close enough. Any other snake could glide silently under this dense green mat and I would never know it.

The woman made polite conversation the entire time. Initially, her questions were of a general nature: How long had I been doing this? Was this my full-time job? Etcetera. Gradually, her inquiries became more personal. Was I married? Did I have kids? What did I do for fun? She then started sharing information about herself.

Her husband, she claimed, was in Iraq, and had been there for nine months. She wasn't much of a socialite and didn't have a lot of friends. I was beginning to get uncomfortable, changing the subject to explain that there wasn't much chance of finding a snake in foliage as dense as this.

As I prepared to leave, she placed a hand on my shoulder and asked if I wanted to come inside. Did this lonely housewife really intend to seduce me? She could always tell her neighbors that the car parked out front belonged to the snake removal guy. It was a perfect ruse.

She wasn't unattractive and I should have been flattered I suppose. But even though I'm a single man, or maybe because of it, I like to keep my life uncomplicated. Neither of us found what we were looking for that day.

Sometimes you find the snake, sometimes you don't. Sometimes there is no snake, and sometimes you'll never know for sure.

I performed a brief, free-of-charge inspection of the grounds at a hotel near the airport one evening. A woman from Guam had seen a snake near the front entrance and parts of her went back to Guam without even boarding the plane. All I found was a shed skin and a lot of prime snake habitat.

A few days later, Jordan and I removed a good-sized rattler from under Rick and Christine's deck. Afterward, they served us lemonade in the waving shade of a dozen large trees, and the neighbors, who were previous customers of mine, came over and brought cookies. It was a regular party!

Jordan did the dirty and dangerous part, crawling under the deck with a headlamp, stick, tongs and bucket, while I drizzled water on the snake from above to keep it from retreating further and becoming inaccessible.

This snake had the largest string of rattle segments I have ever seen on a wild snake — 14! Segments usually break off well before the strand gets that long.

Public access became hugely problematic as more land was placed off-limits, making it difficult to meet the state's requirements for a short-distance translocation. We hopped a 10-foot privacy fence and released the snake on uninhabited private property.

A call came from Carol who had a beautiful female Great Basin rattlesnake in her yard. By the time I arrived 20 minutes later, the snake had moved to the neighbor's yard where she was poised majestically in shafts of dancing sunlight among a bed of flowers in a grove of birch trees. This serpent had found her own Garden of Eden! She barely resisted as I picked her up with tongs, carried her down a set of stone steps and placed her in a bucket on the sidewalk.

It didn't take long for the neighbors to congregate along with their children. The mail carrier stopped to look at the snake, as did the UPS guy. Everyone took pictures and asked questions. I always enjoyed those teaching moments.

Due to the lack of hiking trails or other public access to the mountain in this particular neighborhood, I knocked on the door of the state's most preeminent family and spoke with the matriarch. (The wrought iron security gates were open to accommodate a service van and the guard dogs were kenneled.) Her husband founded a phenomenally successful chemical corporation and a world-famous cancer hospital. One of her sons owns the Salt Lake Tribune, and another son was, at the time, the U.S. ambassador to Russia, a former governor of Utah, and a candidate for president.

The only access to wild habitat was on the mountain above her very private property, which is fenced off with no public access. We chatted about snakes for a while, and I told her that the last time I saw her in person was when she and her husband spoke at my brother's commencement at Dixie College more than 35 years before.

She summoned her personal representative/emissary/attaché to unlock the gate to the private canyon and escort me to a suitable place to release the snake. In the future, I allegedly had permission to hop the fence with a reasonable degree of assurance that I wouldn't be shot, arrested, or have a pack of Doberman's sicced on me, but it wasn't terribly reassuring.

Due to a worsening eye condition, I've never enjoyed night calls, but when the Webb family called me after dark on a Friday night to say that there was a rattler coiled placidly on their front porch, I knew I had to help them. They were expecting their two youngest girls to come home barefoot from a swim party down the street and were understandably nervous about a rattler in the yard.

I arrived not knowing what to expect or whether the snake would evade me in the clandestine darkness. The snake was in the open and seemingly oblivious to my presence at first, but the moment I tried to tong it the game was on!

With dad holding a flashlight and me with a flashlight in one hand and a snake stick in the other, mom and the kids watched the adventure unfold through the living room window as I pursued the snake back and forth through the front yard shrubbery. The wily snake propelled itself along the ground as though it was being pulled by an invisible string. The kids were delighted by the antics of the funny snake man as I weaved and dodged my way among a maze of unusually tall, grassy stalks and other non-native xeriscaping, eventually trapping the stealthy trespasser in a corner by the porch where the chase first began.

I didn't want the kids to be traumatized by the experience of having a rattlesnake in their yard, but my worries were unfounded. I introduced them to their snake, removing the lid from the bucket and shining my light on it. The kids were cute and extremely excited by the whole adventure, huddling over the bucket and asking thoughtful questions. Far from being afraid, it turned out to be a positive learning experience for all of them.

It was my third rattlesnake of the day, but instead of releasing it in the dark, I waited until the next morning to put the wayward serpent back on the mountain.

In all humility, I am truly the world's greatest snake removal specialist. I got a call to remove a snake in Eden. (That's right, a snake in Eden. What are the odds?) If someone had made that call way back in the beginning, snakes might not have been blamed for everything and the world might not be so screwed up today.

Because Eden is well outside my service area, the woman (I couldn't help but ask if her name was Eve) wanted to know how to get a big gopher snake out of her garage. She was tempted to kill it (tempted, get it?), but I gave her how-to instructions on do-it-yourself snake removal using a leaf rake or a push broom. I never heard back from her. I hope the serpent didn't beguile her and that she didn't eat any forbidden fruit.

Jana called me about an escaped ball python in her home. It belonged to a houseguest who didn't tell her she had a snake until after it escaped. Jana doesn't like snakes.

The Only Good Snake . . .

Jana tore her house apart, but still no snake. She was sleeping with a towel jammed under her bedroom door so the snake wouldn't visit her during the night, and she was scared to use the bathroom. Basically, she was afraid to be in her own home.

Snakes can stay hidden for long periods, and these issues aren't always resolved quickly. With mostly hardwood and tile floors in her home, I suggested that she sprinkle a light coating of flour on the floor near any suspected hiding places. If the snake came out at night or when no one was home, it would leave tracks in the flour and reveal its location.

Jana called back to say that the flour trick worked and the snake was found. I told her I'd been doing this a long time and that I had learned a thing or two. She must have told me 10 times how wonderful I am. Aw, shucks!

Garter snakes were a fact of life every spring. March usually brought the first snake calls of the year, which were always for an overly optimistic garter snake, and usually more than one. After giving my best sales pitch, I was often able to broker a peace deal and the snakes were allowed to stay.

The next garter snake call was in the backyard of a residential neighborhood in the southeast part of the valley. The Middle Eastern family I met that afternoon was extremely hospitable and gracious, but being from a part of the world where cobras are common, they were also terrified. Even my best sales pitch had no effect on them whatsoever.

The three little kids were entertained as I probed the flower-beds, peered under shrubbery, and lifted paver stones. They even got excited each time I found a wiggly little snake, but I could not get them to touch one. Maybe it was their mother's stern gaze as she watched from the kitchen window, wagging her finger and shaking her head back and forth emphatically. Or maybe it was the smell.

Garter snakes are stinky beasts. They emit a pungent musk from scent glands at the base of their tail as a defense mechanism against predators. I refer to them affectionately as three-striped stink noodles. If you want to be left alone, or if you want to commit social suicide, just put a little dab of garter snake musk behind each ear and no one will bother you for days. Guaranteed!

Another Indian family called about a garter snake in their yard. I searched for an hour but couldn't find it, and I didn't feel right about charging them a service fee without actually helping them because they probably wouldn't call again.

I thanked them for not killing the snake and told them it wouldn't hurt them. It would eat the pests in their garden, it was their friend, and to please call me if it came back. I'm not sure I was terribly convincing because they didn't exactly look reassured when I left.

The state only condoned the relocation of harmless snakes under extreme circumstances, and I only moved them for customers who were truly afraid or who threatened to kill them. A 70-year-old woman was afraid to leave her house because two consenting adult garter snakes had homesteaded her front porch and were practicing planned parenthood. Yes, those amorous serpents were doing the horizontal mambo in order to produce the next generation of three-striped stink noodles. Averi removed the amorous pair and received a generous tip in return.

A woman called about a gopher snake in her yard. Casey found the gopher snake, but it escaped into a rock pile. In a more thorough search of the area, he discovered a little rattlesnake that the homeowner wasn't aware of. This is why you want licensed professionals to deal with the snakes in your yard. We know what we're doing and we're good at it.

Public Works called one afternoon about rattlesnakes at a pump facility in one of Salt Lake's most prestigious neighborhoods. Neighbors were complaining of an "infestation" of snakes. Someone beat me there because two rattlesnakes lay bludgeoned and beheaded in the gravel.

I met the nicest lady. Wendy called to say that her gardeners quit after they saw a snake in her yard. Averi and I performed a yard inspection and Averi spotted the culprit critter, a gopher snake, just as it went under a fence and into an overgrown area. Wendy was happy to have the snake around once she knew it wasn't a rattler. But that fact didn't satisfy the gardeners. She called the next day to say that the wily critter was back and hanging out near a drain spout. I raced back up to Tomahawk Drive and that time I caught him. That kept the gardeners happy and gainfully employed.

I took a call from a whiney woman 30 miles away who claimed to have "tons" of garter snakes in the lot where her new home was being built. I told her I would check it out.

Working with Jamison, we managed to find and catch a total of six wandering garter snakes in an hour and a half. The last time I checked, six garter snakes fell slightly short of a ton.

The unfortunate snakes, which had done absolutely nothing wrong, were taken away and released in a marshy area further north. It exceeded a standard translocation distance by almost three miles, but it was the closest viable habitat without placing them in another neighborhood. How much better things would be if we could learn to live with nature instead of making her the enemy.

I should have left the snakes where they were and dumped the whiny woman in the marsh. It would have been more satisfying and there would have been greater harmony in the universe.

Just because someone fears snakes doesn't mean the snakes should have to leave. A short-distance removal isn't nearly far enough to placate most homeowners, but it increases the odds that the snakes will survive. Otherwise, what's the point?

A man called from an adjacent city to say that there was a snake in his window well. Because he lived in the foothills, it could have been a rattler. When he texted a photo, however, it was a tiny baby garter snake as big around as a piece of fat spaghetti and about ten inches long.

"I can't have it here," he said.

I told him there were two solutions; I could send someone to remove it or he could save himself the cost by simply putting a branch in the window well so the snake could crawl out on its own.

"You need to send someone," he told me.

"I can do that," I replied. "Our fee for removing a harmless snake is $75."

"That's fine," he said.

Jordan took the call and released the snake at a nearby canal. It was the easiest $75 he ever made.

It's sad that so many people are so afraid of a harmless little animal that the free option isn't worth considering. But if the snake had gotten out of the window well by itself, he wouldn't have known its whereabouts which would have compounded his anxiety even more.

I have seen levels of fear that vacillate between mild apprehension and incapacitating terror. It's sad that people's lives can be so affected by an irrational fear, and disturbing that in this information age we fail to inoculate ourselves against our own false perceptions of reality. It should be an easy cure, but very few people are willing to take the medicine.

A local caller complained of a rattlesnake that someone caught and put in a bucket. Knowing that it was virtually impossible, since rattlesnakes in the valley were eradicated decades ago, I asked him to text me a photo. The alleged "rattlesnake" turned out to be a very handsome baby racer. How does anyone mistake a racer for a rattler? (Sometimes all I could do was shake my head and try not to beat it against a wall.)

I was so mad at myself one night that I wanted to kick my own ass. I left my phone in the car, so when the call came from Officer Don with County Animal Services about a "giant snake" at an apartment complex, I missed it.

Two hours later, I was walking around a strangely silent cluster of scary, low-end apartments looking for an unknown species of snake. When I hear the words "giant snake," I picture a serpent at least eight feet long. For the average non-snake-loving individual, however, it could describe any snake over 18 inches.

After much sleuthing, I finally found the guy who placed the initial call and he had taken a picture. It was a handsome gopher snake about three and a half feet in length but skinnier than normal. I looked for that snake for well over an hour until it got completely dark, but the only critters I found were a feral cat and its pet skunk. Or vice-versa.

There was a sneaky rattlesnake under a porch slab at a home in a nearby canyon, and an hour of trying to flush it out with water had no effect. I told the family not to let the kids go barefoot in the yard until I could catch the snake and to call me when they saw it again.

The Only Good Snake . . .

The homeowners called back the following day to say that the snake was on the lawn but was headed back toward the slab. I told dad to block the hole if possible, or to get the hose and spray the snake with water, keeping it away from its hiding place until I could get there. He did a great job and I caught the snake.

Whenever someone called about a snake in their yard, I prided myself on a quick arrival time. Snakes didn't always wait for the snake man, and homeowners were afraid to use their yard until I could catch their snake, sometimes taking drastic action if the situation wasn't resolved quickly. I could be at most locations within 20 to 25 minutes on average, depending on whether I was at home, at work, or somewhere else. That day, however, I outdid myself.

I had just caught the slab snake and was ready to leave. As I was backing down the driveway, my phone rang with another snake call. It happened a lot. The caller said he had a large rattler in his yard and wanted to know how soon I could get there.

"Where are you?" I asked, thinking that he was probably on the other side of the valley.

"Emigration Canyon," he replied.

"That's convenient," I responded. "I'm in Emigration Canyon right now."

"Where in Emigration Canyon?" he asked.

"I'm in Emigration Place. I just picked up a snake at a house on Marysvale," I said.

"No way! I'm on Wyndom, just around the corner."

"I know where you're at," I told him. "I'll be there in 60 seconds." And I was. He was in his yard when I pulled up, phone still in hand. The look on his face was priceless.

I caught the large female rattler that was sleeping contentedly under a pine tree in the side yard and released both snakes away from the neighborhood.

Yes, I was the world's fastest snake man, and while I probably could have made a lot more money delivering pizzas, it wouldn't have been nearly as much fun!

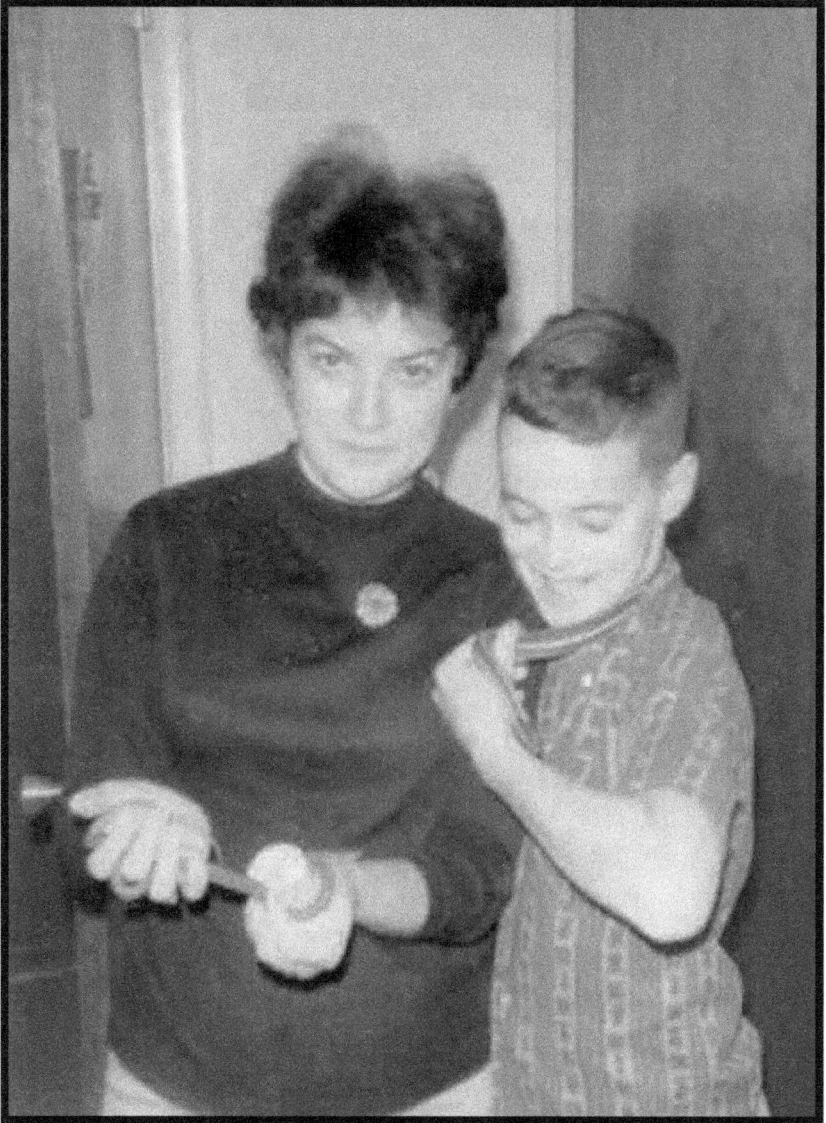

The author at 11 or 12 years old, with his mom and two
of his early pets — a Wandering garter snake and a Valley
garter snake.

Due to their relative scarcity in Northern Utah, Long-nosed snakes are always fun to find!

Moving snakes away from traffic is a fun and worthwhile way to spend a summer night with friends.

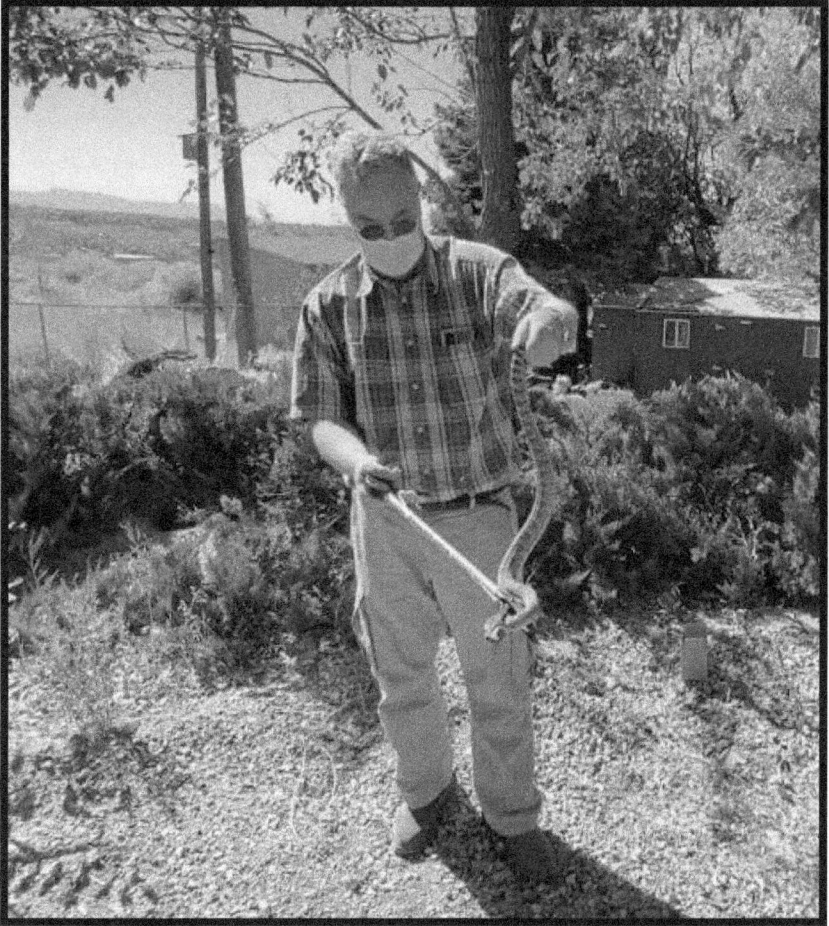

The author captures a Great Basin rattlesnake at a residential yard during Covid. Like all snakes, it was released into the nearest suitable wild habitat using a short-distance translocation protocol, ensuring that it remained in its home range but away from human habitation.

Great Basin rattlers have docile temperaments and rate low on the venom spectrum, making them the teddy bears of the rattlesnake family.

This young rattlesnake was looking for its dinner at the museum. For the safety of the snake and museum guests, it was relocated to nearby habitat.

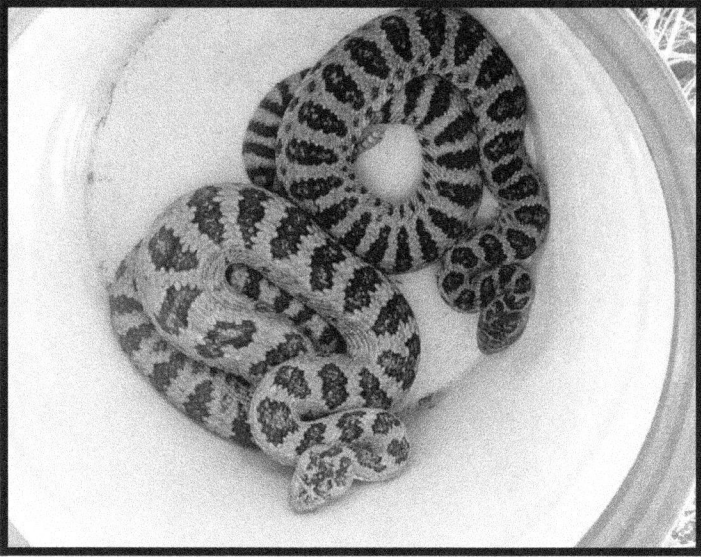

Averi removed these Great Basin rattlesnakes (above) from a residence in a local canyon. This shows the high variability in coloration, contrast, and patterning of this species, and may help explain why many people believe there is more than one species of rattlesnake along the Wasatch Front. She located the extremely dark (melanistic) specimen below at the museum. Despite obvious differences in appearance, these are all Great Basin rattlers.

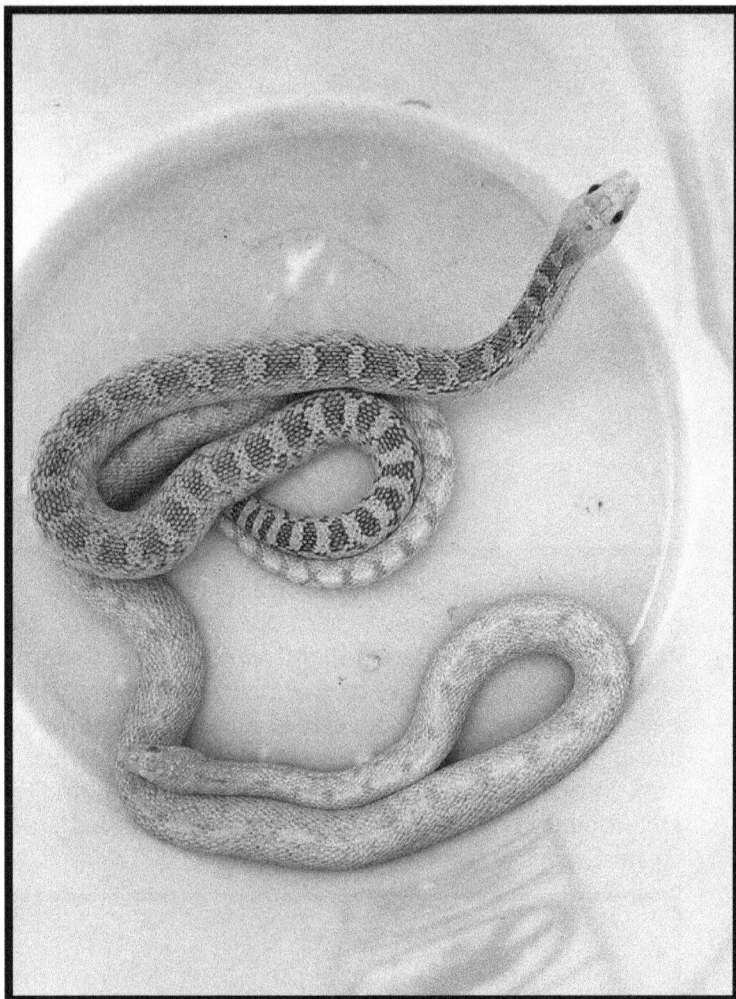

Homeowners in different locales reported both of these highly unusual Great Basin gopher snakes in or near their yards. Pinky (top) is a hypomelanistic gopher snake with a form of dwarfism, and a true genetic anomaly. She was found by a farmer in central Utah in 2020, and may be the only one of her kind. TLKM (pronounced Tilkum) is a wild born lavender albino gopher snake. This mutation occurs in nature only once in 20,000 to 100,000 births. She is currently on breeding loan with a friend in Nevada, and we hope to see her equally beautiful offspring within the next few years.

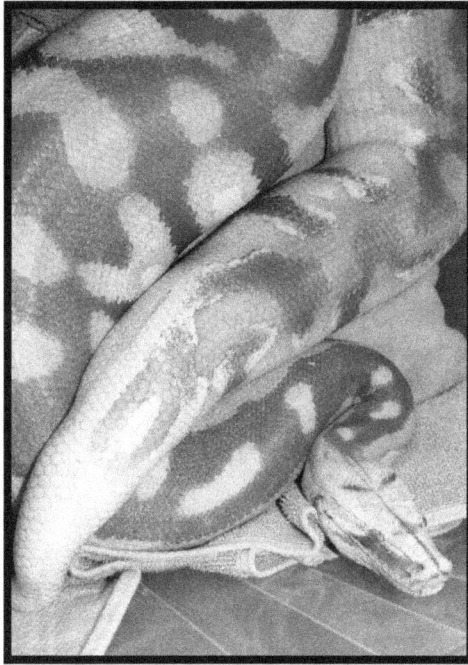

In two of the most unusual and exotic snake calls Wasatch Snake Removal ever got, this Blood python (above), a native of Sumatra, was found outside on a cold, rainy day. The Golden Child Reticulated Python (below) was removed from a toilet on Halloween night at a residence. Both animals were rehomed with qualified keepers.

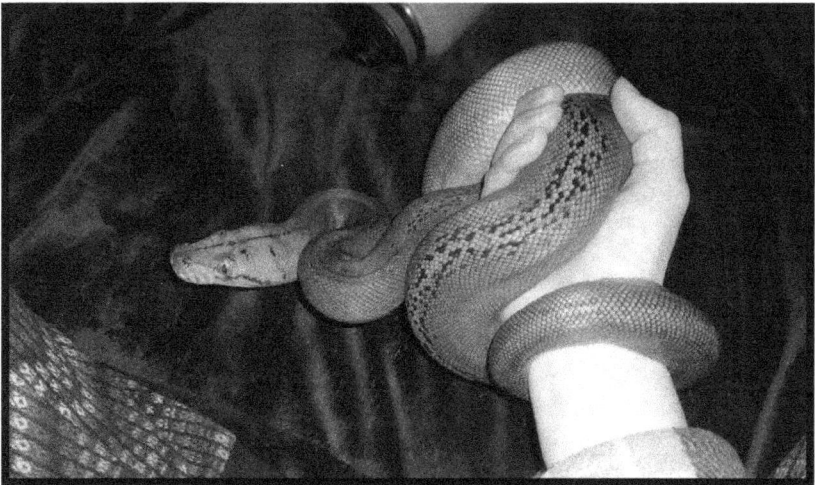

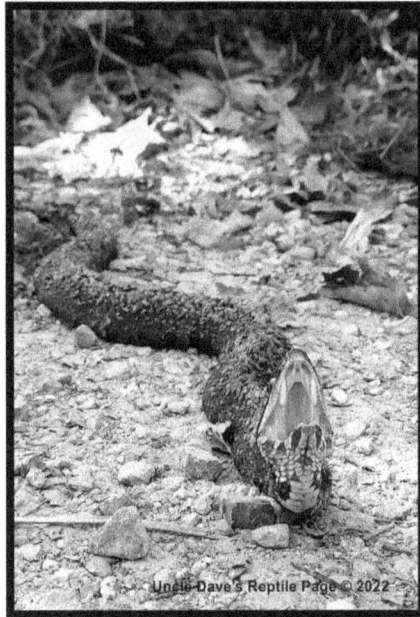

A duckweed-covered cottonmouth smiles for the camera on Snake Road in Illinois. These snakes are not the aggressive people-chasers that urban legend would have us believe. They are extremely docile and want nothing to do with humans.

College students from a local University look for snakes on Snake Road.

CHAPTER 11

Buzzer Butts and Beemers

"Life doesn't come with seat belts, air bags, or guarantees. That's what makes it worth living." –Optimist Quarterly

I picked up a rattlesnake on a sunny afternoon from a house I visited regularly.

Bart and Cindy's yard was a smorgasbord because Cindy fed the squirrels that lived in a retaining wall that surrounded the backyard, making it a haven for rodents of all sorts and a popular dining spot for local snakes.

The first time I met Bart and Cindy it was to remove a large rattler from their backyard. Bart answered the door wearing full motorcycle regalia: leather pants and jacket, boots and helmet. In his gloved hands, he menacingly gripped a 5-iron. He looked like a demented Hell's Angel who was about to play nine holes. His plan was to catch the snake himself, contain it somehow . . . and that's where his plan fell apart.

He invited me in, leading me through the large living room and kitchen, and out the sliding glass doors that opened to the backyard. Removing his helmet and gloves, he pointed at the snake.

There, coiled on the shady side of a large cedar planter box with brass straps was one of the biggest Great Basin rattlers I had seen in a while. The contented snake was easily four feet long, fat, and full of squirrel. She twitched her sizable rattle just enough to say, "Hey, what's up?" Arching her iridescent tongue over her wedge-shaped head, she calmly tasted the summer breeze. Like most Great Basins, I could tell she was a sweetheart and that we were going to get along just fine.

"I saw it and didn't know what to do," Bart said. "I guess I look a little silly in this getup."

"You may have overkilled it a little bit," I chuckled, "but your intentions were good. You weren't going to hurt it, right?"

"No," he assured me. "If I had been going to do that, I wouldn't have called you." I liked him already.

Then he asked me about my own attire. I was in my usual Saturday snake call uniform: Khaki cargo shorts, a Wasatch Snake Removal t-shirt, socks, and hiking shoes. I was holding a former golf club shaft as well, but mine had been converted to a snake stick with the addition of an aluminum hook where the head used to be. Bart thought I was underdressed for the task.

Ordinarily, Cindy enjoyed standing at the kitchen window watching the squirrels cavort on the wall, gorging on the tempting charcuterie she provided for them daily. Long before then, however, Cindy had disappeared, and I learned that whenever she saw a snake in the yard, her first inclination was to lock herself in a basement bedroom.

Bart watched with nervous apprehension as I tailed the snake. He was doing the dance of those who just can't comprehend interfacing with an animal like this.

"Would you like to meet your snake?" I asked, as he skittishly moved toward her and then away. He was as intrigued as he was terrified.

"I'll hold her behind the head so you can touch her."

I pinned the large, lazy snake and grasped her behind the head, turning 90 degrees so her head faced away from Bart, presenting her body and tail instead.

"Go ahead and touch her if you want to. It's perfectly safe," I reassured him.

Mustering all his courage, Bart stepped forward cautiously, extended his arm, and ran his index finger along her dry, scaly body before retracting it quickly.

"Hey, that's cool," he said, as a broad smile crinkled his face. "I had no idea what they felt like. I don't think I'm as afraid of them now."

I responded to lots of calls from Bart and Cindy's house, mostly from Cindy, who was home all day while Bart was at work. She put me on speed dial. When I'd answer there'd be nothing but the sound of hyperventilated breathing. In her deeply panicked state she couldn't form words. I knew she was locked in her basement safe room waiting for me to come and move a snake. This was problematic because without her telling me where the snake had been, I often had to patrol the entire yard until I found it.

Late one night after catching another buzzer butt (much smaller than the first), Bart and I sat in lawn chairs shooting the breeze on the patio. At about 1 am he asked if I wanted to go for a drive.

"What do you have in mind?" I asked.

"I want to show you what my Beemer can do on the S-curve," he said excitedly.

"Sure," I said. "Sounds like fun!"

He told me all about his BMW M6 racing class sport coupe and how it cost $116,000 new, but he bought it three years old with 23,000 miles for "only" $57,000. Cash.

The car was black, sleek and low. It had seven forward gears and could do 200 mph on a track without even breathing hard. The convertible top was down and when it rumbled to life it sounded like a big cat growling.

"What kind of music do you like?" Bart shouted as we sped down the boulevard headed for Big Cottonwood Canyon in the dark.

"I'm kind of partial to classic rock!" I yelled, trying to be heard over the sound of air rushing past our ears.

Bart tuned the radio to a station playing Led Zeppelin's "Black Dog" and cranked the volume to ear-bleed levels. We roared up Big Cottonwood Canyon doing 85 on the straightaways and only slightly slower on the curves. I was certain that a deer was going to step in front of us at any moment, sending us careening into the creek.

Storm Mountain was just a blur. Then we hit the S-curve. The car clung to the road as tenaciously as a spider clings to its web. Once above the curve, Bart spun the car around and headed back down. I think he took the curve at about 45 mph, but I was too busy watching my life pass before me like a short parade to notice the speedometer.

Back at the house, Bart handed me $80 for coming to get the snake. As I drove home in my Santa Fe, I thought about trading it for a Beemer, but I knew I'd probably live longer if I didn't.

Bart and Cindy split up the following year and I heard she moved to Nevada to be closer to family and to get away from the "snake house." I didn't have the heart to tell her that there were a lot more snakes where she was going than in her backyard in Salt Lake. And that's how I lost two of the best customers I ever had.

Having Wasatch Snake Removal and my phone number prominently displayed in the back window of the snake mobile, along with a rattlesnake graphic, led to some interesting calls when I was in traffic.

"I'm in the car behind you," one man told me. "Do you really move rattlesnakes?"

"I really do," I told him.

That's cool," he said. "I was wondering if you were for real."

Then there were the good old boys who just couldn't resist pranking me.

"Yeah, I got a snake for ya," some guy would announce, doing his best hillbilly impression. "It's in my pants!" Then he'd laugh maniacally and hang up.

I enjoyed the rare occasions when someone would actually honk and wave in response to my HONK IF YOU HERP bumper sticker. I assumed most of them knew what it meant, or maybe they just appreciated having permission to honk for any reason whatsoever.

But the most fun I had in traffic was at red lights. I'd watch in my rearview mirror as the people in the car behind me tried to phonetically sound out my license plate, SNKRSQR. There were usually two people in the front seat attempting to enunciate each consonant while filling in the missing vowels. They'd mouth something, look at each other and shrug.

Even people who knew what I did would ask what my license plates said. I enjoyed chiding them.

"What do you think they say?" I'd ask, and they'd come up with some goofy speculation. SNICKER SQUARES was the most popular, followed closely by SNAKE OR SQUIRREL. SNAKES R SQUARE was a frequent contender, along with SINK RESCUER (as though I was the Roto-Rooter guy). The weirdest interpretation I ever heard was from a woman I used to work with. Her guess? SNEAKERS QUEER. Sorry, no. Try again. (For those who may still be wondering, it's SNAKE RESCUER.)

I was performing a yard inspection in the Boulevards on a Saturday morning when a car pulled up behind mine. He had seen the stickers on the back of the snake mobile.

"Do you move snakes?" he hollered from the road.

"I sure do!" I replied.

"Rattlesnakes?" he asked.

"Especially rattlesnakes," I told him.

"Well, I've got one in my yard right now if you want to follow me home." I apologized to my first client and told him I'd be back. I didn't want to miss that snake in case it was on the move. I drove to snake guy's house, caught the snake, got paid, and drove back to my yard inspection customer.

He had seen two rattlers in his yard in the past two weeks. He ran an Airbnb and having buzzer butts on the premises was bad for business. I could look for snakes in a yard, but it was more important to mitigate the likelihood that snakes would return or become comfortable enough to stay. I made recommendations for the removal or storage of yard items, locating woodpiles away from the house, pruning or removing thick shrubbery, taking pet food and water bowls inside at night, sweeping up birdseed and anything else that might attract rodents.

Because snakes like to shelter under things, moving non-permanent items like lawnmowers, coiled hoses, kiddie pools, and garbage cans periodically is a good idea. These are the best remediation procedures for preventing recurring snake sightings. Snakes aren't the real problem, however. Rodents are. If you don't have rodents in your yard, you won't have snakes either, at least not for long.

The 2019 snake season began with my first engine compartment snake removal. A gopher snake had hitched a ride on the skid plate of Katie's Mazda 323 for almost 150 miles from her family's cabin. Someone at her gym noticed it peeking out from under the car. Getting it out took nearly an hour, five removed screws, a snake stick and a garden hose. I had never gotten so wet catching a snake, but I was under the car holding the snake by the neck so it couldn't retreat while Katie sprayed us both with cold water.

I expected to find a burned or badly scalded serpent but he was perfectly fine! (No, I didn't take him back where he came from.) I had to bushwhack my way up the side of a mountain on a barely discernable trail to release him in his new urban home. He's a city snake now, patrolling a grassy hillside overlooking the overpopulated metropolis below.

Another call took me to the underground parking terrace at a large office complex where someone saw a snake hanging out of the right front wheel well of a client's VW Jetta.

Dressed in slacks, shirt and tie, I had to don coveralls I bought when I was skinnier. It was like squeezing into a straitjacket.

I had the owner jack his car up and remove the wheel where the snake was allegedly seen. An employee dragged a hose over. With a probe and a flashlight, I spent an hour flushing the engine compartment, firewall, top of the skid plate, behind the grill, under the car, you name it, but I saw no sign of a snake.

Soaking wet and cold to the bone, I presented the company with an invoice and drove my soggy self home.

A nice Hispanic man named Juan brought his car to me because he saw a snake by the gas pedal. And then it was gone. He didn't know where it went and was afraid to drive his car. Based on pictures I showed him, he said it was probably a garter snake. If he had scooted it out of the car when he first saw it, he wouldn't have had a problem.

After looking under the front seats and removing the back seats, I could only assume it went into the dashboard where it was not only invisible but completely inaccessible. There's so much stuff in the dashboards of modern cars that there's barely room for even a small snake to fit. Still, if anything can, a snake can.

I looked everywhere for that snake, and if I could have seen even a portion of it, I might have known how to proceed, although I wasn't about to dismantle someone's dashboard.

It was a Mustang convertible, which may explain how the snake got in. I told Juan to leave top down and a door partly open so the snake could escape on its own. If the car got too hot and the snake died, he'd be stuck with a car he wouldn't want to drive and couldn't sell due to the stench. I hope he listened to me. Having the dashboard dismantled and the dead snake removed by a mechanic would not be cheap.

I took two rattlesnakes out of a doctor's yard where they were living their best lives and fulfilling their little snake dreams in the crevices and cubbyholes of a retaining wall made of stacked boulders. I named them Fred and Wilma and let them go about a half-mile away in accordance with state regulations. First, I gave them the standard lecture about avoiding kids, dogs, cats, cars, bikes, lawnmowers, big birds, hungry mammals, shovels, and anything with two legs. It's not easy being a rattlesnake on the outskirts of suburbia.

A guy at work saw a rattlesnake while hiking with his wife and kids. His wife's reaction was, in his words, "Gasping, hyperventilating, three-to-five-foot backwards long jump followed by pointing and speechlessness." I know, right? I get excited when I see a rattlesnake too!

I arrived at one home in time to see the back end of a rattler disappear into a thicket just as the sun dropped. I wasn't going after it in the dark. It would wait till tomorrow.

I had to extricate a cranky little buzzer butt from the inner workings of a hot tub where it took a defiant stand among the maze of tubes and wires in the pump compartment. Most Great Basin rattlesnakes are kittens with scales, but this snake was in pre-shed condition and was not a happy camper. If a snake can have a chip on its shoulder, this one did. What he lacked in size he made up for in ferocity. It took two people, two snake sticks, two flashlights, a broom handle and a garden hose to finally extricate and bucket him.

Cramped quarters and a pissed off snake made this one of the more technical and potentially dangerous removals I ever did. Although he wasn't big (20 to 24 inches), he was locked and loaded and ready for action on his terms. He struck at me multiple times before, during, and after capture, and once during release. Can't say I blame him; he was living in a really nice neighborhood until I evicted him.

Huge thanks to the homeowner for the call, the root beer, and for joining me on the hike to release the snake. The dog can go back in the yard, the family can use the hot tub again, and the snake can live happily ever after on his own private hillside.

I made a rattlesnake mad at me by using tongs to grab her by the tail before she disappeared under the front deck of a cabin at a summer camp for people with special needs. I grabbed her harder than I meant to, but I only had one chance because I wasn't about to follow her under the deck.

I can usually catch a rattlesnake without inciting so much as a buzz, but this otherwise shy girl swung around, fangs bared, ready to do business. I felt bad and hope I didn't hurt her.

Another residential customer had a rattler that was contentedly patrolling her backyard in the dark. It was necessary to crawl on my belly under a pine tree where it hid from me. Before I could tong it, the fleeing reptile took refuge under a railroad tie staircase where I flushed it out with a hose. It helped that there were two attractive young ladies holding flashlights for me.

In the Northern Hemisphere, August through September is the time of year when baby snakes are born. Based on her posterior girth, the snake was likely gravid and I didn't want her giving birth in someone's yard.

Finding baby snakes is one of the few times you're likely to see multiple snakes together. They'll soon disperse to look for food, shelter, and a place to take their long winter's nap. With the possible exception of rattlesnakes in a suburban yard, they do not need rescuing or removal. Just let them be.

I had a second call for a snake that had already eluded me once. When she wanted to feel safe, she merely crawled out of the short retaining wall where she hung out, scooting back into the scrub oak and blackberry brambles where I couldn't go. I hadn't seen the snake yet but the homeowner took pictures so I knew she was real. Maybe the third time would be the charm.

Not to brag, but I was pretty darn good at my job. If there was a snake within a hundred yard radius, I could usually find it.

That day's snake moved in the time it took me to get there, but I found him. He was on the other side of the fence in the neighbor's yard, sticking his tongue out at me as if to say, "Neener, neener, neener!" It was rude. I knew if I wanted to get paid by the people who called me, I had to coax him back through the fence, which I did.

I couldn't hook him in the thick vegetation and I couldn't grab his tail. He made a beeline back to the rock pile where he allegedly was when the homeowner first saw him.

I could feel him under a large, flat boulder, but I couldn't see him. Water from a hose should have sent him shooting out from under the rock like a scaly projectile, but he vanished. If there was a burrow, it should have filled with water. I spent the next 45 minutes looking for him with no success. Smart snake! In the end, it was a freebie call because the homeowners were no better off than when I got there.

A lady with a wonderful Russian accent thought she had a snake in her yard and maybe one in her house too. I asked her if she had seen a snake in the house. "No," she said, "but there are poops on my carpet and I think they're snake poops."

I asked her to describe the poops, which wasn't terribly helpful, so I asked her to text me pictures of the poops. Those didn't help either. All I knew was that they weren't snake or lizard poops which have a uric acid component, nor were they small mammal poops which are well defined and have specific shapes and colors. They were mystery poops! With his biology background, Jordan said the droppings were most likely those of a bat, which makes perfect sense. They weren't from a bird, rodent, reptile, or domestic pet, and there isn't much else in-between.

I had a call one morning asking if I could remove an impaled deer carcass from a fencepost. I kid you not. How does someone confuse snake relocation with deer carcass removal? Sometimes I just shook my head and wondered if I should start drinking.

I had a text request about a small rattler that a man hit with a shovel. The snake was contained so I sent Casey over to determine the extent of the snake's injuries and hit the homeowner with a shovel. It seemed only fair.

I picked up a beautiful little ball python that was left on the doorstep of some nice people who don't like snakes. It was in a Styrofoam container with no explanation. Weird.

One Sunday night I picked up a baby boa constrictor that had been abandoned in a third floor condominium. As far as anyone knows, the snake didn't belong to anyone in the building. Thanks to all the good folks who called us when these strange things happened. Remember, when you're nice to snakes, the karma always comes back to you.

Three snake calls before 11:30 am was unusual, but none of them involved having to go anywhere. One lady had garter snakes in her yard. All sizes. When I asked her if she also had mice, she said, "No, probably because I have snakes." BINGO! Remind me again why you want the snakes gone.

On a warm September day, a nice guy from a county up north had a clutch of baby gopher snakes hatch in his yard. Lucky guy! He said he feels the same about snakes as Indiana Jones. I told him I'd be happy to come up and catch as many as I could, but I assured him that they would disperse on their own and that by the end of next month they'd be headed for the hills to hibernate. He seemed comfortable with that.

I would have given someone a hundred dollars for a snake call one afternoon just to get me out of work for a while, but the call from campus police didn't come until I was driving home. A roaming rattlesnake had found itself a nice shady spot in a grove of trees next to a parking lot and a grassy place where students eat their lunch, so he had to go back up the mountain. He wasn't bothering anyone; he was just a happy, friendly rattlesnake savoring a perfect summer day more than most of us do.

I was releasing a snake one evening when I met a young couple on the trail with their baby and dog. I welcomed these random encounters because they provided opportunities to share information. The couple was intrigued by my bucket and asked what I was doing. I unscrewed the lid and produced a handsome adult gopher snake I had just removed from a laundry room at a nearby home.

The woman asked to hold the snake, commenting on how attractive it was, and asked me to take their picture. We talked about snakes for a bit, and just before we parted ways, her husband told me how refreshing it was to talk to someone who is so passionate and obviously enjoys what they do. It was an extraordinary compliment.

11 | Buzzer Butts and Beemers

What do people do who don't have a passion in life? We have to have a reason to get out of bed in the morning — some ember of purpose that sparks passion and makes rising feel less like a chore and more like an adventure.

A few years ago I was on my nightly walk with a snake around my neck when a car stopped behind me, its headlights illuminating the road in front of me. I just kept walking. The car went past and stopped a short distance ahead. Again, I just kept walking. As I got closer to the car, the driver's window went down and a voice said, "Is that a snake?" I affirmed that yes, it was indeed a snake.

"That's awesome!" said the 20-something young man at the wheel. His friend sat in the passenger seat. The two of them acted as though they'd never seen a snake before. (Or maybe they had just never seen a lunatic walking alone with one in the dark.)

"Can I take its picture?" the driver asked, as he activated the camera in his cell phone. Then he thoughtfully asked if the flash would bother the snake. I assured him that it wouldn't. I stepped up to the window and he took a picture. Then I answered their questions.

"What kind of snake is it?" (Corn snake.) How old is it? (She's at least 12, maybe more. I don't remember.) "Does she like to go walking?" (She has never protested.) What's her name? (Cinnamon.)

They thanked me, then drove down the street, leaving Cinnamon and me alone in the dark once more.

I frequently trekked around the neighborhood with Durango, my six-foot bull snake. One night I passed a family that was also walking, and the dad said, "There's something you don't see every day," and I suppose it's true. It's not every day that you see a snake taking a human for a walk.

Durango was usually in control, wrapping around my head, shoulders and arms, sometimes pinning one arm to my chest and forcing me to walk like a zombie. People watching from a distance probably thought I had some unfortunate affliction.

Another night, I slung Durango over my shoulders and off we went, up the hill and into the neighborhood just as the sun was setting.

The Only Good Snake . . .

Those evening forays provided more than just exercise and fresh air. They were opportunities to educate people, or at the very least, give them something to think about. They could be either moments of connection or contention.

That night a lone car approached. The woman behind the wheel slowed, her headlights catching sight of Durango as he draped me like a muscular rope. Then she stopped completely. I nodded and smiled in acknowledgement, ready to answer any questions she might have. She returned my invitation with a glare of intense disdain, her curiosity thwarted by a closed mind.

For those of us who understand snakes, the work is never truly done. Not while fear still outruns knowledge, myth eclipses truth, and beauty is mistaken for threat. The most ludicrous aspect of this behavior is the trivialization of the life of a snake — an animal considered expendable by its very nature and existence — mostly because humans can always justify a need for monsters.

Whether you find them sinister or seductive, snakes are intriguing creatures. Most people have strong opinions about snakes. Sadly, these are often steeped in superstition and compounded by an unfortunate and unnecessary fear.

It was always refreshing to see intelligent people who would allow themselves to be educated, or who were willing to educate themselves. Sadly, too many people forgo this opportunity because they have already made up their minds that the only good snake is the one that has been dispatched and disposed of. Such an act is a crime against nature and proof of a significant human deficiency to coexist with a fellow being.

I didn't relocate snakes for accolades or attention. I did it because misunderstanding has a price. Because educational moments don't always have immediate results, but they still matter. Once someone has a positive snake experience, it can change their life forever.

CHAPTER 12

Hollywood Calls

"Well, it's a lot less dangerous, working with snakes and mountain lions and dangerous animals, than working in Hollywood. Hollywood will kill you." –Bernie Krause

Utah has long been a haven for the movie industry. Filmmakers the world over have flocked here since the invention of the movie camera to make use of our stunning scenery, diverse landscapes, talented locals, tax incentives, and low production costs. Dozens of iconic (and some not so iconic) films were made here including *Butch Cassidy and the Sundance Kid*, *Dumb and Dumber*, *Footloose*, *High School Musical*, *The Sandlot*, *Thelma and Louise*, *127 Hours*, *City Slickers*, *Indiana Jones and the Last Crusade*, *Galaxy Quest*, *John Carter*, *Con Air*, *Independence Day*, *Wind River*, and hundreds of other familiar movie and TV titles.

During Hollywood's golden era of the '40s and '50s, director John Ford partnered up with box office legend John Wayne. Together they brought Hollywood to Utah, choosing Moab as their go-to spot for epic Westerns like *Stagecoach* (1939), *Fort Apache* (1948), *She Wore a Yellow Ribbon* (1949), *Rio Grande* (1950), *Wagon Master* (1950), *The Searchers* (1956), *Rio Bravo (1959)*, and *The Comanchero (1961)*, among others.

Back in 1990, on a road trip with my intrepid hiking and mountain biking friend Darrel, I drove us up the long and winding road that leads to Goblin Valley State Park. Visiting the park is like stepping onto another planet — one sculpted by time, wind, and a touch of whimsy. Tucked away in the San Rafael Desert of Southeastern Utah, this surreal landscape is famous for its thousands of mushroom-shaped rock formations called goblins. These sandstone hoodoos, formed over millions of years, cluster together on the valley floor like a gathering of ancient gnomes — stony sentinels performing secret rituals under the hush of an endless sky. The effect is both eerie and enchanting, especially when the shifting light of sunrise or sunset creates an eerie, otherworldly backdrop.

Goblin Valley's surreal landscape is the result of more than 170 million years of geological artistry. The valley's iconic "goblins" — those bulbous, mushroom-shaped rock formations — were carved from Entrada Sandstone, a sedimentary rock deposited during the Jurassic period when the region was part of a vast tidal flat and desert system. Over time, layers of sand, silt, and clay were compacted into rock, then uplifted as part of the San Rafael Swell, a massive geologic dome in central Utah.

What makes the goblins so distinctive is the interplay between hard and soft layers within the Entrada Sandstone. Softer layers erode more quickly under the relentless forces of wind and water, while harder capstones resist erosion, creating the bizarre, top-heavy shapes we see today. The result is a natural sculpture garden that looks like it belongs on another planet — one of the main reasons why Utah is so popular with filmmakers.

Spanning nearly 10,000 acres, the park offers more than just a visual feast. Visitors can hike narrow slot canyons like Little Wild Horse and Ding and Dang, bike the Wild Horse Trail system, or even rappel into Goblin's Lair — a hidden chamber that feels like nature's secret amphitheater. When night falls, the park's designation as an International Dark Sky Park means the stars come out in uninhibited, dazzling brilliance.

Darrel and I couldn't help but notice the nearly mile-long caravan of trailers that clogged both shoulders of the narrow road. It was obvious that a movie was being filmed. At the entrance station where we paid our admission fee, the ranger told us we were free to explore anywhere we chose, but not to cross the yellow tape.

Curiosity is a strange and compelling force. As we neared the yellow boundary tape, we could clearly observe the organized chaos of a closed movie set. Stepping carefully over the tape, Darrel and I ambled covertly over to where the action was taking place. Giant reflective umbrellas bounced light into shadowy alcoves of sandstone. Light and sound technicians scuttled to and fro like sand crabs, the walkie-talkies on their belts crackling with staticky commands from invisible voices.

Directly in front of us, two men sat in director's chairs with their backs to us. On the canvas backrests, neatly stenciled, were their names: Daniel Stern and Billy Crystal.

We couldn't believe it! We were standing less than six feet away from two of Hollywood's biggest stars! Did we dare to introduce ourselves? We had already overstepped our bounds, both literally and figuratively, so what did we have to lose? Just as we were about to approach them, a voice summoned "Mr. Crystal" to his rehearsal spot, and he got up and strode away. What lousy timing!

As I stepped up next to Daniel Stern's chair, he stood up and we introduced ourselves. He was cordial and polite. He told me that the movie they were filming was called *City Slickers*, and that it would most likely be released the following year. At that moment, he too was called away, abruptly ending our conversation.

Before Darrel and I could melt into the background, an attractive young woman asked us if we belonged there. I smiled and asked what her definition of "belonged" was, before admitting that we were just a couple of curious bystanders. She explained that she had no problem with us being there, but that she could get in trouble if we hung around. We thanked her and left.

At that time, I had absolutely no way of knowing that 25 years later, I would be working on sets very similar to that one as a snake wrangler.

In 2009, filming began on *127 Hours*, starring James Franco. Franco portrays Aaron Ralston, an intrepid canyoneer whose harrowing tale of amputating his own arm with a dull pocketknife in a gruesome act of self-preservation made headlines worldwide.

Even though I had no connection to that film, the kid at the end of the movie was at my house in April of the following year. He was the friend of the son of a friend of mine from work. His name is Jeffrey, and he was 10 when filming began. They gave him $750 for each day he spent on the set. The interior scenes were filmed in an empty furniture warehouse in Salt Lake, which included a fiberglass mockup of Blue John Canyon, where Ralston's ordeal took place.

One of the perks of being an urban snake relocator is that movie productions are inclined to hire a snake wrangler for their outdoor sets, and with so many productions underway at any given time, I made sure to register Wasatch Snake Removal with the Utah Film Commission early on.

My first real dalliance with celebrity began in the summer of 2015. It was my second year in business. On August 15, ABC TV called. They were filming a new Sunday night drama called *Blood and Oil* and needed a snake wrangler on the set near Kamas that very afternoon. I was there within the hour.

A driver shuttled me from the base camp to the set, and after filling out the requisite paperwork to get on the payroll, I spent the afternoon near a posh cabin on the Weber River. California film crews do not want to see snakes, not even harmless ones, not even little ones. I was sent out into the lush green foliage along the riverbank to scout for any malicious garter snakes that might feel inclined to sabotage the production.

From a distance, I saw Don Johnson, star of the show. And Amber Valletta walked past me in a slinky black swim suit. Utah's premier location catering company, Pig Boys, provided dinner, and no, there wasn't a snake to be found. This was episode three, which aired on October 11, 2015.

The episode included locations at Smith and Morehouse Canyon (Hap and Karla's house), Echo frontage road (truck chase), Oakley (Koala Rig), Woodland (McCutching Ranch), Echo (café), etc. I was at all of them, often close enough to hear the actors' dialogue, even being doused by the fake gusher that was filmed in a local farmer's field.

The days on set were long, lasting anywhere from 10 to 16 hours or until the director was happy. The job kicked off early, often before sunrise and not wrapping up until well after dark. It was hot, tiring, often boring work, but the food and money more than compensated.

There are two types of snake wranglers — those that provide snakes for productions that require them, and others, like me, whose job it was to prevent wild snakes from disrupting a shoot in snake-prone locations for the safety of the cast and crew. Wasatch Snake Removal didn't provide snakes, mostly because my license didn't allow for the keeping of venomous snakes in a residential dwelling, and because the need for snakes in movies was infrequent enough that I left that aspect of it to my friends Shane and Rindy, whose license allowed them to keep rattlesnakes in a secure commercial building.

Because they were filming outdoors in Utah, where snakes are present almost everywhere, my job was to inspect every location for snakes before film crews set up their equipment in a new location. Wild snakes would be contained until shooting ended or relocated a short distance away.

Being a snake wrangler on a movie set is what you might call responsible monotony. Once the actors were in place and filming began, I was to remain vigilant, ensuring that a curious snake didn't try to make its Hollywood debut by performing an impromptu screen test. From that point on, it was a matter of being present and available while staying quiet and out of the way. This often meant sitting for hours at a time, in the heat, hopefully in the shade, trying not to go silently insane. Books and crossword puzzles were my only therapy.

Between takes, I did double duty as an educator, reassuring anxious crewmembers that they didn't need to worry about ninja snakes leaping from bushes or dropping out of trees.

Even though the probability of seeing snakes was low most of the time, most crews appreciated having a snake wrangler on set. Others however, assumed that by sitting on my snake bucket most of the time, I wasn't performing a useful task. "Now we know where all the money goes," I heard one of them say. It was a real issue for some of them. They didn't understand why I wasn't walking around catching snakes. (Because that wasn't the job description and I would have only been in the way.) Apparently, those folks weren't there when I swept the entire area for snakes before filming began, and I was constantly on the alert just in case an especially stealthy snake violated the set perimeter.

In spite of being in prime rattlesnake habitat, no one saw a single snake. That was okay with the crew, but at some point, it would have been nice if I had found something just so they knew I really was a professional. It would have been a pauper's gig if I was being paid per snake, but the beauty of it was that I was paid well, snakes or no snakes.

The Only Good Snake . . .

The following week on the set of *Blood and Oil* saw a land auction in a farmer's field. It took more than eight hours just to film the auction scenes, which were several short scenes spliced together and lasting only a couple of minutes in the episode. Before filming began, I inspected the area for snakes, including the trees in the background and a rocky area just behind the auctioneer. Between scenes, I walked the perimeter fence (it was a large paddock), to see if anything had crawled in from the sagebrush on the other side. Nothing did.

After a six-week hiatus, I was back on set. Only Hollywood would hire a snake wrangler in Utah, in October, at 6000 feet above sea level. I tried to explain that to the location manager, but he insisted, so I showed up and graciously took their money.

It's a liability issue. Contractually, for insurance purposes, studios have to have a snake wrangler on all outdoor sets, along with a paramedic and a security guard. That way, they can't be sued if someone gets injured, property gets stolen, or someone gets bitten by a snake, no matter how unlikely the odds might be. It was still silly at that time of year, however, but the scenery was beautiful, the sets were impressive, the people were nice, and the food provided by Pig Boys was haute cuisine.

My last day on set, I witnessed a fenestration when Gary (Paul Rae) went through a window and was chased through a grove of aspen trees by Billy (Chace Crawford) and Wick (Scott Michael Foster), and when he fell into a ravine and was impaled. It was overly dramatic (typical TV fare) but a lot of fun to watch.

That morning, the last van leaving the staging area for the set was carrying the stars of the show, with the exception of Don Johnson (whose ego insisted on its own van), and I caught a ride with them. I had met Max Theriot once before at the snack cart. He's a down-to-earth guy, easy to talk to.

Once we arrived at the filming location, the assistant director had me introduce myself to the cast and crew. He told them that in no uncertain terms were they to kill a snake or anything else while they were there, and to call me if they saw one. No one did, including me. All I wanted was one snake, just one, to make an appearance so I could impress these Hollywood folks, but I think the snakes in Summit County were conspiring against me.

12 | Hollywood Calls

Blood and Oil premiered on ABC TV on Sunday, September 27, 2015. With a disappointing debut and a smarmy story line, the show was canceled after less than one season. Critics hated it and viewership tanked with each successive episode. The original 13 episodes were cut back to 10 and the coffin lid was slammed down and nailed shut. Somehow, it seemed doomed from the very beginning, but it was the most lucrative part-time job I ever had. How else am I supposed to make that much money doing practically nothing? At least I got my little slice of the Hollywood pie before it was swallowed up and spat out.

In Skull Valley, in July of 2017, Jordan and I kept the rattlesnakes at bay for a movie crew for 17 hours under a blistering sun. It was hotter than the Devil's doorknob. All we really had to do was be there because the snakes were smart enough to stay hidden until the sun went down, at which time several of them were pressed into road jerky by departing crewmembers and studio trucks.

The production was a teaser for *Sonic the Hedgehog, The Blue Blur*. Sonic is a blue animated (and at the time, invisible) hedgehog. His stand-in and stunt double was a plush blue Cookie Monster doll with an equally blue vocabulary when the actors got bored. The set consisted of a large, dilapidated road sign that read, "Welcome to Green Hills South Dakota." Hiding behind it was a cop car with a single, bored police officer. A long, straight stretch of road pointed to distant horizons in both directions.

It was Jordan's first day on a movie set and he was excited to meet director Tim Miller, who also directed *Terminator, Borderland, and Dead Pool*. (Miller didn't direct *Sonic*, just the teaser.) I wanted as many of my team members as possible to have this experience and to earn the kind of money that only the world of make-believe could offer. Over the next several years, Jordan, Averi, Bebe and Jason all became experienced on-set snake wranglers.

After two-and-a-half years in post-production, *Blue Blur* was finally released to mixed reviews, and although it isn't a film that would have registered as even a tiny blip on my radar screen, I had to see it strictly out of curiosity.

The movie is a frenetic romp of ridiculous proportions, aimed primarily at fans of the video game. It is everything you'd expect from a movie about an animated refugee rodent from a distant galaxy (voiced by Ben Schwartz) and an obsessive-compulsive mad scientist hell-bent on his capture, played convincingly by the ever-maniacal Jim Carrey.

Carrey's performance as a sinister rogue agent from an undisclosed branch of the military with an unlimited budget ("Ever wonder where your tax money goes?" he asks, sardonically) is fun for a while, but in my humble opinion, it won't be hailed as one of his more memorable roles. To be fair, there are plenty of belly laughs, and kids in particular are bound to find Sonic to be an engaging, blue-quilled, mischievous dynamo. He is also a true-blue (pun intended) friend and sidekick to a small town police officer (James Marsden) who befriends and protects him from Carrey's sadistic mad scientist, who is described at one point as a "psychotic tire fire."

In the film, South Dakota morphs into Montana, new sign and all, and if the footage from Utah's west desert was used in the final film, it was so adorned with computer-generated greenery that it became almost unrecognizable. (And no, Wasatch Snake Removal does not appear in the credits. Bummer.)

On July 11, 2016, I was hired to be country singer Kelsea Ballerini's personal snake wrangler at a photo shoot for a national boot manufacturer. Kelsea's star was rising, and while I don't know of any connection she had to Utah, the foothills behind the museum were chosen as the backdrop. It was a small crew consisting of Kelsea, her manager, a makeup artist, a famous woman photographer from Los Angeles, a drone operator, and me. There was also a horse, a dog, and their trainer. (You might say it was a real dog and pony show!)

Because the museum grounds are a hotspot for snakes, it was my job to keep everyone safe from stepping or sitting on a rattlesnake. We spent most of a day near the rocky cairns where the likelihood of seeing a snake was high before moving into tall grass. I would have loved to show them all a snake, but try as I might, I could not conjure one.

It was a pleasant day, everyone got along well, and the animals performed flawlessly. When it was over, Kelsea gave me a big hug and told me how much fun it was having me there. Hey, the pleasure was all mine!

Kevin Costner's *Yellowstone* series was shot in multiple Utah locations. Despite the story taking place in Montana, many of the outdoor scenes used local people and places as substitutes for Montana's majestic mountain wilderness. Airing on the Paramount network, Costner's tale of the Dutton family cattle ranch and their ongoing battle against unscrupulous land developers poured $81 million dollars into the local economy over three summers and became a major hit for Paramount.

One of my team or I were present for many of Yellowstone's iconic scenes, watching Costner and other cast members rehearse their lines, sometimes only feet away from the actors. Industry rules discourage engagement with "the talent," as the actors are called, unless they spoke to us first. Despite numerous close encounters with Costner, I never actually met him. Then, in the fall of 2020, after filming at various locations all summer, I was summoned to a *Yellowstone* set just outside of a small town in the Uinta Mountains.

The air temp at 9 am was 36 degrees. It snowed earlier that morning and it didn't hit 50 all day. It was a little surreal donning wool socks and a fleece jacket to wrangle nonexistent snakes. I told them they didn't need me in those conditions, but the safety coordinator said it was due to an "overabundance of caution" because there was a child actor who had to run into a field. It didn't change the fact that rattlesnakes can barely function at those temps and wouldn't be out by choice. Besides, we were working on the shoulder of a road and not in actual habitat.

A later scene included live vultures. There must have been 200 people there. Everyone was wearing jackets, gloves and hats, and there I was, walking around with a snake stick and bucket. I felt like an idiot. In spite of the cold and the ridiculousness of the situation, it was an interesting day.

At one point, I was walking along a row of parked vehicles when a truck door opened and a man's voice said, "Caught any snakes yet?" It was Kevin Costner. I told him that any snakes unlucky enough to be outside last night had already frozen solid. "It's a little cool," he chuckled. I told him it was a pleasure to meet him. He reciprocated the greeting and closed the door.

It was the antithesis of a day in August when filming lasted for 13 hours in 97-degree heat with barely any shade. I could feel my brain boiling in my skull. The snakes didn't come out then, either. Can't we find a happy medium?

When the series ended, I bought all five seasons on DVD so I could watch it over the winter. That was five years ago, and so far, I've only seen bits and pieces on TV.

Jamison started watching it early on. He texted me to say he may have to stop based on principle. Apparently, someone kills a rattlesnake in an early episode.

That's bad enough, but it gets worse. The location is prairie rattlesnake habitat, but the snake that gets killed is a Western diamondback. Until it's dead, that is. Then it turns into an Eastern diamondback.

Why is it so hard for moviemakers to depict snakes realistically and responsibly? Come on, Hollywood, get your act together. Literally. This is why it's so confusing for people to correctly identify snakes and not fear them.

Usually it's because they can't tell a story without hyper-sensationalizing it for dramatic effect. But mostly it's just laziness. On the other hand, maybe they're too cheap to hire consultants.

I'm hoping that the dead snake was a prosthetic. If so, they should have painted it to look like the live snake, although it would be better if there were no depictions of snake killings at all. Think of the impact it could have on millions of people if a character in a movie saw a rattlesnake, acknowledged it, took two steps backward, and left it the hell alone. But that's not the Hollywood way. A rattlesnake encounter that mundane wouldn't be relevant to the story so it would be omitted as an unnecessary distraction, being replaced with a boudoir scene or a car chase instead.

While on set one evening, I learned the hard way that my headlamp was woefully inadequate for finding a rattlesnake in the dark in tall grass. That's why my new headlamp has 1500 lumens. This sucker will catch the grass on fire if I'm not careful!

Following the success of *Yellowstone,* Costner began a new series called *Horizon - An American Saga*, which filmed almost exclusively in Utah, depicting true stories from a 12-year period in the history of the American West. Averi and Bebe each spent considerable time on multiple sets in beautiful locations under oppressive heat, as wagon trains and scenes of a bygone century passed before them.

I'm proud of the work my team and I did. We met nice people and had a lot of fun. Today, when I watch a show like *Yellowstone*, I know how much time and hard work went into creating those scenes.

A typical *Yellowstone* workday lasted 13 hours beginning at noon, because there were usually night scenes involved. It was my first experience on a nighttime shoot, but by 10 pm temps had dipped into the low 50s, again, too cold for snakes, and they cut me loose, but not before Pig Boys served New York steak for dinner. Another night, I sat high above a canyon escarpment, freezing my butt off while eating tortilla soup on the side of a lonely road, waiting for the director to yell, "Cut!" There were no snakes of course, but it was an unforgettable experience just the same.

Most television today is a deep morass of malignant swill, assaulting us with some astonishingly bad entertainment over the years. For example, in 2013, I watched about 10 minutes of *Snake Salvation,* lacking the fortitude necessary to watch any longer than that as I felt my brain cells begin to die.

Snake Salvation's plot (if there was one), was the sensationalizing of snake-handling religious cults based on a single line of Scripture from Mark 16:18, "And they shall take up serpents . . ."

It's more like bad performance art than a demonstration of faith or a spiritual pursuit. That one fragment of scripture has been stretched into a doctrine that elevates danger to new heights of zealotry, often with tragic consequences. As someone who handles snakes without fanfare, it was hard to watch as animals were used as props for spiritual bravado instead of living creatures that deserve respect.

The Only Good Snake . . .

This wretched series was the latest offering from the desperate producers at the National Geographic channel, who will put anything on TV as long as it includes stupid people, an element of danger, and doesn't actually involve feeding Christians to lions. In that event, they should start with the cast of this show.

Whether people will actually watch or not remains to be seen, but I'm sure there are devotees of the *Turtle Man* who will feel right at home with these hillbilly zealots who consider it their divine mission to free-handle venomous snakes for God. The rest of the time, they're busy demonstrating some of the most despicable techniques possible to capture the needed snakes for their blasphemous rituals.

The snakes, not the delusional cultists, are the real victims here. Apparently, gassing snake dens is still legal in Texas, but so is marrying your sister, I think. (No offense to any nice, normal, snake-loving Texan who might read this, but get out while you still can!)

Naturally, the promo for the show featured a photo, not of a rattlesnake, cottonmouth, or copperhead, which might actually test someone's faith if they were to handle one, but of a harmless garter snake.

It's no wonder people don't know which snakes to avoid and which ones are their friends. Oversimplified media narratives condemn curiosity and feed fear. Even documentaries don't always distinguish between a rattler's rattle and a gopher snake's bluff — painting every serpent as a slithering menace and turning every nature encounter into a confrontation with evil.

By partnering with the film commission, my ultimate goal was to have Wasatch Snake Removal listed in the credits of at least one major motion picture, but it hasn't happened yet. Most of the locally filmed productions were for television only, and the really big ones often flew their own snake wranglers in from Los Angeles, even though it cost them more.

There's still hope, however. As of this writing, the summer of 2025 is already turning out to be a banner movie year. In May, Jordan spent nearly a week beating the brush for location crews on a production starring Sam Rockwell, John Malkovich, and

Parker Posey. Nondisclosure agreements prevent me from divulging the title at this time.

In August, Averi and Jordan worked on the pilot episode of *Y: Marshalls*, a spinoff of the *Yellowstone* series.

These days, a progressive eye condition keeps me from interacting with venomous snakes, and my doctor and I agreed that my driving days are done. It's a huge shift in my paradigm, not just logistically, but to my very freedom and identity.

When life's rhythm is disrupted, stepping away from something you love feels like a silent void in a place that once resonated with purpose. It's like a bad plot twist in an otherwise good movie.

CHAPTER 13

The Venom Factor

"There is no way to catch a snake that is as safe as not catching him." –Jacob Braude

If there was a worst day in the history of Wasatch Snake Removal, it was June 30, 2020. Covid was in high gear, racing through the population like the flu at a sneezing festival and mask mandates were in effect everywhere.

It was moving day. My sibs and I had sold our parents' home due to the impracticality of it being a split-level with too many stairs and no bathroom on the main floor. Now in their 80s, it was time to swap the house for a first-floor apartment.

The moving truck had already left with mom and dad following close behind. My job was to clear out the fridge and the freezer, putting all the perishable items in an assortment of coolers and hauling them to the new place. This would be the last trip from the house.

About an hour earlier, I had dispatched Averi to an affluent home in a highly populated local canyon and a source of frequent snake calls. A five-year-old boy playing with his dog had seen a rattlesnake in the yard. His mother, Leah, ushered them both into the house and called me. Being unavailable myself, I called Averi. With her typical good-natured enthusiasm, Averi took the call. I informed Leah that someone would be there to move the snake within a half-hour or so and resumed loading my car with food.

An hour later, as I was about to drive away, my phone rang. It was Averi. Thinking that she may have an issue with a particularly uncooperative snake or a question about pricing, I didn't have any reason to be concerned. After all, Averi had never been in a relocation situation she couldn't handle on her own.

"Hi Averi, how's it going up there?" I asked. That's when I heard the words I never wanted to hear from any of my people.

"I got bit," she said, matter-of-factly. The words punched me in the gut like brass knuckles. My mind was racing but I needed to stay calm for her sake.

Choosing my words carefully I asked, "Are you okay emotion-ally?"

"I think so," she replied. Then she began to cry.

So she wasn't okay emotionally. That was perfectly normal under the circumstances.

"You need to get to the U of U Med Center," I told her. "But don't even think about driving yourself. Is there someone who can take you?"

"Yes," she said, regaining her composure, "the homeowner will take me."

"Good." I said. "But don't wait till you get there to tell them what happened. Call and tell them you're on your way so they can be ready for you. I'll get there as soon as I can."

Hauling four large coolers back into the house, I began to un-load them like a maniac. Frozen stuff was shoved in the freezer; everything else got dumped in the fridge. There was no time for neatness. I barely remembered to lock the door on my way out.

Midday traffic wasn't bad and I arrived at the hospital in rec-ord time. The woman at the reception desk handed me a mask. "Oh yeah," I stammered, "I almost forgot. I'm here to see Averi," I explained. "She was bitten by a rattlesnake."

Looking up from her patient roster, she said that Averi had been admitted about 45-minutes ago.

"Can I see her?" I asked, completely forgetting once again that we were in the midst of a pandemic and that the world wasn't normal anymore.

"Are you family?" she asked.

"I'm her boss," I told her, telling only half a lie. (My team members were contracted agents and not actual employees.)

"It doesn't matter," she said. "Under pandemic restrictions, no one is allowed in patient rooms."

Then why the hell did she ask?

"Is anyone else here? Her dad or her boyfriend?" I inquired impatiently.

"I'm not sure, but they wouldn't be allowed to see her either."

Was this woman trying to irritate me? I only had one nerve left and she was stomping on it with golf cleats.

The Only Good Snake . . .

The snake house was only 20 minutes away. When I arrived, Averi's car was parked out front and her snake stick and bucket were in the driveway. Leah answered the door. Her husband hadn't yet returned from the hospital.

"Did you see what happened?" I asked Leah. There were so many scenarios flooding my mind that I needed someone to give me the facts.

I'll skip the details and cut to the chase. Averi had arrived at the house as expected and the owners showed her where the snake was hiding in a four-foot-high rock retaining wall that ran the length of the driveway. Coaxing the snake out by gently touching its tail with her stick, she hooked the snake and placed it in the bucket.

"She made it look so easy," Leah told me. "It was kind of amazing!"

"Yeah, she's good at what she does," I said. "Then what happened?"

Leah went on to explain that they had only seen a single snake, but there were actually two. After bucketing the first snake, the second buzzer butt attempted to retreat into a crevice in the wall. Thinking that it was escaping into a hole, Averi grabbed its tail. Letting the snake escape would mean making another trip to the house, leaving the owners in the meantime as nervous as before about letting their son and dog out to play.

But the snake wasn't going into a hole. The crevice dead-ended, leaving the snake no choice but to make a U-turn and come back out. Also, to see what had hold of its tail.

Reacting as it would toward any threat to its safety, the snake bit Averi on the back of her left hand between the joints of her pinky and ring fingers.

The first snake was still in the bucket. The second snake, a two-and-a-half-footer, lay segmented in the gutter in front of the house where Leah's husband had gone full gonzo on it with a shovel. It was the only time a homeowner had ever killed a snake in the presence of a relocator. I released the first snake on the mountain above the neighborhood and drove back down to the valley to resume my moving duties.

194

I didn't blame Averi. Even though I told my people repeatedly not to take unnecessary risks, it didn't change the fact that we had a job to do. As paid professionals, our customers expected results. While I never took overtly ridiculous risks, I can't count the times I took hold of a rattlesnake's tail without knowing exactly (or even approximately) where the snake's head was. I wasn't being cavalier; it was simply a side effect of working with a species known for its mellow disposition. But risks are risks, and none of us could say that we didn't understand the potential consequences of screwing up. If the snake had truly been going into a hole, she could have used the garden hose technique to flush it out.

Averi spent three days and two nights in the hospital with no visitors. Her phone died on the first day, making it impossible to communicate with anyone until her boyfriend gave her charger to a nurse who gave it to Averi. She texted me a picture of her arm. From her left wrist to her elbow, she looked like a weightlifter.

"Look at my Popeye arm!" she wrote.

"That looks ridiculous," I responded. "You need to pump up the other arm or else you'll be lopsided."

My only concern for a long-term prognosis was that she might suffer some diminished dexterity in those two fingers, which could have spelled the end of her career as a piano teacher.

That was more than five years ago, but like most snakebite patients, she was just fine within a week or less. Like nothing ever happened.

Averi received an unknown quantity of Anavip, one of two brands of antivenin (antivenom) for treating North American pit viper bites. A week after being discharged from the hospital, I visited her at home, giving her an eight-foot plush rattlesnake with googly eyes and a rattley tail. "When someone asks you what happened to the snake that bit you," I told her, "tell them you had it stuffed."

"That should impress them," she laughed.

Averi took a sabbatical from moving rattlesnakes for the rest of that year, but like the trooper she is, she went right back to it the following spring. Repeat customers would request her. They'd call and say, "We have another rattler in our yard. Can you send that cute little red-headed girl over to move it?" As a school teacher, Averi had her summers free, and I could always count on her to take a call and make a good impression.

Much of The Salt Lake Valley's malignant sprawl lies along the highly urbanized western slopes of the Wasatch Mountains which form the eastern perimeter of several valleys. The only rattlesnake along these burgeoning population centers is the Great Basin rattlesnake. These guys are small and quite benign. They are reluctant to strike, but will defend themselves from an impending threat. Staying on trails and away from rocky or brushy areas will reduce your chances of meeting one of these shy snakes.

There have been only five snake-related deaths in Utah in the past 175 years. Of those, only one is considered a legitimate bite resulting from an accidental encounter with a rattlesnake, and one wasn't a Utah bite at all. In the second scenario, the 'victim,' an Arizona man, was playing with a Western coral snake (*Micruroides euryxanthus*) when it bit him. He was transported to Utah where he later died. It remains an Arizona statistic. The rest were snake-related deaths resulting from hysteria. A woman, upon simply seeing a snake, became so frightened that she miscarried her unborn child. A man bitten by an unknown species of snake, perhaps even a harmless one, panicked and beat his head against a rock. These are classified as illegitimate deaths instigated by humans and not by anything a snake did. This is why an unreasonable fear of snakes, and not snakes themselves, is so dangerous. When we let fear control us, we become our own worst enemy.

Major U.S. hospitals in snake-prone areas stock antivenin based on estimated need. With a high production cost and short shelf life, it is not inexpensive. Antivenin is cheaper in spring when supply exceeds demand, usually around $3,000 per vial. As summer wears on and availability drops, prices soar, sometimes exceeding $10,000 per vial (most often due to hospital markups), with some bites requiring up to 12 vials.

There are two brands of antivenin for treating North American pit viper (rattlesnake, copperhead, and cottonmouth/water moccasin) snake envenomations: CroFab and Anavip.

CroFab is made in Australia and has been a staple of North American snakebite treatment since 2000. Processed from venom extracted in America from multiple species of rattlesnakes, it is derived from immunized proteins in the blood of sheep that were injected with venom for this purpose.

Anavip is a newer option, receiving FDA approval in 2020, and is manufactured in the U.S. from horses immunized with venom. It is less expensive than CroFab, probably because it doesn't have to travel half way around the world twice, and has a stable shelf life of four years at room temperature.

In a recent Facebook post, I mentioned that rattlesnakes and other venomous snakes save lives, and a gentleman responded with this valid question: "Excuse my ignorance, but how does a rattlesnake save a human life?"

This was my reply:

> *Excellent question! Snakes (both harmless and venomous) save lives by consuming rodents that act as vectors for a variety of diseases like hantavirus, Lyme disease, tick-borne encephalitis, tularemia, and about a dozen others, including the plague. They also prevent house fires by eating rats that chew on wiring. (Surprisingly, this is a big problem in some parts of the country.)*
>
> *Snakes prevent the decimation of our food crops by controlling rodent populations, and various venoms and their components are known to have medicinal properties that can treat conditions ranging from Alzheimer's disease to cancer, stroke, and multiple sclerosis. Copperhead venom prevents blood clots and keeps cancer cells from sticking together, while cobra venom is used to treat Parkinson's disease.*
>
> *Snake venom saves far more lives each year than it takes, while people kill far more snakes than snakes kill people. Coincidentally, snake venom, properly processed, is the cure for venomous snake bites.*

In this country, fewer than five people die from snakebite each year, often because they don't seek treatment, whereas, hundreds of thousands of harmless and beneficial snakes are killed out of ignorance or fear, on highways, by pesticide use and habitat destruction.

Many people are interested in knowing how to identify "poisonous" snakes. Without getting into semantics, there really is no such thing, at least not in most places.

But rattlesnakes and most other venomous snakes are just that — venomous. Venom is injected. Poison is ingested. In the most basic terms, if it bites you and you die, it's venomous. If you eat it and you die, it's poisonous. This is overly simplistic, of course, but it's an easy way to remember the difference.

Yes, there are snakes that are poisonous because their bodies sequester toxins from their prey, but they're only dangerous if you eat them. As toad eaters, Eastern garter snakes are one of these. Between being toxic and emitting a foul-smelling musk from two anal glands, almost nothing eats garter snakes. Not more than once, anyway.

When I talk to kids about snakes, I ask them if they've ever seen a poisonous snake. It's a trick question, and most of them raise their hands. Then we discuss the difference between 'poisonous' and 'venomous,' and I tell them there's no such thing as a poisonous snake bite. This single fact makes them more knowledgeable about snakes than most adults. There are a few poisonous snakes in the world, meaning that if you eat one, you might get sick. This includes some species, like garter snakes, whose 'venom' has no significant potency even if they bite you.

Then we talk about what to do if you see a snake and don't know what kind it is. Leave it alone! That way, it doesn't matter if it's venomous or not.

Because there's an exception to almost every rule, there are snakes that can be considered both venomous and poisonous. The Tiger keelback (*Rhabdophis tigrinus*) of Southeast Asia is one of a very few snake species that is actually 'poisonous' due to its ability to secrete a non-lethal poison from the nuchal glands on its skin that serves as an irritant to predators that may want to eat it. Its bite is also venomous but not lethal to humans. It is a serpentine conundrum!

13 | *The Venom Factor*

Snakes that can harm us by biting us are venomous and venom can only do its job in the bloodstream. It can be swallowed with no ill effects as long as the person doing the drinking doesn't have an ulcer or some other way for the venom to enter their circulatory system. A number of venomous snakes pose a minimal threat to humans even if they bite us. My hognose snake, Harley, is one of them.

I was informed on a regular basis by people with zero snake knowledge that baby rattlers are more venomous than adults because they can't "control" their venom. Well, sometimes I can't control mine either, but I tried to be nice and educate them without being too condescending or snarky. It wasn't always easy.

"Did you know . . ." they'd say, and I already knew where they were headed, "that baby rattlesnakes are more dangerous/poisonous/venomous [these words are used alternately and synonymously] than big ones?" Then they'd beam proudly, confident that they had just handed me the gift of an epiphany, waiting for me to see the light and commend them for their brilliance.

People spouted this erroneous bit of trivia as though it was God's gospel. It was on par with their story about the diamondback rattler they saw in Utah. I don't know how this particular urban legend began, although it probably has something to do with the fact that young snakes are more inclined to strike than larger snakes, mostly because everything wants to eat them when they're little. In this regard, smaller snakes can be more dangerous, yes.

However, small snakes have a smaller venom yield than larger snakes. When it comes to venom in your body, less is better. However, there is no evidence to indicate that a young snake's venom is more potent than an adult of the same species. Therefore, if a small snake injects a small amount of venom and a large snake injects a larger amount of venom, wouldn't it be better to be bitten by a smaller snake?

When I try to explain this to people, they act almost resentful, as though I'm trying to steal their thunder. I suppose an exciting lie is more interesting than a boring truth.

A snake may inject a little venom, a lot of venom, all of its venom, or no venom at all, depending on the circumstance, but it's probably not a conscious decision on the snake's part. A snake that strikes in self-defense doesn't need to inject any venom, but it still happens.

If a venomous snake bites you, there is a small but not insignificant chance that the snake didn't envenomate you. This is known as a "dry bite." A dry bite is the most anyone can hope for, but they account for less than 25 percent of venomous snakebites. These odds aren't in our favor, but they're better than nothing. If a bite happens, stay calm and get to a hospital or call 911. Do not attempt treatment on your own.

It isn't advantageous for a snake that's striking defensively to deliver its entire venom yield because it needs venom to subdue its prey, otherwise it can't eat for a while. This applies to large snakes and small snakes equally, although it's highly doubtful (though not impossible) that individual snakes 'learn' to control the amount of venom they inject as they get older.

Regarding the learning factor, noted herpetologist Dr. David Steen explains it this way:

> *For learning to occur, there must be positive or negative reinforcement. If we state that a snake may keep venom on hand in case a prey item (or one that appears shortly after the first prey item) requires a second bite, this snake must have experienced a number of incidents where they injected a fraction of the venom they had into a prey item only to have this prey item escape. Over time, they may learn that it's beneficial to keep some venom for a successful attack later. This may make sense superficially, but one might think that it would be more likely that the snake learns to inject more venom with their first bite and increase the chance of a fatality than saving venom just in case they experience another opportunity to bite their intended food again . . . there are a number of other potential scenarios we need to consider as plausible.*
> *–Dr. David Steen (source unknown)*

There are two issues at stake here: are baby snakes more venomous than adults, and are baby snakes less able than adults to regulate the amount of venom they inject? Here's what another doctor has to say:

> *Are Smaller Venomous Snakes More Dangerous? Several times each year someone asks in class about the relative danger of an envenomation from a small versus a large [pit viper]. Some people are insistent that smaller snakes are more dangerous. This idea has always felt counterintuitive to me. The explanations seem fanciful at best. Usually, people argue that larger (and therefore older) snakes possess some sort of volume control. They argue that larger snakes hold back venom against humans because we are not food for them. These larger snakes want to warn us with a strike but preserve venom for when it matters, like a meal. I have been unable to find any science and none of the experts that I have spoken with can give a definitive answer one way or the other. With the publication of a recent study, perhaps this theory will disappear. –David Johnson, MD (source unknown)*

While it's true that baby snakes are more inclined to strike in self-defense, small snakes inject a much smaller volume of venom, and they inject it less deeply into tissue. As an additional benefit, clothing and other barriers more easily deflect a strike from a small snake. Even if a small snake had more debilitating components in its venom, the lesser volume makes it a preferable bite over a larger snake that will deliver more venom more deeply into the body, thereby making it more systemically significant and difficult to treat. For these reasons, I'd rather be bitten by a baby rattler than a big one any day of the week.

Of the 7,000 to 8,000 people who are bitten by venomous snakes in the U.S. each year, only about five of those bites are fatal. Most of them were messing with a snake, so the snake is not to blame. At least as many people per year (on average) are killed when heavy furniture and TVs fall on them. More people die from falling out of bed. About 400 more. Pet dogs, horses, cows, deer, bees, and even ants kill more people than venomous snakes. Far more. According to the Texas Health Department, the non-animal list includes lightning, tornadoes, frying pans and peanuts.

Defensive strikes are another matter. If you taunt, torment, or try to kill a snake and it bites you, let's be honest, you had it coming. Most venomous snakebites in the U.S. are not random occurrences, but are the result of deliberate interactions with snakes. These are known as illegitimate bites because humans being stupid instigated them. Others are the result of unlucky encounters.

It should surprise no one that snakebite victims are typically young males and alcohol is often involved. Like drunken monkeys, inebriated young men will try to demonstrate bravado by showing off with a venomous snake — often to impress friends or girlfriends — stunts which don't always end as intended. These incidents are often preceded by the exclamation, "Hold my beer!" or "Look what I can do!" But testosterone, venom and booze don't mix, although these "stupid human tricks" are usually quite entertaining after the fact, especially if someone filmed them.

In 1988, two doctors at the University of Southern California Medical Center analyzed 227 cases of venomous snakebite, covering more than a decade, and found that 44 percent occurred during accidental contact, such as stepping on the animal. More than 55 percent, however, resulted from the victims grabbing or handling the creatures, and in 28 percent of these cases, the victims were intoxicated. The doctors' conclusion was that the typical snakebite victim is a male under 30 years of age, with a blood-alcohol concentration of more than 0.1 percent at the time he was bitten. Yet only 0.2 percent of all snakebite victims die each year, due mostly to not receiving medical treatment or first aid. (Steve Grenard, August 2000)

It seems that testosterone, alcohol, and stupidity are far more dangerous than rattlesnakes, and they always have been.

Rattlesnakes are somewhat fragile, have stout bodies, relatively weak musculature, and crawl much slower than most other snakes. Without venom, it would be virtually impossible for them to subdue prey or defend themselves against predators. Even a small mouse would prove a formidable and potentially dangerous opponent to a rattlesnake without venom.

13 | The Venom Factor

Unlike most harmless snakes whose heads are narrow and blend into the neck, rattlesnakes have a broad, wedge-shaped head and a narrow neck with an obvious difference in diameter between them. Most (but not all) harmless snakes have round pupils, while a rattlesnake's pupils are vertically elliptical like a cat. (Many people have informed me that they do not intend to get close enough to look at the pupils. Fair enough.)

Vertical pupils are not always an indication of a venomous snake. Round pupils do not always indicate a harmless snake. Arizona, New Mexico, and Texas have coral snakes with red, black, and yellow bands that encircle the body. There are other red, black, and yellow-banded snakes in the U.S. that are not coral snakes, but laypersons don't typically take the time to learn the difference. Subsequently, milk snakes and some king snakes are killed needlessly despite legal protections in most places. Trust me, you'll know if you are bitten by a coral snake and not a harmless milk snake (although you'd literally have to be handling it), and killing the snake at that point is a waste of your time. Get to a hospital!

Killing the snake that bit you is never recommended. You run a greater risk of being bitten again by interacting with a defensive snake. It's much easier and safer to take a picture of the snake with your phone for identification purposes, although in Western states, the antivenin used to treat every rattlesnake bite is the same polyvalent blend of native venoms.

To reiterate, any snake in Utah (and most of the West) that doesn't have a rattle is harmless to humans. For the sake of argument, there are other species that are considered venomous based on being rear-fanged (as opposed to the hinged, forward-facing fangs of a pit viper).

These species, however, are small, secretive, disinclined to bite, and completely benign even if they do bite a human. In this instance, venomous means venomous to humans, and in the Western U.S., only rattlesnakes have that distinction. All others are harmless unless you're a lizard or a mouse. Still, as a way to dodge responsibility for their actions, some people try to justify killing every snake they see, harmless or otherwise, which makes no sense whatsoever.

The Only Good Snake . . .

I always told my customers that the only snakes in Utah that are potentially dangerous are rattlesnakes. It's true, and that was all they needed to know. Anything beyond that is just confusing. They're never going to remember the exceptions anyway because they don't care and it will probably never affect their lives.

It makes me crazy when newbie herpers want to spew all their newfound knowledge by telling everyone they know that garter snakes (and a few others) are venomous, when in reality, they pose no threat to humans. All they accomplish is causing people to fear garter snakes who may not have feared them before. When people hear the term "venomous snake," they automatically assume that the snake is a danger to *them*, making them more inclined to kill it. We don't do anyone a favor by telling them that all these harmless snakes are venomous. We most certainly don't do the snakes a favor.

Venom, which is an absolute necessity for the rattlesnake's survival, is ironically also the primary reason for their demise. Too many humans, despite having arms, legs, opposable thumbs, vastly superior intelligence, and the ability to make and use tools, still wrongly identify the rattlesnake as a life-threatening enemy.

The most popular option for the ignorant and ill-informed is to kill them, but it's time to call a truce to our one-sided war against snakes. Whether in a battle of wits, speed, or strength, the odds are stacked heavily in our favor. Isn't it funny that rattlesnakes, even with their primitive brains, know this? For a rattlesnake, biting a human means almost certain death, meaning they will do it ONLY in self-defense and ONLY as a last resort. We have made the terrible mistake of overestimating the danger of these snakes and wildly underestimating their value as allies in pest control and medical cures. Rattlesnakes save many more human lives in a single year than they have taken in decades.

Venom is a complex, bioactive substance that varies from species to species and even within different populations of the same species. Composed of countless combinations of enzymes, proteins, peptides, and molecules that are continuously evolving alongside the rest of nature, it is used in research and medicine and cannot be easily reproduced in a lab. The life-saving drug Integrilin (Eptifibatide) is a glycoprotein platelet inhibitor that prevents blood clots or heart attack in certain conditions. Made from a protein that was discovered in the venom of the dusky pygmy rattlesnake, it is one of many treatments extracted from snake venom, or the many synthetic derivatives made from compounds found in snake venom.

There are many more opinions on the subject of snakes and venom, most of them siding with the premise that these wives' tale assumptions are false, perpetuated by the same people whose indoctrination causes them to believe that snakes are evil and out to get us.

The final and most important aspect of venom and envenomation is what to do if you get bit. Those of you who spend time outdoors should already know the proper precautions for avoiding snakebite, and those of us who deal directly with venomous snakes have to take even greater care not to get bit. But what should you do if it happens?

There isn't one item in most snakebite kits that is useful in a snakebite situation. Whether the kit costs $5 or $50, it's worthless. Don't buy one. If you already have one, chuck it.

Forget everything you ever heard about snakebite treatment. Forget what your Scoutmaster told you, forget what the Red Cross used to say, and forget every snake scene in every Western movie you ever saw, especially True Grit (both versions).

The last thing you want if you get bitten by a venomous snake is for someone with little or no medical knowledge cutting you with a scalpel, especially in a field situation. Venom cannot be sucked out of a bite, tourniquets aren't recommended for pit viper bites, and Band-Aids are the least of your concerns if you've been envenomated.

There are only two items you need in your personal snakebite safety kit: a cell phone and car keys. But don't try to drive yourself to the hospital.

If a snake bites you, determine whether it's a venomous species. If the snake is harmless, clean the bite thoroughly with soap and water. There are rarely any significant side effects from a harmless snakebite, although there have been instances where sensitive individuals have experienced anaphylaxis and/or a secondary infection.

If the snake that bit you is venomous, there is a chance that no venom was injected. If envenomation did occur, symptoms may include pain at the bite site, swelling, nausea, muscle tremors, sweating, weakness, dizziness, hemorrhagic bleb (blood blister) and tachycardia (rapid heartbeat).

Time is of the essence, but you have hours in which to get medical help. In the meantime, do these four things:

1. Keep the bitten extremity elevated above heart level. (This protocol replaces the old recommendation of keeping the affected limb lower than heart level.) *Never* use a tourniquet on a pit viper bite.
2. Do not panic or exert yourself.
3. Get to a hospital or call 911 and have help come to you.
4. Contact National Snakebite Support. They will connect you with competent medical professionals and assist with proper protocols. Let the doctors do the rest.
   NOTE: This information is not intended to replace competent medical intervention or advice.

The following are basic common sense precautions for avoiding snakebite:

1. Make noise or walk with heavy steps when hiking. This gives snakes time to get out of your way. If there's a snake on the trail, go around it.
2. If you're not sure what kind of snake you're looking at, don't touch it or try to pick it up.
3. Never poke a snake with a stick or tease it. Don't be a show-off or try to impress your friends.
4. Let a snake get away from you. That's all it wants to do.
5. Don't place your hands anywhere you can't see. This includes ledges, shrubbery and burrows.
6. Don't forget about your dog!

If you hike or trail run with your dog in rattlesnake-prone areas, consider putting it through a rattlesnake avoidance training course. Nature has endowed dogs with a high level of resistance to snake envenomation, perhaps as a holdover from their wolf lineage, but small dogs don't fare as well as larger breeds, and all dogs can suffer long-term health effects if not treated promptly and properly. Rattlesnake vaccines are ineffective and can be administered only once or twice in a dog's lifetime. Prevention is always better than treatment. It's also far less expensive.

There are local people almost everywhere who offer this service, but the good folks at Get Rattled! provide the best dog training by far. Based in Reno, Nevada, I first met John and his team a little more than 10 years ago when he called to ask if I would sponsor a clinic in Salt Lake. The Get Rattled! team travels extensively during the summer months, offering their unique and invaluable training methods to dogs and their owners all across the Western states.

By using live snakes in a controlled situation, this affordable training has saved the lives of hundreds of dogs, not to mention the cost savings of prevention versus treatment. More important, it has shielded dog owners from the pain of losing a beloved fur person to a preventable death.

Wherever you live, there is probably a snake avoidance program that can provide this service for you and your dog.

In an enlightened age, it's time to start seeing snakes as the valuable and vulnerable creatures they are. Show them proper respect, take precautions in snake habitat, and learn to get along. It's not hard to do.

Whatever you think of them, snakes really are more afraid of us than we are of them. The next time you meet one, enjoy the experience and allow it to continue on its chosen path. This will ensure that all parties go home safe at the end of the day.

CHAPTER 14

Journey to Snake Road

"Those who find beauty in all of nature will find themselves at one with the secrets of life itself." –L. Wolfe Gilbert

Normal people vacation in places like Hawaii, Sea World, or Disneyland, and that's fine for them. Snake people, however, go where the snakes are.

There's a 2.7-mile ribbon of double-track dirt road in Union County Illinois, not far from the town of Murphysboro, just east of the Mississippi River. Known as Snake Road, this backwater byway serves almost no purpose most of the time, but for four months each year, it's heaven on earth for herpers — the place snake lovers go when we die. But I suggest not waiting till then.

Wedged between the east bank of the Big Muddy River and the adjacent limestone bluffs, the road isn't wide enough in most places for two cars to pass. That doesn't matter since foot traffic is all that's allowed during April and May, and again in September and October, when the semi-annual snake migrations occur.

As I discovered by asking around, most local folks are completely unaware of the road's existence, perhaps because its real name is Larue-Pine Hills—Otter Pond Research Natural Area. But to snake enthusiasts like me, this rural backroad is known far and wide as Snake Road — the ultimate snake-lover's dream destination and a field herper's paradise.

The area is lush and green and parts of the road are canopied with trees. In places, the rocky bluffs give way to deep forest where armadillos grunt and snuffle, their flexible snouts probing the leaf litter in a relentless quest for insects. In a wetland area, duckweed on tranquil water looks like a welcoming green carpet just waiting to trick you into strolling on it. Another spot resembles the fire swamp from *The Princess Bride*, where dead stumps protrude from stagnant water and rodents of unusual size (ROUS) wallow near the fringes of quicksand pits, eager to make a tasty meal of a passing herper.

The first thing an old desert dog like me notices is the humidity, which is something we don't deal with in the desert. Back at home I have to exert myself to work up a sweat. We call it a "dry heat." In Illinois, I remain permanently damp. As a nice lady in a local convenience store reminded me, October isn't even the humid season. "You should have been here in August, hun," she said. I'm glad I wasn't.

The idea to visit snake road had rattled around in the back of my brain since I first heard of it around 2010. The only person I knew who had been there was Jamison, and his experience was less than stellar due mostly to inclement weather.

I put the idea on hold for a few years. Then Todd contacted me. Todd Michael Cox is an author and the administrator of The Snake Anti-Defamation League (SADL), a Facebook page devoted to snakes, snake awareness, and the elimination of the prevalent and perfunctory human ignorance that surrounds them. "Protecting the reputation of the noble serpent" is the page's motto. I was the administrator of Uncle Dave's Reptile Page, and Todd and I had corresponded once or twice. Like-minded folks have a way of finding each other. Todd's invitation came in 2014, but it took another year for our plans to materialize.

I met Todd and his wife Heidi at a campground near Carbondale, Illinois on October 8, 2015, after flapping my way from Salt Lake to St. Louis the day before. This gave me a chance to scope out the road before they arrived from Wisconsin. Snake people are never at a loss for words because we can always swap stories and lies about the snake adventures we've had or hope to have in the future, and we hit it off right away. At that moment, we were only an hour's drive from a serpent-lovers paradise, and we eagerly headed there the following morning.

The first snake you see on Snake Road will likely be a cottonmouth. I heard one little girl exclaim, "There's a cottonmouth over here and I found him first!" Indeed she did.

Too many people can ruin any pursuit, but a reasonable number of people on Snake Road isn't always a bad thing. More people mean more eyes for finding snakes, and most of them are more than happy to share their finds with you. Too many people, of course, could destroy the experience even if they are fellow snake lovers.

One woman took advantage of her time on the road six months earlier, posting a photo of her two young daughters enjoying a picnic lunch. Sitting on a blanket in the middle of Snake Road on a perfect spring day, the girls are unfazed by a cottonmouth casually cruising by several feet away. I wish I could show you the photo, but here's what she said about the scene:

"I like sharing this picture. I took my kids to Snake Road for spring break. Here they are having a picnic while a cottonmouth just passes by, minding its own business. My girls loved it! They like telling the story of this vacation where they learned that snakes, even the 'bad' ones, aren't as scary as people think they are."

The accompanying commentary from a snake group had this to say:

"What a great moment, and it encompasses everything we are trying to teach. There was no chasing, no hysterics, no bites, no calling 911, no snake getting killed through fear and ignorance. It's just a cottonmouth minding its own business while a group of people observe it. We all can learn from this."

I met my first Northern cottonmouths (*Agkistrodon piscivorus*) on Snake Road. Lovely serpents, and very tolerant, they are nothing like the delusional fabrications of those histrionic individuals who claim to have been chased, harassed, and even attacked by "nests" of vigilante cottonmouths, also known as water moccasins. As long as a human doesn't jump around and pose a threat to these mellow snakes, they have absolutely no reason to be defensive. Feet and legs that don't move are just tree stumps or rocks to a snake, and snakes don't bite those things. When you dance around and act hysterical, that's when you put yourself in danger. Stay calm. It's just a snake and it couldn't care less about us until we get in its way.

Nevertheless, according to generations of urban folklore, these mercenary serpents, angry and fueled by homicidal rage, allegedly chase boats, cars, even helicopters and space shuttles, insatiable in their quest for human prey that run screaming frantically away, steadfast in their brain-addled, hyperventilating assertions of reptilian vendettas. Someone please tell me where these people come from and why we allow them to reproduce. There ought to be laws against it.

There I was face-to-face with one of these supposed agents of destruction on its own turf. Would I live to tell the tale? I had heard redneck ramblings of demon cottonmouths, and maybe I'm a bad judge of character, but it didn't seem to me that these indolent snakes were engineered by nature to wipe out the entire human race. But hey, don't ever let reality get in the way of a good, overly dramatic and possibly liquor-induced legend, right?

The truth is, cottonmouths are so complacent that I was inspired to write this limerick:

> *I need a moccasin to chase me*
> *Just to see if it can outpace me*
> *This new generation*
> *Has no motivation*
> *I can barely even get one to face me!*

Well-fed after a summer afield, hordes (herds? scads?) of Northern cottonmouths make an eons-old pilgrimage to ancestral hibernacula in Snake Road's limestone bluffs as their kind have done for millennia. I followed one of them. He knew where to go as surely as a bird knows to fly south. I watched in rapt fascination as the robust reptile clumsily dragged his lethargic body up a dry incline and slowly disappeared into the well-worn entrance of a crevice accessible only to snakes. He'll spend the winter underground with a few hundred of his closest friends, living off fat reserves from his summer buffet of fish and frogs.

It was my first time herping east of the Mississippi and I wanted more. Finding snakes is a serendipitous venture at best, and luck is always a welcome companion. But herping the verdant green forests and wetlands of Illinois was infinitely easier than the dusty desert herping I was used to, not to mention there were snakes I had never seen. Even finding a Common garter snake (*Thamnophis sirtalis*) was a thrill because it's a taxonomically different animal than the Wandering garters of the Great Basin, and a fairly rare find even on Snake Road.

The Only Good Snake . . .

In addition, we saw rough green snakes (*Opheodrys aestivas*), a DeKay's brown snake (*Storeria dekayi*), Western ribbon snake (*Thamnophis proximus*), North American (black) racer (*Pantherophis spiloides*), two species of water snakes; the Plain-bellied (*Nerodia erythrogaster*) and the Mississippi green (*Nerodia cyclopion*), a Red-bellied mudsnake (*Farancia abacura*), and a Common worm snake (*Carphophis amoenus*) which Todd flipped that morning near the campground. These were all new species for me.

The next day produced another cornucopia of serpents, with repeat sightings of many species, but it didn't matter. Finding any snake, anywhere, is always a thrill, and finding so many snakes in one place was like winning the serpent lottery.

In the middle of our third day of herping Snake Road (and the best herping day of my life at that point), I had to flee that ephemeral Eden or miss my flight back home. Looking back on it, I should have stayed. There's always another plane, but snakin' days like that are few and far between, especially where I come from. At 2 pm I had just three hours to return my body and my rental car to St. Louis. I bade Todd and Heidi a reluctant farewell and apologized for leaving right at the apex of an extraordinary trip. I swore never to make that mistake again if I returned. I also swore that I would return, which I did the following year.

Jordan and I spent our vacations there in 2016, allowing him to escape dad duty for four days, and granting us both a well-earned reprieve after a busy summer moving rattlesnakes in Utah.

The drive from St. Louis on Thursday was pleasant enough, but Friday dawned cold and wet. We awoke in our campsite at Giant City State Park to drizzly skies the color of battleships. We had flown 1,500 miles and burned a week of vacation time only to witness an unseasonably soggy mid-October storm pattern. It did not bode well for finding snakes, but we were determined to salvage the day.

While waiting for the clouds to break, we stopped at a natural attraction in Jackson County called Little Grand Canyon — a deep box canyon eroded by water from the exposed sandstone of the Shawnee Hills. Even though it was raining, we looked forward to a scenic hike in a deep gorge adorned with sculpted rock and cascading waterfalls. But we didn't make it that far.

Only a quarter-mile into the hike, the soles on my new boots proved useless on wet limestone, skidding and slipping like bowling shoes on melting ice. I was literally standing still when both feet shot forward as if an invisible force had kicked them out from under me.

I reacted in an instant, swinging my arms behind me, palms down, to brace my fall. My right arm absorbed most of the impact. In that moment, I heard a loud *pop* as something in my shoulder tore loose.

Abandoning our hike, we headed for Snake Road and herped it intently — the way detectives might comb a crime scene. But the weather was better suited to finding frogs than snakes. Fortunately, Snake Road has a healthy population of amphibians as well. We amused ourselves by shining our headlamps into shallow cubbies where surprised alien faces of bulgy-eyed salamanders peered curiously back at us from their comfortable condos in the dank recesses of the cliff face.

That night we stopped for dinner at a festive Mexican restaurant along the highway. It had lots of ambience and great food. When I tried to take a drink, however, my arm trembled and water sloshed as I struggled to lift the glass more than four inches above the table. The pain in my shoulder was exquisite. Something was definitely wrong.

Saturday and Sunday were cool and cloudy, yet the road was strangely devoid of people. There was no one there, not even a snake. This was normally the right time for the main migration, but we had already lost a day due to lousy weather. Or had we?

By making the most of each break in the clouds, Jordan found three Timber rattlesnakes (*Crotalus horridis*) at different times and places, each one tucked securely under a protective ledge where they remained dry but inaccessible. This was one of the species we most wanted to see. To this day, I haven't seen a Timber on the crawl, but standing tiptoe on a slippery cliff face, I've looked one in the eye from inches away. Based on his superhuman snaking skills, Jordan earned the title, Timber Man.

The Only Good Snake . . .

The next three nights in a tent were pure agony. Most of me loved being in this snake-infested Xanadu, having fallen in love with the area the year before, but my shoulder only wanted to go home.

I toughed it out, let Jordan do the driving, and kept an eye on the forecast. After the shoulder incident, my right arm was little more than a floppy, useless appendage. It still worked, but not very well. Dangling at my side like a broken pendulum, it served mostly as a counterweight for my left arm.

Over the next three days, the snake gods smiled on us, perhaps out of pity, granting us nice but intermittent herping weather.

After the storm, the air was crisp and fresh, carrying the organic fragrance of Petrichor and the muffled hush of whispering trees. A golden canopy arched over us where the trees leaned toward each other from both sides of the road, forming a tunnel. Sunlight filtered through orange leaves in a warm, ambient glow. Dying leaves fluttered like nature's confetti, a celebration of the shifting season. With every step, our boots pressed softly into the unfolding blanket of autumn's last hurrah.

The road quietly pointed the way through a forest of deciduous trees, stately as sentinels, inviting us further along its painted path. A breeze rustling through the branches sent even more leaves tumbling and twirling to the ground. The refugees of summer. Birdsong was the only accompaniment to the serenity.

Stepping carefully along the gentle rise and fall of the road, our eyes scanned the ground like laser beams, searching for any movement against a motionless backdrop. Slowly, almost imperceptibly at first, the road began to yield up her treasure. The warming rays of the midday sun lured creatures from their nooks and crannies and the road began to wriggle. Amid the quiet calm, we caught sight of a subtle shape — a sleek ripple of motion gliding silently between patches of dappled sunlight.

It was a ribbon snake, its yellow stripes weaving their way through the carpet of leaves like golden threads. It stopped in a sunlit patch just long enough for us to take its picture. Then, in the immortal words of Emily Dickinson, ". . . it wrinkled and was gone."

Nearby, the sound of rustling signaled another presence as a slender, dark-colored serpent disappeared into verdant undergrowth. We only caught a glimpse. What was it? A racer? A gray rat snake perhaps? We searched, but we were outmatched by this master of hide and seek.

The following day, another ribbon snake darted swiftly in front of me, daring me to catch it in a stand of nettles. Habit overtook common sense as I thrust my zombie arm into the thorn bush. The snake escaped, leaving me nothing to show for my effort but an arm covered in crimson droplets.

At that moment, a man appeared seemingly out of nowhere and we exchanged pleasantries. "What happened to your arm?" he asked. I decided to have a little fun with him.

"Snake," I told him.

A look of concern crept over him. "What kind of snake?"

"Ribbon snake," I replied, trying to remain serious.

"Whoa!" he exclaimed as his eyes grew three sizes. He went on his way, treading carefully to avoid those bloodthirsty ribbon snakes.

Later that day, I caught a Diamond-backed water snake (*Nerodia rhombifer*) despite knowing exactly what the result would be. Water snakes aren't mean; they just don't work and play well with others. After catching him by the middle of his body as he tried to escape under a log, he delivered four enthusiastic bites to my left arm between my wrist and elbow. This happened in about two seconds. Still not satisfied that he had made an impression on me, he swung the forward part of his body back and forth, hoping to bite anything that came within range of his open mouth. (I need to point out that handling snakes on Snake Road is illegal and I only did it with the intention of getting a photo. That's no excuse, of course, but when it comes to snakes, I can resist everything but temptation.)

I released my cranky friend as blood trickled down my arm. My *other* arm. Jordan stared at me as if I was the biggest moron he had ever met. I prefer to think that my mind isn't twisted, but rather, it's strategically bent in several places for maximum efficiency. But I'm open to all possibilities.

Each rise in the road brought new potential, causing eager anticipation for what lay ahead. Our senses were attuned to the hushed stirrings of life beneath the disappearing awning above us. In the rhythmic swaying of the trees, nature payed tribute to summer's final breath.

As we strode carefully down the forested road, the autumn air carried the scent of dying leaves and living earth. Our eyes scanned the ground, perpetually searching for signs of subtle movement — seeking motion in rustling foliage or a serpentine ripple on a duckweed-covered marsh.

A Rough green snake caught our attention, its sleek, emerald-colored body gliding smoothly across the trail, literally vanishing into a tuft of green grass. Not far off the road next to the bluffs, a mound of leaves concealed a tiny secret. A Ring-necked snake (*Diadophis punctatus*), expertly camouflaged in a plain grey suit, except for the yellow bandana around its neck, inched slowly along the rock face. At our approach, it coiled the bright, citrus-colored underside of its tail in a halfhearted display of intimidation before vanishing with an imperceptible flick.

On a Tuesday afternoon in October 2022, while Jordan was off doing his own thing, I had the pleasure of meeting Jim and Nan from Chicago. We spent the afternoon strolling the road. We saw scads of snakes, but the biggest thrill of all was the juvenile copperhead Jim spotted. For me, it was a lifer. It had taken four trips to Illinois to finally find a copperhead, and I'm glad Jim and Nan were part of that experience. It was a first for them too. From that point on I called them "Copperhead Jim" and "Snake Road Nan."

We gave the little Eastern copperhead (*Agkistrodon contortrix*) our utmost attention. In the mottled afternoon light, the repeating pattern of chocolate kisses along its copper-toned sides blended perfectly with the rust-colored leaves, making it nearly invisible until a slight movement betrayed its presence. Barely a week or two old, it was only as long as a dollar bill. The tiny serpent assumed a dignified stance — still as a stick — watching, waiting, and wanting only to flee for its safety. Lying on our bellies for a photo op, we documented this exquisite little creature before allowing it to escape into the road's ragged edge.

Every step down Snake Road felt charged with possibility. This road, normally a hazard to snakes, brimmed with life as serpents of all types rippled intermittently over its undulating surface in a ritual as old as time. We documented 11 species in two days — less than half of what lives there — including an Eastern milk snake (*Lampropeltis triangulum*) only five feet inside the north gate.

Large snakes were easy to see. Smaller snakes, on the other hand, disappeared and reappeared like shadows among leaves of curled parchment, scales glinting in stark contrast to the remnants of autumn's demise. We proceeded with cautious vigilance, fearful of treading on snakes so small that only their movement allowed us to see them.

Jordan's eagle eyes spotted a Smooth earth snake (*Virginia valeriae*), one of the world's tiniest snake species, with adults reaching lengths of less than 15 inches. This one was only five-inches long and slender enough to crawl through an uncooked macaroni noodle.

Cottonmouths moved with confidence, wending their way among rocks and fallen branches, undulating across the road like fat black ribbons unfurling toward the bluffs, slow and deliberate. Cottonmouths are the most common and congenial species on Snake Road, revealing broad, toothy grins whenever you get too close, and vibrating their excited tails as if to say, "Welcome to Illinois!" If you can't find a cottonmouth on Snake Road, you need to find a different hobby.

Meeting so many cottonmouths gave me a new respect for people who live where these snakes are common. Out West, where the only pit vipers are rattlesnakes, you generally hear one before you see it. In cottonmouth country, you have to pay attention to your surroundings, ever on the lookout for that white, welcoming smile. Gaping is a cottonmouth's defense mechanism. Rattlesnakes rattle and cottonmouths gape. Gaping isn't as effective as rattling because you have to remain alert or you could easily step on one.

Stepping off the road in a thick section of forest, I stood before a large tree to pay the water bill. In that moment, at the base of the trunk, the wide, welcoming yawn of a surprised cottonmouth gaped open in stark contrast to its dark body and the tree's shadow. I didn't see him until that moment. I could make a joke about being pissed off versus being pissed on, but I think I'll let it slide. But a rattlesnake wouldn't have let me get so close without sounding an alarm.

Back at home, the last rattlesnake of the year was a three-footer that slithered through a grate at the Museum of Natural History, falling four stories into an airshaft onto a concrete floor. That is, unless he found another way in that the museum doesn't know about. Or maybe he used the ladder. Who knows?

The call came while we were in Illinois. I really thought the Salt Lake snake season was over, but there's always a straggler or two. After an unscheduled (and uncompensated) night in Phoenix, we made it home a day later than planned. Jordan and I stopped at the museum on our way from the airport to rescue the unfortunate buzzer butt. I was expecting a busted up snake with internal injuries, but its locomotion was normal and it didn't appear to need rehabbing. It didn't want to eat, however, due to the lateness of the season. With my right arm dangling limp at my side, I hiked him back up the mountain the following day. Cold weather was already here, leaving him little time to seek shelter.

Then I called my orthopedic surgeon. He had already seen me for a cervical spondylosis when turning my head felt like someone had shot an arrow through my neck, and he would later scope both knees.

According to an ultrasound, my shoulder was a mess, with the muscles and connecting tissue having detached from the joint. That explained why it hurt like hell, especially at night, and I became a prime candidate for shoulder surgery.

My orthopedic surgeon: "Congratulations, Dave, you have a complete tear of two major muscles and tendons with retraction."

Me: "Will I be able to bench press 300 pounds after surgery?"

Him: "Could you before the injury?"

Me: "No, but I was hoping to after you rebuild me."

Him: "You will probably never regain full strength or mobility in that arm."

Me: "Party pooper."

He explained that he'd be going into my right shoulder arthroscopically, drilling holes, then tying the ends of the muscles back where they belong using screws. Healing time would be four to six months with some extremely uncomfortable physical therapy along the way. Oh goodie.

After explaining the procedure to me, he asked, "Have you voted yet?" I told him I had. "Good!" he said. "Your surgery is on Election Day."

I couldn't think of a better day to be under anesthesia and stoned on opioids, especially the way the 2016 election turned out.

I had a dead arm for the three weeks leading up to surgery, which was a two-and-a-half-hour, multi-part procedure, including a tenodesis. My biceps muscle is now attached about an inch and a half lower on my humerus than nature intended.

In addition to the tenodesis, the surgery consisted of an arthroscopic rotator cuff repair, distal clavicle excision, and subacromial decompression. I don't know what any of that means but it sounds impressive, all held in place with five nylon screws with metal tabs. I wouldn't wish the ensuing pain and recovery time on anyone.

My right arm was strapped to my shoulder for 58 days and I had to sleep sitting up for that entire time due to the pain. When I could finally lie down, I couldn't sleep on my right side for more than five months. Don't even get me started on the physical therapy aspect. I never knew what real pain was until then.

It was a lot of damage from one little fall, and I'm really not that fragile. I believe that a series of incremental injuries over many years, including bike crashes and other accidental impacts contributed to the tearing of my shoulder muscles a little at a time, and one slippery hike in Illinois was all it took to finish the job. If it had to happen, I wish it had happened closer to home.

Twenty weeks after shoulder reconstructive surgery and 16 weeks of physical therapy later, they finally kicked me out. Initially, I had only 47 percent use of my right arm, but thanks to a great team of professionals (and a lot of work on my part) I have 83 percent today. Due to the extent of the injury, it will never be

100 percent, but I went back to catching rattlesnakes the following spring and that's what really mattered.

While waiting for my shoulder to heal, I also had surgery to fix my funky knee. In medical terms, the unilateral thing-a-ma-jig was torn in two places, with separation of the whatcha-ma-call-it from its primary doo-dah. And there was fluid retention. Even worse, my surgeon said there was also something going on behind the kneecap. I hope it was a party.

Jordan and I have returned to Snake Road a few more times since that first trip. We're happy to report that there are snakes on Snake Road. Lots of them. All sizes and species. Twenty-three species to be exact. It's like God's own garden for snake lovers — but you have to time it right — something we're getting better at.

Thanks to all the people we met on Snake Road; professors and undergrads from the local university, photographers, videographers, bloggers, writers, Facebookers and families. Everyone was more than willing to share their knowledge and discoveries.

We hope to see you all on Snake Road someday soon!

CHAPTER 15

Media Matters

"Social Media is like jail. You sit around wasting time, writing on walls, and getting poked by people you don't know."
–Unknown

July 16th each year is designated as World Snake Day. For those of us who celebrate this auspicious occasion, it's like the summertime version of Christmas. The only thing better than World Snake Day is when it falls in the Chinese Year of the Snake, which it did in 2025. The last time it happened was in 2013.

That was the year I blitzed local print media with World Snake Day articles and letters to the editor, sending op/eds to seven newspapers including the Salt Lake Tribune. Beginning in May, I asked the editor if he would consider publishing a snake article to commemorate World Snake Day in July. His reply made me chuckle: "I will carefully consider what I assume will be our only World Snake Day-related submission." Only? Why would it be the only? Doesn't everyone celebrate World Snake Day? In my world, World Snake Day is bigger than the Fourth of July and National Bikini Week combined!

When all was said and done, only two of them printed an article. The Trib wasn't one of them. Being a snake ambassador isn't always easy.

As an editor myself, I read sentences that couldn't be more convoluted if the author had written them poorly on purpose. As a writer, I hope I've never written a sentence that made an editor consider quitting the craft.

Ernest Hemingway said to write drunk and edit sober. Personally, I think Hemingway had it backward.

I spend many hours each month vigilantly slaying the dragons of bad grammar, poor punctuation, run-on sentences, split infinitives, subject-verb agreement, wordiness, etc. The magazine I write for told its writers to avoid difficult words and use shorter sentences because a certain percentage of readers only want to look at the pictures. Website statistics show that if the photos accompanying an article don't grab them, they're unlikely to read beyond the captions. If they do, they're unlikely to engage with unfamiliar vocabulary.

I love writing. It's my preferred method of communicating with people because I can make sure everything I say is correct before the recipient sees it, leaving no excuse for grammar errors, Freudian slips, and so forth. The only problem is that we live in an age of short attention spans while simultaneously valuing entertainment and devaluing education, resulting in a dumbing down of society. It's pointless to write something if no one wants to read it or take the time to understand it. This is why writing about snakes is so frustrating. I can give readers great information but I can't make them read it. No writer can.

We live in a clickbait culture that wants to consume information in small, quick, digestible bites, but as a writer, I don't cater to those people. I write for those who like to read and who aren't afraid to learn a new word now and then. Short sentences and small words have their audience, but I am opposed to dumbing my writing down for the lowest common denominator in any demographic. Is this really where we want to go as a society?

When I was a kid my grandfather used to say "Let's went" whenever we were about to go somewhere. He was joking, of course, but it made me think about the power of words, their meanings, and their effect on people.

Words are invisible and intangible, but they can whisper comfort to the dying or incite wars among the living. They can invoke a healing blessing or mutter a damning curse. And once they've been uttered, they can never be recalled. Words have power and we need to choose them wisely. Nowhere is this truer than on social media.

In 2012, I climbed aboard the social media bandwagon and set up two accounts on a popular social media platform. One was my personal page while the second was dedicated to reptiles. After using a couple of faulty names, I finally settled on Uncle Dave's Reptile Page. This allowed me to use my familiar moniker which gave the page a friendly feel. It must have worked because the page grew in leaps and bounds — exponentially outpacing itself every year for the next 11 years while establishing a global fan base that exceeded 200,000 followers.

(To avoid any issue with corporate entities, I'll avoid using the name of the particular social media platform, but it has the words *book* and *face* in it, not necessarily in that order. Going forward, I will refer to it as "The Platform.")

One fan of Uncle Dave's Reptile Page gave this unsolicited endorsement: "Uncle Dave has vast reptile knowledge and shares it at levels everyone can understand. And it's not just snakes that he shares about, but all manner of reptiles, and how they fit into their various environments and food chains. (With amphibians tossed in here and there.) You'll learn about endangered species, newly discovered ones, and fun & fascinating facts about these beautiful, ancient, misunderstood animals that share our planet. Enjoy all this page has to offer! You won't be sorry!"

Uncle Dave responded, "Wow! That's really nice. Thanks!"

Another loyal follower had this to say: "I enjoy this page more and more every day. Thank you for helping me educate people about snakes and how valuable they are to the world. I share a lot from this page and if it helps one person not harm a snake it was totally worth it."

A comment from Vern went into greater detail: "I like your page. I've tried a few other pages and they are frustrating because it's either a bunch of know-it-all's, or it reminds me of all the old herp symposiums I used to attend; one big show and tell/sell. Happy to be part of something honest, humorous, and just plain real.

"I'm an old retired herp keeper from Denver who now just works part time at the Arizona Sonora Desert Museum and sits on the board of the Tucson Herp Society. Keep up the good work, Uncle Dave."

Cody, in New York State, sent me this message: "First, I have to say I love your page. I love seeing other people care about snakes and teaching people about them. You sir, I have the highest respect for, and would love to talk about rattlesnakes and anything about reptiles with you. Thank you for sharing your respect and passion for these amazing animals."

The Only Good Snake . . .

The most overwhelming comment about Uncle Dave's Reptile Page said this: "Following Uncle Dave's Reptile Page has been the best decision of my life so far."

Gee, no pressure there!

Accolades like those kept me motivated even after 11 years.

Fans of the page asked lots of questions, many of which pulled me out of my comfort zone. I was not the reptile expert they presumed me to be, forcing me to research matters I knew nothing about. This was irritating in one regard, namely that they had access to the same internet I did and could easily have done their own research. The result, of course, was that I learned more than anyone else, and that was okay.

Many requests came from people, often friends of friends, who wanted to friend me on my personal page. I had no problem with that except that most of them were reptile people. For that reason, I steered them to Uncle Dave's Reptile Page where it was all reptiles, all the time. (They were welcome to follow my personal page as well, where they reaped the additional benefit of my witty social repartee and insightful political commentary.)

A co-worker once told me I posted too many political memes on my personal page and not enough funny stuff. Well excuse me! Many of my political memes are quite funny if you have the right sense of humor. But not everything in life is funny. There is some serious stuff going on in the world and not everyone is aware of it. I also understand that we need an escape, so I try not to get too heavy-handed.

It wasn't long after I started Uncle Dave's Reptile Page that I opened Wasatch Snake Removal, so I made a page for that, too.

Relocating rattlesnakes is an endeavor that catches people's attention, and I was soon dragged into the spotlight of real media despite my reservations and the fact that I've never been comfortable as the center of attention, especially when it involved having cameras and microphones shoved in my face.

On the upside, by being on TV or the radio, I could reach people who may never read a snake article or watch a snake documentary. On the downside, I quickly learned that media's goal isn't to inform but to entertain, or to create some strange blend of infotainment. We already know this as viewers, but it becomes painfully obvious when you become the infotainer — especially when the role is forced upon you.

I made my television de-butt (oh wait, it's pronounced day-byoo) on the local Fox affiliate after I picked up a ball python in a park and Fox thought it was newsworthy. (I have no idea who called them.) 'If I sound too dumb,' I told myself, 'I'll just have to move out of state.'

Later, a local country radio station contacted me after I had removed a rattler from the yard of one of their corporate executives. A trio of morning show DJs was going to call me at a designated time to ask questions for the benefit of their listeners. Knowing that I would only have a few moments to state my case, I was prepared with notes and a brief outline. That way, I reasoned, they couldn't derail my train of thought and I could make at least a few salient points no matter what they threw at me.

I couldn't have been more wrong.

Interviewers, I discovered, don't want you to be prepared. They want to catch you off guard. They want you to balance on a ball with one foot while juggling flaming knives as you do your best to dodge ludicrous and irrelevant questions from sadistic clowns.

It wasn't live so I don't know how they edited the interview. Because I was at work, I never heard it despite being told that it would be replayed throughout the day. All I know is that I resent how the media doesn't even try to promote intelligent, cogent thoughts and info; all they want is a damn sound bite, and the more controversial and less informed the better. I had a list of bullet points — info that could have truly helped people by making them less afraid. Instead, they asked whether removing snakes was my full-time job, and other irrelevant fluff. It was pathetic.

Social media platforms are revolutionary in their ability to connect people, allowing us to share information in ways that were unimaginable just a short time ago. The highest and best use for such a pervasive and influential medium should be the sharing of thoughts, ideas, philosophies and aspirations for our collective and cultural well-being and enlightenment.

Despite this loftier capability, social media platforms remain nothing more than mass delivery systems for cat photos, jokes, rants, proletariat propaganda and political drivel — proof of the prevalent social trend that drives us toward hollow entertainment. It's sad that so many people can have access to something with so much potential, yet still manage to reduce it to its most trivial and banal purpose.

Even at its highest and best use, it's doubtful that we'd ever agree on many of the same thoughts, ideas, philosophies and aspirations, but agreement isn't the objective. No one learns anything if everyone agrees. But it's not supposed to be a shooting gallery either. Want to start a culture war? Simply express an unpopular opinion on social media and wait for the character assassination to begin. This may explain why people share cat pictures, stupid jokes and unsubstantiated political opinions instead.

The Platform is the visual equivalent of X (formerly known as Twitter), meaning that it doesn't allow for a thorough explanation of an issue, which makes it more like emotional bomb-throwing than an educational forum. People don't want long explanations or in-depth analyses of a subject. We want short, quick bits of info before moving on to the next chunk of trivial gossip or inflammatory innuendo. Sadly, it's also how some people get their news. In the information age, we can learn about anything if we will take the time to research it, but we choose to remain woefully ignorant of the reality that surrounds us and bombard each other with cute little memes and trite witticisms instead.

More than once I found myself in The Platform's jail with my account suspended, sometimes without even knowing why. Seriously. They wouldn't always show me the offending content so that I might remain infraction-free in the future. To the best of my knowledge, I didn't violate community standards either by accident or on purpose, but I still managed to displease his holiness, Lord Zuckerberg and his Kindergarten Kops, ending up in solitary confinement with little hope for clemency.

"Guilty until proven innocent!" is their credo, and I suppose I should feel fortunate that they didn't convene a firing squad.

We've all been there. Nemo the Wonder Cat sat on the keyboard one Saturday morning as I was trying to compose a reply on someone else's page. He posted 23 nonsensical comments. The Platform thought I was a spammer and temporarily blocked me from posting. (Nemo always was a poor button pusher.) Bad kitty!

In May 2023, Uncle Dave's Reptile Page was placed on a temporary suspension while they decided what to do with me. With no Miranda rights, no attorney, no judge or jury, and no chance to plead my case, the obtuse, fatuous twits that rule over The Platform with unchallenged impunity disabled Uncle Dave's Reptile Page so that neither I nor my peeps could post on it.

The offending content was a meme, a simple meme, and it wasn't even mine. I had reposted said meme in prior years without complaint, and yet it was suddenly offensive and intimidating. This was strange because I also posted it on my personal page where it was not deemed offensive, so apparently there is no consistency, uniformity, or logic where The Platform grannies are concerned. I wasn't even allowed to plead my case before a live person.

On at least one occasion, Uncle Dave's Reptile Page reached 939,000 people in a single week. Those craven overlords of the digital domain didn't seem to realize that my page brought them viewers (i.e., customers), and that by punishing me, they also harmed themselves, inhibited the free flow of information and ideas, and infringed on my followers' rights to express themselves. The page wasn't monetized and I never made a dime from it.

The Platform said, "We removed your content. We can't show this content. Your content goes against our community standards."

The Platform has standards? When did that happen?

"You're temporarily restricted from doing things like posting or commenting in groups or creating new groups until May 14 at 3:10 pm. If you think this doesn't go against our community standards, let us know."

In an appeal to The Platform's oversight board, I tried to explain to their prudish overlords that it was merely a contextual issue. This was my argument:

The Only Good Snake . . .

Humor and sarcasm are not threats of violence!

I run a page for reptile enthusiasts and I rotate certain posts each year as they show up as memories from previous years. The one that [The Platform] currently has a problem with is a meme showing the actor Liam Neeson from the movie "Taken," with the caption, "If you send me another picture of a dead snake asking for an ID, I will hunt you down and I will kill you."

As every film buff knows, "I will hunt you down and I will kill you" is a famous tag line from the movie.

As a snake relocation specialist, I get texts from people showing me the snake they killed and asking what kind it is. Others in the reptile community experience the same phenomenon, and as snake proponents, we are appalled by the stupidity of the act. However, the meme is not a violation of community standards on violence and incitement for the following reasons:

1. It is humor from a pop culture source that nearly everyone is familiar with.

2. It is said in a sarcastic way. It is not a threat of intimidation or violence against any specific person or group of people.

3. It has specific relevance to a specific group of people who understand and appreciate the humor and the sarcasm behind it.

4. I have posted this meme each year for the past several years. Why is it offensive now when it wasn't offensive before?

5. I didn't make the meme, I only shared it. Who are the puritanical censors whose tender little feelers get hurt by things that normal people aren't offended by? Your moderators must be a group of hypersensitive, senile grandmothers with no concept of real-world scenarios and no sense of humor. They were also offended by an Easter meme showing a photograph

228

of a Komodo dragon (a large Indonesian lizard) wear-
ing bunny ears and standing next to an Easter basket.
Who are these people, and what gives them the right
to decide what's funny and what's truly offensive or
violent in its intent? How is anyone supposed to sec-
ond guess your arbitrary censorship when the rules
aren't applied consistently?

I do not promote or endorse violence of any kind
and neither do the people who follow my page.

For these reasons, I wish to protest the decision to
remove the "offending post" from public view.

Best regards,

Uncle Dave's Reptile Page

When I tried to send it, I was told they couldn't process my request. Not only does The Platform consider you guilty until proven innocent, they remove your ability to declare your innocence. You can't even interact with a living, breathing being, or even an algorithm because the "Help Page" doesn't work.

After the warning and losing my argument (assuming they even saw it), my page was scheduled to be blocked beginning on June 1, 2023 and lasting until the end of July.

Shutting down a reptile page in the middle of summer is beyond unreasonable. This was how I reached people. This was how I made a difference. It was how I made the world a better place for animals and the people who love them. I couldn't even commemorate World Snake Day with my peeps.

After the temporary block, I told my followers I wasn't ignoring them, and that I wasn't disinterested or dispassionate about their posts, likes, questions and comments. I told them about the decision and that I'd see them again in 60 days. However, after 70 days my page was still inactive. It was inactive after 90 days, and after 120 days. I never did get it back. That was in 2023.

Even after paying the penalty, The Platform's draconian censors shut down Uncle Dave's Reptile Page permanently due to an infraction I thought was resolved, leaving thousands of devoted followers in the dark. Without a page, I couldn't even tell them what happened. There was no one at The Platform to contact, no way to file a complaint, and no recourse. Eleven years' worth of photos, memes, questions, answers and advice simply disappeared into digital darkness as if they never existed. I took a more active role in administering The Snake Anti-Defamation League page, and many of my former followers migrated there as well, but my disdain for The Platform hasn't wavered.

Despite a less than congenial relationship with local media, there were also several positive experiences, including an invitation to appear on the Doug Wright Show. Now retired, Doug Wright was a local celebrity commentator with a weekday radio program that ran for nearly 30 years. He was known for his easy-going personality and good-natured delivery. His producer called less than 24-hours in advance of a live broadcast from the zoo. The show would be about snakes, of course.

On June 29, 2016, I arrived at the zoo at the appointed time, was fitted with headphones and a mic, and awaited my turn in the hot seat. I would be on following a woman who was a reptile curator at the zoo. During a commercial break, Doug and I chatted briefly to break the ice. He asked if it was okay to refer to me as a snake whisperer. I told him he wouldn't be the first. All of a sudden, the commercial ended and we were live on the air.

With a broadcast radius that covered several states, I tried to calm my nerves by not thinking about how many people were listening and convince myself I was having a one-on-one conversation. There were only six minutes left in the show, but Doug, professional that he was, made good use of them all. It was the single biggest audience I'd ever had, and I was more than pleased with the outcome.

At the opposite end of the spectrum, in the single worst on-air experience I ever had, I was invited to be the guest on a call-in radio show. The host introduced me to the staff and fitted me with a set of headphones. He explained that when the green light in front of me came on, it meant my microphone was on, or "hot" as they say in the industry. A producer would point at me, indicating it was my turn to speak.

Several interesting people called and I did my best to answer their questions. Things were going well until the final call. A man claiming to be a Scoutmaster proceeded to regale listeners with a gruesome tale of idiotic proportions.

He explained that he and his scouts were on an overnight campout when a "seven-foot 'diamondback' rattler crawled into camp." I bristled at the comment and couldn't wait to set him straight. (At most, it was a three-foot Great Basin rattler.) Then the story took a flaming nosedive into lunacy.

The father of one of the boys was a cop. Drawing his sidearm, he shot the snake multiple times, after which the boys were told to chop it into pieces. They didn't eat it; they didn't even skin it. They just butchered it with the zeal of adolescent savages. Or, being civilized kids, they may have caved in to the expectation that it was the 'manly' thing to do. Peer pressure and approval from respected adults will cause kids to do things they wouldn't normally consider. I imagined a scene straight out of *Lord of the Flies*, but with adult supervision. The wanton, needless killing of any animal is barbaric, but encouraging children to participate should be considered a criminal act.

I was incensed! I was prepared to deliver a scathing reprimand about the importance of respecting nature, setting a good example for impressionable youth, and the flawed mindset of visiting nature with the intention of killing the things that live there. Those boys deserved better role models. I waited for the green light to come on and the producer to point at me.

"That's all the time we have for today," said the host. Was he serious? Were they really going to let this moron have the final word? I shifted gears from irritated to apoplectic in a nanosecond. As a snake educator, it was one of the most frustrating moments of my life.

It reminded me of my own similar experience with scouts.

Once, at a lakeside scout camp, I made the mistake of leaning my snake stick against a picnic table within the confines of our campsite, putting it in plain sight of anyone passing by. I suppose it was too much temptation for some kid to resist because it disappeared on the first day of a weeklong camp.

After grilling my boys thoroughly and stressing the importance of honesty, I was convinced that none of them was the culprit. I had the camp director announce a cash reward for the return of the stick. Anyone who returned the stick would get $20 with no questions asked. It wasn't that the stick had any real monetary value, but for me it was a necessary tool (and the only one I had with me at the time), and besides, these kids were on their honor to be trustworthy — an essential attribute for a Boy Scout.

On the second night, an hour or two before sundown, I had nine 12- and 13-year-old boys in bare feet and sandals playing on the beach and frolicking in the dry scrub 50 yards from the water's edge. Our camp was situated in-between. Two more boys sat mesmerized by the fire, poking glowing embers with scraggly sticks. The other leader and I sat planning the next day's activities.

Abruptly, a shrill voice cried out, "Dave, there's a rattlesnake over here!" I got up and went to where the boy was pointing. There, between two tents, a two-foot buzzer butt cruised calmly on the warm sand. "Good spotting, bud!" I told him. His startled face melted into a satisfied grin. The other boys stopped what they were doing and came running over. I looked directly at one of them. "Tanner," I said firmly, "I need you to run to your tent and bring me your pillowcase."

Tanner was the only boy in the troop with a snake of his own — a large Burmese python named Monty. He scampered away like a rabbit, returning a moment later with a red plaid pillowcase.

"Hold it open," I told him. I bent down and caught the surprised viper by its tail. Tanner's eyes got wide and suddenly his arms weren't long enough. He stretched them out as far as he could, grimaced, and turned his head. I lowered the snake into the bag's narrow opening and withdrew my arm. Then I took the bag from him, twisted it and tied a knot at the top.

It was unusual for a snake to be so close to the lake, especially with so much activity going on. And it had to cross a road to get there.

"Put your boots on, Tanner, we're going for a hike." Tanner and I trekked the wayward reptile across the paved highway that encircles the lake and released it a few hundred yards up the hill

232

on the far side. It was a lucky snake. Of the two dozen or more campsites on the beach, it found its way into ours.

I don't contrast these two stories with the expectation that everyone would, should, or could resolve a similar situation the way I did. That would be unreasonable. And I most certainly don't do it to blow my own horn. I merely mean to point out that there are always alternatives to a hysterical overreaction.

I understand the concern for the safety of children, especially other peoples' children. It's a huge responsibility and one not to be taken lightly. But firing a gun into the ground could result in severe injury from a ricocheting bullet. Doing it in the presence of children sets a negative and traumatic example of idiocy. Not to mention hacking an animal to pieces. Those boys are damaged for life, scarred with a reinforced fear and subject to their own loss of emotional control in an unfamiliar situation. Using logic and reason, one of those 'leaders' could have simply carried that snake out of camp on a stick.

To the extent that fear can put us in greater danger than it can save us from, I maintain that irrational fear is almost never our friend. In many cases, neither is the media.

After World Snake Day a few years ago, I stumbled across one of my online letters to the Tribune where one of the commenters had accused me of trying to solicit business. He was upset that the letter wasn't flagged as 'sponsored content.' It was he, not the Tribune, who posted my website link. (Thanks, by the way.)

Someone who calls himself EG1984 said this in reply:

"There's no reason to have a 'sponsored' tag on it. It was submitted as a letter to the editor by a concerned citizen and there is no mention of the author's business. By the way, I had a snake issue on my property last summer. I called this man and he came out and took care of it in the most humane manner. I would not hesitate one second to recommend him to others."

I wish I could remember who he was.

I'd like to mention that even after increasing the reward, I never did get that snake stick back.

And before I forget, "The Platform" sucks!

CHAPTER 16

Legends and Lies

"People are funny. They'll demand ironclad proof before they'll change an opinion they formed with no proof at all."
–Unknown

"Sometimes people hold a core belief that is very strong. When they are presented with evidence that works against that belief, the new evidence cannot be accepted. It would create a feeling that is extremely uncomfortable, called cognitive dissonance. And because it is so important to protect the core belief, they will rationalize, ignore, and even deny anything that doesn't fit in with the core belief." —Frantz Fanon, West Indian psychiatrist and philosopher

People are constantly claiming to believe or not believe in things as though their belief makes it so. We can choose to believe (or disbelieve) in desired proportion to anything we want, including delusions of all sorts, but beliefs are not facts. Without facts to reinforce them, beliefs are just opinions, and you know what they say about opinions, right? The same is true of theories. Don't believe everything you hear. It's intellectual laziness to remain misinformed in the presence of truth.

If all I had done was relocate snakes, I would have only done half the job, because education is vital. I appreciated my customers who didn't want to see those creatures harmed. Or perhaps they were too afraid to get close enough to kill one. Either way, by calling me, the result was a win/win.

That's why it frustrates me when people start telling me things about snakes as though all my years of study and experience are worth less than their opinion. Giving them factual information can be difficult because the hardest thing for humans to do is admit they've been wrong most of their lives. It's hard to un-believe something when our very own grandpa/uncle/cousin/friend told it to us. After all, we trusted those people. That's why repeating rumors is such a dangerous thing; we have no way of knowing if what we're saying is true or not, but saying it makes us feel powerful. I can give people a dozen reasons why snakes are beneficial to have around, but I can't make them accept the truth when they'd rather believe a lie. It's pathetic that people who have no understanding of these animals can make up their own 'facts' and other people will choose to believe them.

There was a myth making the rounds many years ago that local gopher snakes (mistakenly called bull snakes or blow snakes) and rattlesnakes were interbreeding to create a hybrid species called a "bull rattler." Not only is it a bald-faced lie, it is genetically impossible.

If true, it would mean that gopher snakes are now at least partially venomous, thereby giving haters an even greater excuse for killing them. This ridiculous assertion even made its way to scout camp, with counselors warning the boys to be on the lookout for these new and instantly-evolving serpents.

Rattlesnakes and gopher snakes have been living side-by-side for eons, even sharing the same hibernacula. If such a thing were possible, wouldn't we have seen this bastardized hybridization long before now? Just because two animals are both snakes does not mean they are genetically compatible. Besides, the hemipenes of male snakes are ornamented with hooks and spicules for attaching to a female. These patterns are species-specific to ensure compatibility. A male rattlesnake couldn't do the horizontal mambo with that cute lady gopher snake next door even if he wanted to. Not to mention that rattlers give live birth and gopher snakes lay eggs. How would nature deal with *that* conundrum?

Dogs and cats are both mammals — they each have four paws, a tail and fur — but they cannot interbreed, and for the same good reason. The same holds true for horses and cows and everything else as well. Have you ever seen a giraffe-a-potamus? Nature prevents the hybridization of significantly different species based on different genetic and chromosomal codes. Think of it as trying to plug an American appliance into a European power outlet. It just won't work. And in nature's case, there's no adapter. That's a good thing, right?

People believe all sorts of things that are far from the truth. That's why we need to listen to science more and politicians less.

And it's why we need to take responsibility and fact check our 'knowledge' before we post it on the internet.

The problem with facts is that they're malleable. Too many people think that believing something automatically makes it a fact. But opinions aren't facts. Even facts aren't facts right off the bat. Science doesn't ever assume it's right until it has exhausted every attempt to prove itself wrong. Science doesn't care what any of us believe, relying on available evidence instead of opinion, and making revisions as newer and better knowledge comes to light.

Author Terry Pratchett said, "Science is not about building a body of known 'facts'. It is a method for asking awkward questions and subjecting them to a reality-check, thus avoiding the human tendency to believe whatever makes us feel good."

My mind is boggled on a regular basis by the almost impenetrable ignorance of people regarding snakes. Adult human beings will stubbornly hold on to an urban legend their grandpa told them when they were children, yet they refuse to accept facts from someone who knows what they're talking about.

This kind of belligerent resistance to knowledge keeps people stupid and fearful and benefits them not at all. As a form of personal growth, overcoming a fear by replacing it with knowledge is one of the most empowering things human beings can do for themselves.

We're not living in the Dark Ages. This is the Information Age. No one has to like snakes, but everyone should take 10 minutes out of their life to educate themselves beyond the point of hysterical, emotional overreaction to a creature they know nothing about except what they've seen in the movies (which are ALL wrong, by the way).

When someone tells me they do or don't believe in something because it does or doesn't comport with their political, religious, or philosophical dogma, I just smile. Show me the proof and I might believe it too. On the other hand, I may dismiss it based on the evidence or the lack thereof, although I do try to keep an open mind.

The media is one of the worst culprits, spreading bad information like rancid butter on moldy bread. In 2015, in an ad for a new series, *Animal Planet* used an image of a cottonmouth — a venomous North American snake, claiming it was a boa — a non-venomous South American snake. This is a departure from the usual propaganda in which harmless snakes are more often depicted as venomous.

In my experience, many people want to believe the snake they saw was venomous, not just because the TV told them so, but because it makes for a better story, allowing them to play the victim card by appealing to gullible sympathizers.

Please don't watch Animal Planet or Discovery Channel believing they are educational. That ended when Steve Irwin died. Today, it's just manipulative exploitation for viewership and advertiser dollars.

Unreasonable people don't respond to reason, they react to emotion. People who watch these shows have a right to be told the truth, but they only know what they're told and they believe it because they want to. They can always deny responsibility for their newfound 'knowledge' because they saw it in a 'documentary.'

I have the utmost respect for anyone who has the courage it takes to break the barriers of traditional Dark Ages thinking and learn the truth for themselves, no matter the topic. The internet, however, that vast bastion of cumulative human knowledge and experience, is not always trustworthy. As a repository of infinite information, its benefit as a harbinger of truth and facts is counterbalanced by an equal or greater amount of untruths — what have come to be known as "alternate facts." For this reason, pursuers of truth must enter this realm alert to the potential for deceit, which may or may not be intentional.

Edward Abbey was one of the most prolific proponents of the American West. In his iconic book, *Desert Solitaire*, in the chapter entitled "The Serpents of Paradise," Abbey waxes poetic about two gopher snakes he met one afternoon as a ranger at Utah's Arches National Monument prior to its eventual dedication as a national park.

"Precisely what did those two enraptured gopher snakes have in mind when they came gliding toward my eyes over the naked sandstone? If I had been as capable of trust as I am susceptible to fear I might have learned something new or some truth so very old we have all forgotten it." (Edward Abbey, Desert Solitaire, Ballantine Books 1971, pg. 21)

He goes on to describe the gopher snake he kept in his shirt, one that randomly popped its head out between buttonholes, much to the delight of tourists.

Abbey was an agent of change; a one-man tour de force. Using only words, he painted the American West as a beautiful, fragile, and dying frontier. Those words still echo in the desert canyons he revered as places of sanctuary and solace, urging the protection of a once vibrant and resilient land now under threat on every side by the destructive forces of commerce, industry, and relentless growth for growth's sake. The ideology of the cancer cell, he called it. Edward Abbey was a prophet.

But this is where Abbey takes a wrong turn into misinformation, referring to gopher snakes by the Latin name *Drymarchon corais couperi*, which is actually the name of the Eastern indigo snake. As inhabitants of the Southeastern U.S., this species doesn't come closer to Utah than East Texas. In the same sentence, he also refers to gopher snakes and bull snakes as the same species [same genus, different species, different locales] while repeating the misnomer that they are "the enemy of rattlesnakes, destroying or driving them away whenever they are encountered." This is a common but erroneous belief, due perhaps to people mistaking them for king snakes. (ibid.)

Abbey goes on to describe the Western diamondback rattlesnake — a species he has no desire to meet — as being "five, six or seven feet long, thick as a man's wrist, dangerous." He doesn't want *them* camping under his trailer. This may well be one of the legends behind the lie that diamondbacks occur in Utah, or that they get seven feet long. (ibid.)

People are constantly telling me about the diamondback rattlesnake they saw on their hike, while they were camping, or even in their back yard, and they usually seem annoyed when I tell them they didn't see a diamondback at all.

Along the Wasatch Front, our only rattler is the Great Basin. Five others live in the southern part of the state, primarily near the overpopulated manmade oasis of St. George in Washington County. Another lives along the borders of Wyoming and Colorado, and an eighth species sneaks into the state via tributaries of the Colorado River.

There are two species of diamondback rattlesnake in the U.S. — the Western (*Crotalus atrox*) and the Eastern (*Crotalus adamanteus*) — neither of which is found in Utah. You have to go well into Arizona to find a Western diamondback. Eastern diamondbacks range along the coastal portions of North and South Carolina, Georgia, Alabama, Mississippi, and through peninsular Florida to the Florida Keys.

Diamondback is a cool name — cooler than Midget-faded rattlesnake, for example (which is found in Utah), and I suppose it makes folks feel smart to toss this erroneous tidbit around like a factual football. Or maybe they've simply seen too many cowboy movies. Still, it doesn't change the fact that there are no diamondbacks in Utah!

We can dismiss these falsehoods as poor research or an editor's failure to fact check, but we cannot excuse them as creative license, only as the perpetuation of bad information. Although he never claimed to be a snake expert, this is proof that even reputable writers like Edward Abbey can get it wrong. But because he's Edward Abbey, people have a right to expect that what he says is the truth.

One of the most common misconceptions about snakes is that they chase or attack people.

Remember that story your eccentric Uncle Fred told you about the snake that chased him away from his favorite fishing hole and all the way back to his truck? Didn't happen. Your Uncle Fred has been brainwashed. And he drinks. But to be fair, he is a victim of the type of social conditioning that has preceded the lowly serpent throughout history and deprived it of any hope for a redeemable reputation.

The snake that allegedly chased your Uncle Fred is still sitting back where he started running, laughing its little snake ass off and wondering what the hell is wrong with that human.

In rare instances, a snake may dart toward the human that is standing between the snake and its hiding place. This is almost always interpreted by the human as, "It attacked me!" Nope.

Again, it was simply looking for a safe place to hide. The human just happened to be in the way.

How stupid would a snake have to be to attack something as large as a human, something it can't possibly eat, and something that could easily overpower it? Although extremely large snakes have swallowed humans, it is a freakishly rare occurrence. Even snakes as large as anacondas and reticulated pythons don't consider humans as prey, so to assume that the three-foot rattlesnake on the hiking trail has homicidal tendencies toward humans is silly beyond belief.

Another common misconception concerns 'nests' of snakes. With the exception of cobras, snakes don't build nests per se, and it's unusual to find multiple snakes at a single location. As solitary creatures, snakes spend much of their lives alone. They don't mate for life, females show little if any maternal care, and with most species, the babies disperse to fend for themselves almost immediately after being born or hatched, with rattlesnakes being a rare exception. Rattlesnake mothers, after giving birth to live offspring, often stay with them for a week or two.

In less temperate climates, snakes congregate to spend the winter months underground, and finding one of these den sites in the fall or spring is one of the few times when you might find groups of snakes. A few dozen to a few thousand snakes may cluster together for the communal purpose of overwintering to survive the cold. Dens can be obvious openings in the ground such as crevices in rock piles or the entrances to small caves or caverns, or they may appear as ordinary rodent burrows.

Every year, thousands of garter snakes gather at the Narcisse Snake Dens in Manitoba, Canada, in the largest gathering of snakes anywhere in the world, with people coming from far and wide to witness the spectacle.

Take some time to understand these primitive, diverse, and highly specialized animals. Learn to identify local snakes when you see them. Many of them are quite beautiful. Teach your children which snakes are dangerous. Put aside old prejudices and replace them with new knowledge. No one is asking you to love snakes, just to appreciate them more and not harm them.

We demonize snakes out of misguided fear and a lack of knowledge. For example, whenever a dog gets bitten by a snake, the reaction of most people is, "The snake attacked the dog!"

No, it most certainly did not. The dog rushed up and sniffed the snake. The snake, for its part, being on the menu for virtually everything, perceived the dog's actions as a threat by a potential enemy. The snake didn't provoke or attack anything. It merely defended itself, which is a fundamental right of every living creature, including you and me. After all, if someone comes after me with a shovel (the preferred execution implement of snake killers everywhere), I'm going to try to defend myself any way I can. And so are you.

"But," people ask, "don't they bite?" Good question! It's partially a species thing. Some species will almost always bite, while others almost never do. But there are other factors too, like whether or not the snake feels threatened. I know they sense fear because I have held wild rattlesnakes that showed absolutely no aggression, and I have seen tame snakes thrash wildly when people who felt uneasy tried to hold them. Snakes however, do not want to bite humans nor do they want us to get close enough for them to do so. Some snakes excrete a musky, slimy secretion from their cloaca to keep animals from eating them. They usually do this instead of biting.

One of the biggest fallacies of all is the notion that snakes show deliberate aggression toward humans. If we apply logic, it would not bode well for snakes to chase or attack humans any more than it would benefit you to attack a giant that was stomping down your street.

Pretend you're in your living room when the ground begins to shake and tremble. Terrified, you look out the window to see a 50-foot-tall gargantuan with unknown intentions thunderously stomping past your house. What would you do? Would you run into the street and bite the giant on his toe? Only if you had a death wish, right? Hopefully, for your own safety, you would run and hide instead. And so it is with snakes.

To a snake, humans are nothing more than large potential threats and a snake will almost always retreat if given the opportunity. If it feels truly threatened, a snake may stand its ground rather than turn its back on you long enough to make an escape. That would make it vulnerable. In that case, just take two steps backward and walk away. No harm, no foul. The snake will not follow you, I promise.

Many years ago, I was with fellow herpers when we cruised a tiny juvenile rattlesnake. As we were setting up to take its picture, the poor frightened snake, not knowing what kind of danger it might be in, and having nowhere else to hide on an asphalt road, hid under the arch of my friend's boot. Unsure of our intentions, it just wanted to be left alone. This shows that even rattlesnakes are shy and reclusive creatures that don't want a confrontation with humans.

After our picture session, we moved the snake off the pavement where it was safe.

Even though I've been teaching people about snakes for more than 50 years, it can still be hard to convince some of them of the truth, especially when they trust their source information more than they trust an expert.

Far too many people feel compelled to tell me about the snakes they've killed and about all the things they "know" about snakes that just aren't true. I wish they could see how silly they look and sound. Like the guy who told me that the baby garter snake in his window well was a diamondback rattler. You sure about that, Ace? Everyone should know what a garter snake looks like, and everyone should know the snakes that live in their area, or at least the venomous ones.

Even venomous snakes are a vital part of a healthy biotic community. Killing snakes upsets the balance of nature and causes rodent populations to flourish, along with the diseases they carry. It's time to stop the ignorance.

If someone was to kill a puppy on television, people would lose their minds, but it happens all the time with snakes. I once turned on the Discovery Channel in time to see a naked man kill a sleeping snake with a stick. My letter to the viewer relations department told them what I thought of their shameless pandering to the same demographic that watches boxing matches and bullfights to satisfy a bloodlust, and NASCAR races hoping for a crash. Just like puppies, snakes are animals, too, and they are vital to a healthy planet.

Whereas I used to be a paragon of patience, calmly and rationally explaining the truth to people, far too many of them refused to listen, preferring to wallow in ignorance instead. I no longer care to engage with those people, finding it frustrating and futile. I've reached the point in my life where I have zero tolerance for the inconsiderate, the incompetent, and the willfully ignorant. If someone falls into one of these categories, I'm doing them a favor by telling them so. They can thank me later. Or not.

A call came from a homeowner to remove a "copperhead rattler." Uh huh. I'd love to see THAT genetic freak of nature. He might as well have said it was a rattle-headed-copper-moccasin. But it was only a gopher snake. Better tie me down before I go ballistic and hurt someone. I have very little tolerance for this level of absurdity, although I suppose my expectations of people are excessively high. I expect to be far less frustrated once I abandon all hope for humanity. To be fair, it may not be his fault. He probably learned it on TV.

Of all the inane urban legends and outright stupid wives' tales that persist in this supposedly enlightened time, insisting that a pet snake lying next to its owner is sizing them up for a meal is perhaps the most ridiculous of all. I even heard of a veterinarian who was promoting this nonsense.

Do wild snakes lie down next to their prey to measure it? What wild animal is going to let a snake measure it before allowing itself to be eaten? It's preposterous!

Most animals won't eat humans. We don't taste good, plus there's that whole clothing thing. Only a 30-foot-long snake could swallow even the smallest adult human, and even if it did, you can bet it didn't stop to measure them first or that the human cooperated.

A three-foot-long, five-pound ball python is not trying to figure out how to eat its six-foot, 160-pound owner. However, a pet snake may lie next to a human to absorb their body heat. Did anyone consider *that* possibility?

Some cities have banned all constricting snakes and others are in the process of doing so. This is ludicrous. People hear the term "constrictor" and they imagine giant snakes from a bad horror movie eating their children.

The fact is, with the exception of venomous snakes and a very few others, most snakes are constrictors, including hundreds of species worldwide that pose no danger to humans.

Dozens of snake species in North America are constrictors, but when was the last time you heard of someone being squeezed to death by a North American snake? It's virtually impossible!

Before jumping to conclusions, people (and cities) should educate themselves about things they don't understand.

You know those pictures of giant, dead rattlers you see on social media? Don't fall for it. They're not really that big. Not even close. They're just close to the camera. It's called *forced perspective* and it's just a sleazy way to scare people. Fishermen use the same technique to make the fish they caught look bigger than it really is.

For most people, seeing a wild snake is a novelty and something that doesn't happen every day, and there are probably as many different reactions to seeing a snake as there are types of people. So you saw a snake. Now what?

Snakes are amazing animals and the best thing to do if you see a snake is to appreciate the experience and leave the snake alone! Especially if you don't know what kind it is.

Do you know the best way to identify a snake? Take a picture so you can ID it later, then leave it alone! There are also internet pages devoted to snake ID.

Do you know the best way to avoid being bitten by a snake? Leave it alone! Even venomous snakes aren't dangerous if we simply go around them or walk the other way. Most bites are the result of people foolishly interacting with a snake.

Don't be the guy who thinks he looks cool by poking a snake with a stick. He just quadrupled his chances of getting bit. He wouldn't have to worry about getting bit if he'd leave the snake alone!

I always loved teaching kids about snakes. Adults won't always admit that most of the things they believe about snakes are wrong, so they hang on to those wrong ideas. But give kids good information and they will know it all their lives.

Do you know the best way to keep your children from being afraid of snakes? Teach them that snakes are valuable members of the natural world and to respect them from a distance. If you're afraid of snakes, please don't pass your fear along to your children. It's not fair. Let them learn about snakes if they want to. Encourage their curiosity.

Do you know the best way to let snakes do their job of eliminating vermin and other pests in nature and around your home? Leave them alone and let them do their job without interference from you. Most snakes are just passing through and will usually leave your yard within 24 hours.

Sometimes it's a neighborhood decision. When a snake leaves your yard, it often ends up in a neighbor's yard. Someone would find a snake in their yard, or perhaps in a park or common area nearby. The neighbors, not knowing what to do, would huddle together for a pep talk before calling me to move it. If it was a harmless snake, I could often convince them of its benefit to the community, always with the caveat that no one would harm it after I left.

Each summer I got dozens of texted photos from people wanting to know of the snake in their yard was harmless. Most of them were not only relieved when it was, but were willing to accommodate a snake that was there to eat the bugs in their garden or the mice in their woodpile. These good folks understood the benefits of mutual toleration and compassionate coexistence with nature's most efficient pest control agents, especially since they'll never receive a bill for services rendered.

Why is 'Leave it alone' such a hard concept for people to understand? Put down the shovel, drop that stick, and realize that snakes are just animals, very much like the other animals you're not afraid of.

If you're afraid of snakes, it may be because everything you know about them came from unreliable sources. Think about it. There are no evil animals, so that can't be it. They're not out to get us, so there goes that argument. And they're definitely not slimy, so guess what? I just dispelled all your excuses. Now you have no reason not to like snakes. You're now happier, more enlightened and less afraid.

And that's the only exception to the 'leave it alone' rule. What should you do if you're afraid of snakes? Learn more about them! Knowledge and fear can't live together in your mind.

Equating snakes with evil is a common but ridiculous concept, and I think we can safely blame Genesis and Hollywood for that mostly successful attempt at character assassination and the resulting ignorance and fear that permeate Christian-Judeo societies everywhere. There are no evil animals, just uneducated people.

Have you ever heard anyone say that kittens are evil? Probably not, and yet I hear people say it about snakes all the time. There is evil in the world, of that there is no doubt. But evil is not a force found in nature. There are no evil animals, trees, plants, rocks or clouds.

Incarnate evil is a trait possessed only by humans. It stems from our conscious and amoral desires within a construct of religious and philosophical ethics based on cultural definitions of good and bad, right and wrong.

Throughout history, serpents have been revered by various cultures as supernatural deities while allegedly being reviled in Genesis as the devil.

Later on in the Bible, however, God sent serpents as a test of the people. After many of them were bitten and died, Moses placed a brass serpent on a pole. Thereafter, when someone was bitten, all they had to do was look upon the brass serpent and be healed. In this and many other Bible stories, serpents were used to represent Christ, and became symbols of healing.

Snakes have played significant roles in the religious, social, cultural, mythological and medical timeline of mankind for thousands of years.

Modern medicine has discovered relief from a host of human conditions within the complex makeup of enzymes found in snake venoms, making snakes more valuable to humanity now than at any other time in history.

Today, two Aesculapian snakes entwined around a winged staff represent medicine and healing in the symbol of the caduceus, although the Rod of Asclepius, with its single snake, is the symbol of the American Medical Association and the World Health Organization.

Animal behaviors are not malicious, spiteful, vengeful, or angry. Rather, they are based on instinctual, survival-oriented biological imperatives such as eating, procreation, and defense. This applies to all animals. These behaviors are essential for an animal's survival, and they are definitely not evil.

Most people perceive animal behavior from the standpoint of human behavior, which is the only thing they can relate it to. This enables them to blame an animal for its "bad" behavior, thereby absolving the human of any responsibility for seeing things from the animal's perspective. In truth, snake behavior (and animal behavior in general) is far more predictable than the too-often random and irrational behavior of individual humans and human nature overall.

We need to stop demonizing snakes. Snakes are no more evil than kittens.

Keeping snakes as pets has become a trend, perhaps corresponding with the rising popularity of field herping. Reptiles long ago surpassed dogs and cats in popularity among urban pet owners in Europe, and the same trend is occurring in other places as well. There are literally thousands of reptiles in private residences everywhere you go. Snakes are living fossils in a way — each species fine-tuned by millions of years of evolutionary pressure to thrive in their respective environments. It's like having your own legless dinosaur. Their instincts are deeply rooted, guiding everything from hunting to survival, offering us glimpses into a primordial past.

For instance, their hunting strategy relies on sensory adaptations that have barely changed since the beginning of time. Whether it's the pit viper's infrared heat sensing ability, or the flickering tongue gathering scent particles, snakes operate on ancient predatory instincts. Even their movement — like the mesmerizing sidewinder slithering across desert sands — is an instinct honed for efficiency.

Consider their defense mechanisms: A cobra's intimidating hood flare. A rattlesnake's warning rattle. A bull snake's blustery bluff. Those are ingrained survival instincts, signaling danger to ward off predators. Some species even mimic the behaviors of venomous snakes despite being completely harmless. For example, many harmless snakes shake their tails. In dry grass or leaves, this type of mimicry can sound very much like a rattlesnake, making it one of nature's coolest methods of passive defense and self-preservation.

Even when it comes to reproduction, snakes follow centuries-old behaviors, like using pheromones to attract mates or laying eggs in hidden locations, ensuring the next generation carries on these primal imperatives.

Their biology may change slightly over time, but at their core, they're still operating on the same instincts that ensured their survival eons ago.

There are so many misconceptions about reptiles in general and snakes in particular that countering them all would be a Herculean undertaking. For those who want to learn more about these fascinating animals, there are scores of reliable resources available to assist you.

Be forewarned, however, that there are also people spewing information that is either inadvertently or intentionally deceptive. Much of what they present as fact is based on an incomplete understanding of the subject matter or perhaps on their insecure need to sound credible.

Avoid second-hand accounts, claims by unreliable individuals, rumors, media hyperbole, pseudo-science, fake documentaries, movies, and any hysterical or illogical claims that don't fall within the realm of scientific scrutiny or your own common sense.

CHAPTER 17

Right vs Happy

"No amount of belief makes something a fact." –James Randi

The perpetuation of myth is a human tribal trait. It's why we tell stories, read books, enact plays, and watch movies. However, at some point we need to discern fiction from fact, because wrong information benefits no one. The deception may not be deliberate, but ultimately, there is one primary reason why people fear and detest snakes and that is because virtually everything they believe about snakes is wrong.

Snakes are such diverse, fascinating and beautiful creatures, it's unfortunate when people react negatively to a harmless snake, or when they make sweeping generalizations like "the only good snake is a dead snake," which displays not only a total lack of knowledge, but a full exhibition of ignorance. It may not be their fault, of course. Ophidiophobia — the fear of snakes — can result from a single childhood trauma or from a lifetime of negative conditioning.

Whatever the cause, the fear is real, making it impossible for these people to see beauty in the beast. Or, like a woman I know who won't go hiking because she might see a snake, it can destroy present-moment happiness.

"All knowledge is wisdom and therefore good." I don't know who uttered that little profundity, but it's only partially true. I would argue that knowledge and wisdom aren't necessarily the same thing. After all, there is a lot of useless knowledge in the world, and a lot of worthless wisdom.

Human beings are gullible creatures, and misinformation bombards us from a variety of unreliable sources. Children are quick to recognize truth and embrace new knowledge, but most adults will cling desperately to a long-held belief system, no matter how wrong, misleading or damaging it may be, invoking the obvious question, 'would we rather be right or would we rather be happy?'

The Only Good Snake . . .

As mentioned previously, I spent many years as a counselor helping Boy Scouts earn the Reptile Study Merit Badge, sometimes in opposition to their mothers' wishes. It's hard to believe that any parent would stand in the way of their child's willingness to learn, but too many adults are resistant to new information because it challenges beliefs they've had all their lives and forces them to admit they're wrong. Human beings, as we've already discussed, aren't good at admitting they're wrong.

Personally, I think people would rather be right than happy, even if being right means being absolutely, completely, stone-cold wrong. If a misguided belief system served someone well most of their life, why would they risk exchanging it for happiness now? For the same reason, most people will not try to educate themselves, and even if they did, there is as much bad snake information on the internet as good. How is a new learner supposed to know the difference?

A nice woman sat in her kitchen one morning and cried until I got there because there was a garter snake on her back porch.

Do I understand hyper-phobic anxiety like this? I try, but no, not really. Do I empathize with it? Yes, to the extent that I'm able. I'm sorry that someone or some event made her so afraid of something that can't hurt her that it now affects her life in a negative way. Do I attempt to mitigate it? Of course. Educating people about snakes is what I do.

When moving snakes, I tried to provide an educational component for my customers, but I was a snake relocator and not a psychologist. At some point, people have to take responsibility for their own irrational fears and behaviors. If there is anything I can do to help, by all means, I'll do it. But I can only lead them to the path. Taking the journey is up to them.

That said, I also believe there are people who use their irrational fears and insecurities to manipulate others, elicit sympathy, and draw attention to themselves. Often, the need for attention is stronger than the phobia they use as a crutch. These people are stubbornly resistant to becoming educated because it would involve taking personal responsibility for themselves and forfeiting a crippling dependence, which they will not do. These 'poor me' folks are too addicted to self-pity, preferring to wallow in ignorance than bask in knowledge because knowledge takes effort. It's far easier to remain uninformed and apathetic. This doesn't apply just to snakes, of course, but to everything in life. Sadly, these people are more numerous than you might imagine.

If your parents taught you to fear snakes, or told you that snakes are evil, malevolent serpent demons with a vendetta against humanity, you're probably going to accept that as a core belief, at least until something more logical comes along to challenge it. Even then, change is hard, truth is elusive, and apparently, happiness is overrated. Knowledge can be hard, but ignorance is easy. After all, acquiring knowledge requires effort and responsibility and who wants more of those?

Mark Twain famously said, "It ain't what you don't know that gets you into trouble. It's what you know for sure that just ain't so." Mr. Twain was a very insightful man. I meet people constantly who have rock-solid convictions — often to the degree that they won't allow logic or even evidence to sway them. That would be fine except that they're still wrong. There is no virtue in being stubbornly stupid, especially when confronted with a verifiable truth.

Refusing to believe in something because it doesn't comport with personal desires or because it's too inconvenient is a worthless and futile concept. A belief or non-belief in any doctrine or theory is invalid in the face of incontrovertible evidence to the contrary.

For example, I may believe with all my heart and soul that pigs can fly, but does that make me right? The density and shape of the porcine form doesn't lend itself to being aerodynamically sound, and the lack of wings makes it impossible for pigs to take flight or even glide safely to earth should they fall from a tree.

Reasonable people accept this as fact even without science to back it up. It's called common sense.

Wanting something to be true doesn't make it true. Hoping that something is true doesn't make it true. Thinking that things are a certain way because you want them to be is just an opinion, and most opinions are worthless except perhaps when they come from someone whose knowledge and experience gives them more validity than the average person.

251

The Only Good Snake . . .

It is the job of science to take a theory and try repeatedly to disprove it. That's the scientific method. When enough experiments have been conducted that the results overwhelmingly contradict the hypothesis, then the original theory is considered either sound or unsound depending on the outcome of multiple experiments conducted under controlled conditions by experts using all available data.

Believing in something doesn't make it true. Conversely, not believing in something doesn't mean it isn't true. After all, people believe all sorts of things that aren't true. This is applicable to everything in life. Politics and religion come to mind. We are free to believe anything we want, but unless we can back it up with irrefutable evidence, it is merely our opinion and not a declaration of fact.

Science is not based on public opinion, political posturing, or the maniacal rantings of controversial talk show hosts or other egocentric pundits who love the sound of their own voices.

Reality is subjective, not objective. Facts can be manipulated, theories without evidence are worthless, and opinions mean nothing at all. Don't tell me what you 'believe in,' tell me what you know to be true. Too many people today don't really want the truth; they just want constant reassurance that what they believe is the truth. As Twain said, "[Be careful of] what you know for sure that just ain't so," and try to keep an open mind.

Case in point: I once met a man who stopped at a booth where I was assisting a local herpetology club with an educational display at a local mall. He attempted to dazzle me with his knowledge of rattlesnakes by informing me that a rattlesnake's venom was stored in the rattle. By cutting the rattle off, he said, the snake would be rendered harmless.

I was stunned! I have heard a litany of lies and half-truths about snakes over my lifetime, but this was something new. Where to begin? I didn't want to offend him, but I had an obligation to give him correct information for his own safety. I pointed out that a snake's rattle is a structure comprised of hollow, interlocking segments made of keratin that, when shaken, produce the infamous maraca sound that warns us that a rattlesnake is near.

If the rattle were full of liquid, like venom, I explained, the sound would be dampened and utterly ineffective.

He was having none of it.

Argument number two was to explain the inefficiency involved in transporting venom from a snake's tail to its delivery system in the mouth where the fangs are located. In the case of rattlesnakes and other pit vipers, millions of years of evolutionary tweaking have produced a highly efficient and carefully refined system of venom injection that does not involve venom having to travel the length of the snake's body to reach its destination. He remained stubbornly unconvinced.

The most obvious argument was to remind him of the triangular shape of a rattlesnake's head, which, while not a defining characteristic of venomous snakes in general, is due to the venom glands being located on each side of the rattler's head and in close proximity to its fangs. This is a scientific fact as inscrutable as any other, and easily provable.

"Nope," he said, "that ain't right."

"Why do you believe that a rattlesnake's venom is in its rattle?" I asked him. I had to know.

"Because my grandpa told me," he said, "and my grandpa wouldn't lie."

Maybe not, but does that mean old grampy was right? Only in his own mind. But he was probably happy!

And there you have it. All the logic and scientific evidence in the world weren't going to convince this guy he was wrong because it would make his grandpa a liar.

Psychologists call this cognitive dissonance — a condition in which there is a disconnect between reality and belief. It is the great barrier that prevents the acquisition of knowledge and the reason why it can be so difficult to change someone's mind despite a barrage of evidence against their erroneous but well-established perceptions. It's what makes them right instead of happy, fearful instead of enlightened, defensive instead of receptive. Misplaced fear and overwhelming ignorance in the midst of truth are perhaps the greatest obstacles to a happy and fulfilling life.

The Only Good Snake . . .

Someone told me that my expectations of others are too high. Really? All I expect from most human beings most of the time is to be civil, responsible, and respectful. And to use their brain as something more than insulation to keep their skull warm. Is that too much to ask?

I used to be a people person, but people ruined that for me. I took one of my snakes outside the other day. One of my neighbors, a woman, saw it and exclaimed, "Ooh, you've got a snake." (She has an amazing command of the obvious.) Then she added, "I can't even look at it!"

How do I counter that? I can understand a reluctance to touch or hold it, but what would actually happen if she were to look at it? Would she burst into flames? Would she turn to stone? Or worse, would she be forced to set aside her preconceived notions and admit what a beautiful animal it is if she would only allow herself to truly see it?

I used to demonstrate infinite patience with people like this, even changing many minds, but life is too short to waste on someone so obtuse. Guess I'm just an old curmudgeon, huh?

But there is good news! In my many years of trying to educate the public about snakes, I have discovered one inflexible, ineffable truth, and it is this: that knowledge and fear cannot coexist. Like the law of physics that makes it impossible for two tangible objects to occupy the same space simultaneously, the same is true of knowledge and fear in the human mind.

The moment a nugget of knowledge is introduced and accepted as fact, an equivalent amount of fear must be displaced. Teaching people about snakes, or any other topic that isn't readily welcomed, is a gradual process of using knowledge to chip away at useless fear until it is slowly eroded and replaced with useful knowledge.

While we cannot force people to accept knowledge against their will, we can introduce it in small enough doses that they are completely unaware of our well-meaning indoctrination. Talking to people about snakes, citing facts, answering questions, and sharing our passion with others in non-confrontational ways, whether in person or via social media, will produce positive results over time, so long as it is genuine and not coerced.

Remember the woman in the crowd at the museum? Few things are more satisfying than explaining a concept to someone and seeing the light go on. There is an actual, factual, physical reaction when someone grasps a new concept for the first time. You can see it in their eyes. You can hear it in their voice. It is the most satisfying aspect of teaching, and while it may require years of patience, it is always worth the wait.

There might even be hope for Rattlesnake Guy.

On a more humorous note, I used to learn a lot from my customers, including some nuggets of genuine wisdom that I gladly pass along to you. This, however, isn't one of them:

Do you know how many snakes it takes to make an infestation? Neither did I. In fact, I never really gave it much thought. Then one day a woman called me to say she had an infestation of garter snakes in her yard. 'Wonderful!' I thought, as I imagined myself filling my buckets with wiggling hordes of three-striped stink noodles and whisking them away from the threats of the human world, especially ignorant people with shovels. This was going to be fun!

Just in case I needed more buckets or an assistant, I thought it wise to clarify approximately how many snakes I might be dealing with.

"Two," she said sternly.

"Two?" I asked, making sure I'd heard her correctly. "Two snakes is an infestation?"

"Yes," she replied. "One snake is too many and two snakes is an infestation."

And now you know.

I didn't realize it before, but apparently I have an infestation of snakes in my house. Do you think they'll leave if I stop feeding them?

As the administrator of the Snake Anti-Defamation League on Facebook, Todd Michael Cox wrote the following refutation of the excuses people give for not liking snakes.

"Now you can counter any excuse that people give you for why snakes aren't every bit as fascinating, beautiful, and (yes, I'll say it) lovable, as other animals. Their answers are, of course, flawed and irrational":

"Because they're creepy." [Creepiness only exists in the eyes of the beholder.]

"Because they're slimy." [Their skin is drier than yours. To them, YOU are the slimy one.]

"Because they're dangerous." [Harmless snakes vastly outnumber venomous ones, and the venomous ones are easily avoidable and don't wish to bite you. Besides, your car is dangerous; more people are hurt by furniture, etc., etc.]

"No, they WANT to bite you. They'll chase you down." [Yes, this is true . . . if you're a lizard, mouse or chipmunk.]

"They move weird, and you can't tell where they're going to go." [Not true if you observe them for even a short period of time. But this IS true of the strange sorts of people you encounter in the aisles of a grocery store.]

"They're ugly." [Ask them to define "ugly" and you will receive silence as an answer. Then show them pictures of the garish greens, the vibrant reds, the eye-popping yellows, and the surprising blues, and ask them what's so ugly about all of that.]

"They don't have legs." ["What the hell does that have to do with the price of eggs?" as my mom used to say. I really don't have an answer for this bit of nonsense. So they don't have legs. They don't NEED legs. And since when did legs become the measure of the beast?]

"They live in weird places." [They live in the beautiful tangled wild mucky messy wet jagged rough quiet and lovely places where we all once used to live . . . back before we decided the worlds of glass and concrete and asphalt were somehow superior. I'd rather live with the snakes than in the poshest of high-rise apartments.]

"They're just . . . icky." [Well, there is indeed 'ickiness' in the world, but it exists in the hearts of foul-minded and abusive humans who would find pleasure in the destruction and torture of innocent lives. I will trust a snake before I will trust any stranger.]

"We all love something," Todd continues, "but some of us choose to love more things. And how can that be bad? And why must a greater openness of spirit and heart be defended? It's the opposite that should be questioned, and the hate and ugliness that should be regarded as strange.

17 | *Right vs Happy*

"In the battle of hatred and killing versus respect and love, I will side with the latter. I side with the serpents."

CHAPTER 18

Fear and Loathing

"Fear is a tyrant and a despot, more terrible than the rack, more potent than the snake." –Edgar Wallace

I don't blame people for being afraid of snakes. In the overall scheme of things, snakes drew the short straw when it came to public perception and they've never been nominated for a congeniality award. This is unfortunate, because the vast majority of snakes are harmless, and even venomous snakes are vital to the health and wellbeing of the ecosystems they inhabit.

Despite the myriad and often overlooked benefits of snakes, there is one primary reason why some people fear and detest snakes and that is because virtually everything they think they know about snakes is wrong. For that reason, I do blame them if they allow fear to control their life, especially in the face of overwhelming evidence that could eliminate an irrational fear and put their minds at ease.

Whether personified in Genesis, presented factually in a responsible nature documentary, or portrayed as man-eating monsters by Hollywood, snakes are a source of fascination and mystery, even if that fascination is the icky, scary kind.

Since the beginning of time, snakes have been deified and vilified by various cultures throughout history, filling dual roles as both gods and devils. But what makes snakes a source of powerful attraction for some and the target of unmitigated hatred for others?

There may be a self-preservation response buried deep within the amygdala portion of our brains that protected our primitive ancestors from the threat of venomous snakes. That fear response is still very real, keeping us safe in stressful or dangerous conditions. But being afraid is still a choice. Modern humans often choose fear and ignorance over knowledge when it comes to understanding snakes.

(It always seemed strange to me that people who fear snakes don't also fear lizards, considering that snakes are just lizards without legs, and lizards are basically hyperactive snakes with four-wheel drive.)

While no one wants to live in a constant state of inescapable fear, it is the most primal form of self-preservation. Fear keeps us from doing dangerous or stupid things like running across the freeway during rush hour or standing too close to the edge of a cliff.

Still, people enjoy being scared within reasonable limits. After all, a good scare can have many health benefits. Fear alerts us to danger by releasing doses of cortisol and adrenaline to the brain, enabling the "fight or flight" response — a built-in survival instinct that can make us stronger and more capable of confronting a threat . . . or running from it.

Taking risks is one of the greatest benefits of fear. Embarking on a new adventure, for example, can trigger an exhilarating dose of spine-tingling fear that provides a natural high and a sense of empowerment. A healthy fear produces dopamine, endorphins, oxytocin, and serotonin, helping your brain work more efficiently. In other words, fear can give you energy and incentive.

But unhealthy fear can be incapacitating. People with severe phobias can be so afraid that they cease to function normally, plunging them into a state of inert helplessness. Or, a phobia can be so debilitating that people may avoid activities they would otherwise enjoy. For example, a person with a fear of flying (aerophobia) may never take that dream vacation to Hawaii. This level of fear can suck the joy out of living.

Human beings like to be afraid as long as it's in a situation where we are in control. This explains the popularity of horror movies and Halloween haunted houses. We go to these places because we want to be scared, knowing deep down that nothing there can actually harm us. The killer is an actor, the chainsaw has plastic teeth, and we can leave whenever we want.

My years of snake experience have taught me that these animals have virtually nothing in common with those allegedly evil creatures from the Bible, cultural myth, urban legend, and that most disreputable source of all, the Hollywood movie.

Even reputable movies have snake scenes that are laughable to anyone with even a marginal understanding of snake behavior.

The Only Good Snake . . .

In the 1969 film *True Grit,* along with the 2010 remake, the young protagonist, Mattie Ross, falls into a deep pit where two rattlesnakes are allegedly sleeping in the bowels of a human corpse. They awaken and bite the girl with unprovoked temerity and are quickly dispatched by the movie's hero, trigger-happy lawman Rooster Cogburn. There are so many things wrong with this scenario that there isn't space to list them all here.

In truth, the relatively placid nature of snakes amazes me. With very few exceptions, snakes are shy and reclusive creatures. They have to be, because everything wants to eat them, especially when they're young. Snakes will defend themselves from provocation, especially if they are unable to escape a threat, but they are not aggressive creatures. They are merely defensive. We all have a right to defend ourselves from danger. Why should snakes be denied that same privilege?

For many people, just hearing the word *snake* makes them shudder. Others cringe, groan, and grimace. Some even do an entertaining little dance. And sadly, I've met more than a few who actually lapse into paroxysms of hyperventilation, often losing physical and emotional control by succumbing to an irrational, phobic hysteria — sometimes even when there's no snake present. For a few poor folks I've met, a photo of a snake, or even the mere mention of one, is enough to trigger a full-blown panic attack.

For me, this deep and debilitating fear is difficult to witness, but its roots run back hundreds of generations, due largely to an indoctrination of primal fear based on primitive superstition, not to mention all the vitriolic hyperbole about snakes that bombards us from cradle to grave. Even Rudyard Kipling's *Jungle Book* implanted doubt in the innocent minds of generations of young people, persuading them that snakes were creatures not to be trusted or befriended.

Fear is a natural component for surviving in a hostile world. While animals rely on heightened perceptions and an acute sense of fear to avoid predation, fear can make people behave irrationally. Unlike an instinctive fear for survival's sake, being educated affords human beings the luxury of making rational decisions based on knowledge instead of fear. In the absence of knowledge, however, fear can result in strange and distorted perceptions.

If you find yourself toe-to-toe with a snake (so to speak), all you have to do is take a step or two backward. There's no need to panic or harm the snake. After all, it's more afraid of you than you are of it. Just walk around it. It's not going to chase you. There isn't a snake anywhere you can't simply walk around. Two or three feet are more than enough distance. If you're in the snake's home, you're just a visitor, and it has an even greater right to be there than you do.

After spending the past 50 years teaching people (mostly children, because they're more open-minded) about the beauty and benefits of snakes and their rightful place in the world, I am fully aware that not everyone appreciates them like I do. But I invite anyone who is fearful of snakes to learn a little more about them. Knowledge and fear can't coexist. Once knowledge replaces fear, the fear goes away. I've seen it and it's amazing.

Children who absorb correct information will know it their entire lives and will perpetuate it by sharing it with others, including their own children, so that maybe, just maybe, each successive generation can be smarter, more compassionate, and less fearful than the ones that preceded them.

A friend stopped by with his five-year-old daughter. I introduced her to Harley, my Western hognose snake, and she said, somewhat distractedly, "I never saw a snake before." She looked at it without apprehension or anxiety, just as she would have looked at a cat, dog, or canary. Then she calmly walked away, bored perhaps, and ready to move on to other distractions.

At the other end of the spectrum, there is a video floating around (no pun intended) of a hysterical teenage girl on a boat with her family when a rattlesnake swims toward their boat. She won't stop screaming. It's obnoxious and pathetic.

I find it extremely unfortunate that anyone has that type of reaction in the 21st century. Shouldn't humans, as a species, be more enlightened at this point in history, or am I expecting too much of my fellow beings?

Yes, it's a rattlesnake. The girl is in a boat. The snake is in the water. It can't climb into the boat. It only wants to get on the boat because it's tired of swimming and it thinks the boat is a log. It doesn't want to hurt anyone.

The Only Good Snake . . .

As much as I'd like to help her, it's probably too late. Sadly, someone else got to her first and the damage has been done. Wouldn't it be wonderful if parents would stop transferring their own fears onto their children? It's okay, even normal, to be apprehensive in a strange and scary situation, but hysteria only puts you in greater danger.

Knowledge is the antidote for fear. This is why we educate children. We can teach them truths while they're young enough to be receptive, and before someone else fills their impressionable heads with lies or hyperbole. It's too hard to teach an adult human anything when they've already been indoctrinated with false information. People embrace comfortable falsehoods like a drowning man desperately clutches a stick. It may provide a small measure of reassurance in the moment, but it won't save him in the long run.

Babies are not born with an intuitive fear of snakes. Studies have been done in which several babies and toddlers were placed in a room with toys and left to play. Once they were actively engaged, researchers brought four or five fairly large and docile snakes into the room, placing them on the floor with the babies. This was done under the watchful eyes of the researchers and the apoplectic eyes of mothers who watched in horror from behind a one-way mirror.

The children, curious about these new playthings, were no more reticent to play with the snakes than with any other toy. After crawling toward the snakes to touch them and satisfy their curiosity, the children soon appeared bored and went right back to what they were doing before. This, and not hysterical fear, should be the normal reaction to seeing a snake, the difference being that older children should be taught not to touch wild snakes, or at least be able to identify them first.

Responding to a snake call at an opulent home in an exclusive eastside neighborhood, I was met in the yard by a woman and her two young children — a boy and girl — both under the age of 12. My understanding was that mom had spotted a rattlesnake in the yard, yet all three were barefoot and unconcerned.

The woman explained that they see lots of snakes and that she usually puts them in a bucket and hikes them up the hill behind the house. But today's snake presented more of a challenge. It was near the front door under the aluminum flashing that covers the top edge of the foundation and she wasn't sure how to get it out. Moreover, the three of them were locked out of the house.

Her husband, in a state of deep and frenzied fear, had locked his own barefoot wife and children out of their own home because of a snake in the yard.

I have seen reactions where individuals were willing to burn their home to the ground because a snake had gotten inside, or, like Bart and Cindy, were willing to move because hungry snakes had the audacity to visit the squirrel buffet in their backyard retaining wall.

From the looks of the home, this man made a good living and was probably well educated, yet his deep-seated fear of snakes caused him to think only of himself while neglecting the safety of his family, who were, for the most part, unfazed by the situation. After all, they knew where the snake was and that it wasn't out to get them. But, I wondered, what if it had been a bear in the yard instead?

Fear can be our friend because it prompts us to identify choices and options, analyze them, and evaluate the best course of action. It can be the framework we need to climb out of the pit of our insecurities and take reasonable chances. This can eliminate the "analysis of paralysis" that might otherwise keep us forever fearful or cause us to take wrong actions.

In an incredible act of self-determination, I watched in amazement as a woman approached my booth at a reptile expo. On that particular day, Durango was in a cage, giving him respite from the throngs of people who were constantly wanting to pet him or pick him up.

I had seen that expression before, and deep down I knew why the woman was there. Durango would have been too intimidating. Harley the hognose was the only other snake that wasn't behind glass, looking like a scaly cow pie in an open Tupperware container.

The woman paused at the edge of courage, afraid to cross that invisible line. Like a bug in a jar, she wore her fear like a glass dome that had entrapped her for most of her life. She had come there that day to shatter it. Her gaze was fixed on Harley, a quiet, gentle snake that was calmly coiled and posed no threat to anyone. But to someone with an intense fear of snakes, every snake is a threat.

She never looked up. She didn't look around. She didn't make eye contact with me or anyone else. She wasn't there to make conversation. She was there for one singular purpose.

Still 10 feet away from the table, she slowly extended her arm as if practicing a dance move, then quickly withdrew it. Advancing a few feet at a time, she did the same thing again, repeating the process until she was within arm's reach of the object of her terror. Her concentration was 1000 percent focused on her task as though she was trying to thread a needle while riding a roller coaster. She was aware of nothing else.

She purposefully extended her arm once again, only to have it retreat on its own, like an involuntary reflex over which she had no control. After several attempts, she finally reached out, ever so slowly, painfully slowly; her index finger pointed at her target, and gently, deliberately, reluctantly touched the snake. In that instant, her arm recoiled and she jumped a little, rising up on her toes as a shy smile broke the statue-like stoniness of her face. I saw her countenance change as a feeling of self-satisfaction enveloped her. She remained for only a moment, then turned and left without saying a word.

Although I stood mesmerized throughout the ordeal, watching her every move with intense fascination, she never acknowledged me. This was something she had to do for herself. In that moment, nothing else mattered.

Had this brave woman come to a reptile expo for the sole purpose of touching a snake? Did she pay a parking fee and an admission fee just to confront and conquer a debilitating and dysfunctional fear? What was her motivation? She wasn't being coerced. I doubt it was a dare. She didn't do it for attention because I was the only observer. I only know it was one of the most courageous acts I have ever had the privilege to witness.

It's important to note that we are not responsible for the programming we received as children, but as adults, we are 100 percent responsible for fixing it.

Then, of course, there are the obvious haters. There is a Facebook page dedicated to the very worst and most ignorant among us, where people are encouraged to run over snakes with lawnmowers and worse. Having a fear that controls you to an extent is one thing, but convincing others that they have something to fear is the epitome of reckless stupidity. The media is notorious for this.

Many educational organizations work hard to provide the public with valuable information and positive interactions with reptiles, bats, spiders, and insects. This is why it is so disturbing when the media insist on pandering to the lowest common denominator when reporting about snakes and other purportedly "scary" animals.

It's embarrassing when newscasters feel obligated to shudder on camera and use phrases like "creepy-crawly," "scary," "icky," or "slimy" in reference to creatures they know nothing about. This is irresponsible on many levels. After all, we rely on these "professionals" to deliver actual news in a factual and unbiased manner — not to editorialize, and certainly not to spew their uninformed personal opinions at gullible viewers.

This trend is particularly prevalent at Halloween time. Even educational TV shows lose credibility when they use show titles like "creepy creatures" and other salacious epithets that appeal to viewers' morbid curiosity. If people actually learn something beneficial from these programs, that's great, but some people will never get past the title, and perpetuating ignorant stereotypes is a form of animal exploitation and human fear mongering.

The legendary Steve Irwin knew how to excite and educate people about these lesser-loved animals without resorting to silly scare tactics. Sadly, Steve is gone, leaving a huge void in the animal education landscape.

A fear of the unknown is normal until we realize that most animals aren't scary at all! The overwhelming majority of the world's snakes are completely harmless, and even the venomous ones pose no danger if we simply stay out of their way and resist the compulsion to annoy them.

You don't have to love snakes in order to appreciate them more. Just ignore the hyperbole and see them for what they really are: beautiful and compelling creatures that really aren't creepy at all once you get to know them better.

Living with an irrational fear is a terrible way to go through life, whereas overcoming that fear is one of the highest forms of self-awareness and discipline, leading to a renewed sense of wonder about the world and mastery over oneself. People can choose to not only cope with their fears, but can also conquer them.

Fear is an interesting phenomenon. According to scientists and anthropologists, humans are born with only two innate fears. One is the fear of falling and the other is the fear of loud noises. All other fears are learned either by direct inference or through observation and imitation.

Fear is one thing, but killing a snake, spider or any other living being that isn't bothering anyone is a choice and not a survival-oriented justification based on primal instinct. Animals are too often the innocent victims of human greed, ignorance, superiority, and fear. Human beings are responsible for most of their own misery, but nature suffers needlessly at the brutal hand of man.

I'm not indifferent to the suffering of humanity, but my allegiance lies with the creatures that are incapable of war, genocide, torture, murder, and the general infliction of misery that humans wreak upon the earth and on each other, often based on unanalyzed and unnecessary fear and hate.

Anyone who can kill a wild creature, not for food or for any life sustaining purpose, but merely for the sake of casually killing another living being, no matter how large or small, or how ferocious or benign, is a person with a severe mental illness or an incurable inferiority complex. Or perhaps they simply have no soul.

One man told me he just had to kill snakes. I told him that he wasn't expected to like them, but it wasn't necessary to kill them.

"Yes it is," he said. "I have to. I can't help it."

This infantile lack of discipline and self-control is an obvious sign of a deep and disturbing psychopathy and arrested development.

Laws in most states and other jurisdictions make it illegal to kill snakes. In addition to being illegal, it is also unethical and immoral. Besides, why would you want to? There is very little justification for killing a snake, anytime, anywhere.

When I tell people it's against the law to kill snakes, they often want to know why. There are several reasons:

1. Wildlife is the property of the state, which means it belongs to all of us. The snake in your yard doesn't belong to you; therefore, you have no right to kill it.

2. Snakes are non-game animals. Only a few states sell licenses to hunt them, and there is no 'open season' on snakes, especially in states where they are protected by law.

3. Snakes are not 'consumption animals.' Although you can eat them, they probably wouldn't be your first choice of wild game.

4. Killing a snake, or even keeping a prohibited or protected species without permission from the state makes you a poacher.

5. It is unethical to kill a harmless and beneficial animal.

6. Snakes are a vital part of a healthy and balanced ecosystem, keeping rodent populations in check and providing food for other animals such as birds of prey. If you have a harmless snake in your yard, leave it there! He'll eat your pests, and once they're gone, he'll leave too.

7. Learning to coexist with other life forms on this planet makes you a better human being.

I tried to convince people to leave harmless snakes where they are and not bother them. Most of them were okay with the concept of free rodent control, but others just sounded annoyed and I couldn't be sure of their actions once they hung up the phone.

I received yet another text one morning from someone asking for an ID on a snake he already killed. It was a garter snake. I try to understand the rationale of someone who is afraid of snakes, but the implication, regardless of circumstances, is that snakes are guilty until proven innocent. But what is their crime? Apparently, they are guilty of merely existing on God's green earth. The problem with a guilty verdict like that is that by the time the snake has been exonerated it has already received a death sentence.

The homeowner lives in an agricultural area with an irrigation canal nearby, so he's always going to have garter snakes. After a long chat, I think he understood the benefits of having these snakes on his property. Maybe he won't kill any more of them, but there's no guarantee.

The state didn't want me moving harmless snakes, and of course, there was absolutely no logical, rational reason for doing so, other than the fact that far too many people aren't logical or rational when confronted with one.

A woman once told me that she was going to take a hoe to the snake in her yard until I told her not to, citing several reasons why she shouldn't. Ignorance pushes people to commit barbarous acts despite the fact that allegedly civilized people should be above killing harmless animals with garden implements.

The most wonderful karmic revenge I can think of would be for snake killers to be reincarnated as mice.

It always annoys me that after finding out I'm a snake guy, the first thing many people do is launch into some macabre tale about the snake that they or their uncle/grandpa/Scoutmaster killed. It may have been 30 years ago or just last week. The weirdest part is that most of them will tell you they're animal lovers.

I have never understood this reaction, but it's clearly a case of cognitive dissonance in addition to a lack of good manners. These stories are often delivered with a sense of bravado or tinged with elements of impending danger. Whether the storytellers are seeking respect or sympathy, they get neither from me.

Can you imagine the reaction if someone told me they have a dog and I responded with, "Oh! A dog came in my yard last week. I didn't know what kind it was so I cut its head off with a shovel." They'd lose their freakin' minds! And they'd be justified. I'd be branded a soulless, psychotic animal abuser and relegated to the outer fringes of respectable society — or prison — someone to be avoided at all cost.

One particularly obtuse individual called to tell me that the five rattlesnakes he found on his property that year "are no longer with us." When I reminded him that killing them is illegal, he muttered something about private property rights. But his confession made no sense. Why did he call and tell me this? It was a verbal middle finger to the concept of respectful coexistence and his egomaniacal need to be in control.

18 | *Fear and Loathing*

I'm not a violent man, but I expect other people to use a modicum of tact and diplomacy in polite conversation. The next time someone tells me "the only good snake is a dead snake," or elaborates about the snake they killed, I may have to exercise considerable restraint not to punch them in the throat.

Much of human understanding is based on superstition and arrogance. This narcissistic superiority may well be our downfall as a species. It may also spell the demise of all other species.

A popular meme on the snake forums shows a woman casually lying on the ground behind an Eastern diamondback rattlesnake. The snake, for its part, is unafraid and unimpressed, perhaps even oblivious to her presence. The message is obvious: snakes are not aggressive, bloodthirsty, angry creatures that want to harm humans. They are reclusive bordering on shy and are non-confrontational until we provoke them.

I'm not advocating that anyone should lie down near a rattlesnake, but if you see a snake, enjoy the encounter. Tell your children how important snakes are in the environment and not to bother them.

There is no point living your life in fear when you can do something about it, and there's no reason for hating or fearing an animal simply because you don't understand it.

My friend Sawyer put it this way: "Snakes will give you the same respect you give them. Venomous or not. The difference between a good encounter and a bad encounter is knowing their triggers and behaviors. Once they figure out that you're not, in fact, a big scary creature trying to eat them, they're usually content with your company."

Well said. I've spent many happy hours in the company of buzzer butts that had no problem sharing their space with me, even sitting with dozens of rattlesnakes at den sites, eating my lunch and taking pictures. Respect is earned, and you get back what you're willing to give.

Some people want so desperately to see snakes as conniving, malevolent creatures that they would rather defend laughable urban legends and justify personal irrational phobias than reconsider their views in an attempt at self-enlightenment.

The Only Good Snake . . .

In October 2024, on the Snake Anti-Defamation League Facebook page that I co-moderate, a man named Frank had this to say:

> *I used to be scared as hell of snakes until I moved to a place where there are a bunch of them, including rattlesnakes. Something I learned about snakes is that they want nothing to do with humans and will make every effort to get away from us. Bites happen if they're caught off guard, but usually they know you're around before you know they're around and will get the hell outta there. In other words, they mind their own business, unlike humans. I recently said in a post that I'd rather be in an area with a bunch of rattlesnakes any day than in a room full of humans.*

Another poster named Christina made this observation:

> *Irrationality is the point of phobias. There are phobias of clowns, books, bodies of water, even buttons. People with koumpounophobia (a fear of buttons and round objects that occurs in almost 1 in 75,000 people) know that buttons aren't out to get them, but rationality doesn't enter into the equation. That's what makes phobias so frustrating. Rationally, they know that buttons aren't dangerous, but the phobia messes with their logical instincts and illogical fear levels. For them it's not a choice . . .*
>
> *Reasons for phobias also aren't a one-size-fits-all proposition. Bad experiences, social conditioning, watching a horror movie like Anaconda, or something with spiders in it when someone is too young or impressionable to fully grasp what's going on, can form phobias. For example, I eventually figured out that my irrational fear of spiders came from my brain struggling with the way they move. Social acceptance of this phobia as normal didn't cause it, but reinforced it. Without going into detail, the combination of things that helped me get over it (and now finding spiders*

extremely fascinating and cool) may not work for someone whose irrational fear is rooted in different causes.

What does this mean for the average ophidiophobiac? For those of us who want to help them, it means there isn't a one-size-fits-all solution to educate people or help them conquer their fears.

Christina continues:

However, if you have a phobia, it's yours to deal with, figure out, live with, or conquer, whichever you choose to do. It is wrong to make your phobia everyone else's problem, and it is cruel and selfish to punish and kill animals (or demand they be killed) because of your irrational perceptions, especially if you, at some level, logically know they aren't a threat.

If that sounds harsh, consider this more compassionate viewpoint from a snake educator named Mark:

Fear is a primal part of the brain, but fear can be turned into fascination through education. You can even elicit fear with stories that may not be true. But fear is a primal part of our survival instinct. This is exactly why most animals, when approached, will flee quickly. They may be curious about us, but they flee out of fear for their safety [and probably as a learned response]. Like people, animals can become more curious after they learn more about what they're experiencing. Curiosity is a choice based on knowledge. Fear, on the other hand, is what is ingrained in all animals as a survival tactic, including us.

People's defenses go up and they become resistant to new knowledge, especially if it contradicts old knowledge. It's a pride thing because no one wants to be told they're wrong. I'll help anyone who wants it, but they have to do it because *they* want to. No one can force them, and no one should. People only overcome phobias if they can see a direct benefit in doing so, or, like the woman at the expo, they're on a crusade for personal improvement, enlightenment, or simply wish to enjoy life without the looming cloud of an irrational fear hanging over them, stealing their sunshine.

For instance, I know a woman who would love nothing more than to go hiking, but she won't. Why? She's afraid she might see a snake.

I asked her, "Sandy, what would be the worst thing that would happen if you saw a snake while you were hiking?"

"It would freak me out," she replied. "And I would embarrass myself in front of whoever I was with."

"It sounds like you're more afraid of being embarrassed than you are of snakes," I said, using my best layman psychology. I assured her that any snake she might see will be infinitely more afraid of a human, and that she has no business walking through the woods scaring innocent snakes.

We shared a good laugh and I think that someday, perhaps in the not-too-distant future, she may work up the courage to visit a hiking trail. I hope so.

Someone on Facebook wants her first pet snake but she's afraid of getting bit. Isn't that like wanting a cat but being afraid of getting scratched? Not only might it happen, it's inevitable.

Her success depends on her intent. Some people buy snakes as a novelty; a way to look cool. She'll buy a snake and eventually it will bite her. This will justify her fear and she won't want it anymore. She'll pawn it off on someone else, give it to a rescue, release it into the wild where it doesn't belong, or it will languish and die. I've seen it too many times. If she's trying to confront a fear, that's admirable, but buying a snake may not be the best way to go about it. Like jumping into a deep swimming pool probably isn't the best way to overcome a fear of water.

Research has proven, and my own observations make it abundantly clear, that a fear of snakes and spiders is culturally conditioned, along with everything else we claim to be afraid of. If you're afraid of spiders and snakes, it may not be your fault, but you can unlearn it along with any other prejudice.

However, where cultural bias is concerned, I do grant extra leeway to people from countries with a higher than normal percentage of venomous snakes, which also corresponds with a higher human mortality rate. But death by snakebite in the U.S. is extremely low. In fact, snakebite fatalities in the U.S. are statistically insignificant compared to other places in the world.

In America, fewer than five people per year die from venomous snakebites, and that's only because some of them (mostly religious zealots) don't seek treatment, relying solely on faith and God's good grace to save them. This can be a fatal mistake. After all, God helps those who help themselves.

By comparison, according to Johns Hopkins University, between 250,000 and 440,000 people die annually from botched medical procedures. This preventable harm to patients, known as iatrogenesis or iatrogenic effect, results from bad medical treatment or advice. In contrast, 6,000 people are killed while texting and driving. Falling out of bed kills another 450 people per year, and domesticated dogs kill between 35 and 50 people. Perhaps it's time to reevaluate where the real dangers lie.

In the most outrageous comparisons, more people are killed by vending machines falling on them than from venomous snakebites, and about the same number are struck by lightning. Yet for some abstract reason, about one-third of Americans are afraid of snakes. I guess people just need something to fear even if it isn't justified.

In many countries, especially those near the equator where the majority of snakes are found, death rates from snakebite are much higher due not only to a greater prevalence of snakes, but to the compounding circumstances of poverty, lack of education, inefficient transportation, and inadequate medical care.

For these reasons, a fear of snakes is definitely a cultural phenomenon. From my personal experience, the most fearful people come from Latin America, India, and Asia. Based on the global distribution of venomous snakes, this makes perfect sense.

I visited China in 2009. While on a river cruise, a gallon jug of "snake wine" was passed around at lunchtime. Four eviscerated cobras floated in amber liquid the color of gasoline. In Chinese tradition, drinking snake wine makes you stronger, and if you're a man, it supposedly works like Chinese Viagra. (Silly, I know, but they really believe it.) I make it a point never to drink anything with dead animals in it, so I politely declined. Besides, I have never been that thirsty. I did sniff the cork, however, and I'm guessing that you could probably run your lawnmower with that stuff.

Jordan removed a handsome gopher snake from a yard one spring morning. The homeowners were Asian and couldn't abide the thought of having a snake — any snake — in their yard. Culture and superstitious tradition are hard to overcome, and it's unfortunate that animals of any kind are killed today based on ancient myths. Kudos to that family for not harming such an attractive and beneficial animal.

A woman I work with told me that she was driving a narrow dirt road in the desert with her husband when they saw a large snake, probably a gopher snake, basking lazily in the mid-morning sun. From her description, the snake stretched from one side of the road to the other, but people who dislike snakes often overestimate their length.

The lethargic reptile was as limp and inanimate as a rope and completely unaware of their presence. My friend confessed that there had been times when they had thoughtlessly driven over snakes in the past, but she saw this one and remembered the brief conversation we'd had about snakes several months before.

She said that thinking of me and how much I respected snakes wouldn't allow her to harm this one, so she told her husband to stop the truck. They waited patiently for the snake to cross, as neither of them was willing to get out of the vehicle and coax it along. For me, this is like saving snakes by remote control and it amazes me how just a little bit of knowledge can change human behavior.

Do you have a fear that keeps you from fully enjoying life? A more logical approach would be to show respect for things that can harm you by confronting them head-on. Talk to professionals and trust them. Knowledgeable people won't steer you wrong.

Please be proactive in educating yourself and others about not killing snakes. Each year as the weather begins to warm, I see pictures of snakes that were unnecessarily killed by people who didn't know any better. Educate your friends, family, neighbors, and co-workers about the many benefits of snakes. You don't have to like snakes, just don't harm them. Live and let live! Nature is fragile, life is precious, and all living things have a purpose.

Life is too short to be lived in fear! This is something I've had to work on in my own life. Not a fear of snakes, of course, but fear of change, a fear of the unknown, and a once-upon-a-time phobia regarding deep water, which I conquered.

Fear exists only in the minds of those people who choose to experience it, but it can be overcome. Don't let fear rule your life.

Be bold and vanquish your fears!

CHAPTER 19

The Off-Season

"In the depth of winter, I finally learned that there was in me an invincible summer." –Albert Camus

Sundays always move at a slower pace, like an old couple strolling through the park. This one was no different. On a crisp fall morning in late October, nervous leaves scuttling across a silent street were the only things moving. There was no traffic, no signs of life at all. It felt like the world had ended and I hadn't gotten the memo. Snake season had drawn to its inevitable close.

When I was a kid, summers seemed about three times longer than winters. Back then, a summer day lasted forever and no school meant there were no schedules or routines to follow. Time meant nothing at all, and its passage was as carefree and limitless as cotton ball clouds in a cerulean summer sky.

Now, winter lasts for nine months, fall and spring are each three days long, and summer is a short series of two-day weekends interrupted by the responsibilities of adult life and the vicissitudes of modern living.

Once snake season was over, I had mixed feelings. After a summer of being run ragged, I welcomed the respite from the interruptions that came at all times of the day and night. On the other hand, I often went into rattlesnake withdrawal long before spring returned. I wouldn't see another rattlesnake for at least six months and I wondered if there was a 12-step program for rattlesnake junkies like me.

During that time, Utah's snakes lie concealed in stony enclaves and deep burrows, avoiding the suboptimal temperatures that render them helpless. During that same period, I lie on my couch in a state if inert dormancy, also avoiding suboptimal temperatures. It is a time of prolonged reflection and quiet retreat.

In Northern Utah, Great Basin rattlers are typically active from mid-May to mid-October, depending on the weather, and during that time, my life was not my own. Calls to move snakes during the summer months kept me busy doing what I loved, and the thought of it ending, even temporarily, was depressing. November through April was always an interminably long slog — a cold and snakeless duration.

A snake man's work is never done . . . not even in the winter. I sacrificed my summers to run Wasatch Snake Removal, making myself available to my customers 24/7 from April through October, and while I loved it, I gave up many other opportunities to do it.

My team and I saved hundreds of snakes each season, educated thousands of people, both online and in person, worked on movie sets, met celebrities, even made a little money, but after nine years it was time to consider moving on. My eye condition was encroaching slowly but steadily and nothing was as easy as it used to be. I could no longer drive at night, and even daytime driving was becoming uncomfortable. Fortunately, I had the next six months to think about it.

Late summer and early fall are the times of year when rattlesnakes give birth to live young. I wanted to move adult snakes out of people's yards in August and September in case they happened to be expectant mothers. Little rattlers are harder to find and harder to catch than larger ones, making life more unsettling for people with children and pets.

The chilly days of autumn are when snakes in the Northern Hemisphere make their way into houses looking for a warm place to spend the winter. After all, why settle for a rabbit burrow or some dark, dank cave when you can have central heat and electricity? One homeowner did not appreciate this information.

This is the advice I gave my customers:

- Check your window wells. Snakes sometimes fall into them and can't get out. It only takes a moment for a snake to slip through an open window, especially if the screen is missing or not latched properly.
- Keep ground-level doors and windows closed. Replace worn threshold seals.
- Keep garage doors closed. Snakes make their way into homes through the garage because garage doors are often left open for long periods at a time.

- Place a wire mesh over outside dryer vents and any other vents or pipes that may provide ingress to your home.
- Check your foundation walls for cracks. Fill cracks with caulk or expandable foam.
- Look for gaps between the foundation and the soil. Contractors often do a poor job of backfilling foundation trenches and the cavities this creates make perfect hibernation burrows for all kinds of critters.

I sometimes got snake calls even on cold, rainy autumn days. One of them was for a Wandering garter snake that was stuck in a window well. (Actually, there's a pretty good chance it was put there by a 10-year-old boy, because it just happened to be his bedroom window. Coincidence? I doubt it.) While the boy may have wanted it there, his grandma did not. She waited until he was at school to call me. It hardly seemed fair.

I didn't usually get snake calls in late November, but some nice folks in Kayenta had a sidewinder rattlesnake on their patio on a chilly Thanksgiving Eve. (Kayenta is a suburb of St. George, and is a little more than 300 miles southwest of Salt Lake.) Sidewinders are common in the area, but it was only 40 degrees in St. George, and the temps were dropping fast. That snake certainly didn't want to be outside. At 32 degrees, it would be a dead snake and the homeowners didn't want that. They also didn't want to pay to have it moved.

I suggested putting the snake in a covered bucket and keeping it in the heated garage overnight then releasing it the next day. The woman was extremely friendly and very worried about the snake. Her husband was willing to try to get it into a bucket but he wasn't thrilled by the prospect. Not only that, they were leaving for Salt Lake early in the morning to spend Thanksgiving with family.

It should have been easy to move a snake so impaired by the cold, but it struck at them as they attempted to pick it up with a leaf rake, which freaked them out. In the interest of safety, Chris, one of my relocators in St. George, left his house and his warm bed to move the snake for them. We've had other customers who balked at paying us to move a snake and chose to do it themselves, but this is why you should always leave the job to a professional. We've done this a thousand times, taking the risks so you don't have to.

Just when I thought we had seen the last snake of the season, I got a call from Marcia. She didn't know what kind of snake was in her yard, and she didn't want to get close enough to take a picture, but I was pretty sure it wasn't a rattler. Sure enough, it was a handsome and somewhat confused gopher snake. It was early December and it didn't want to be out in 50-degree weather, but it wasn't sure where to go or how to get there.

I dispatched Jordan who took care of the situation in his usual professional manner. The problem was where to put the snake now that temps were near freezing at night. Jordan found a hole under a rock and the snake dove right in. It'll more than likely spend the winter there, and there is no doubt that by calling us, Marcia saved that snake's life.

Another December call came from a guy who was afraid to move the trash pile in his yard because there might be snakes in it. Dude! It's December in Utah. If you're going to move the trash pile, do it now! If you wait until spring, all bets are off. February was now the only month in which I hadn't gotten a call.

In mid-November (I don't recall the year), a nice woman phoned from a small town up north to say that garter snakes were appearing in her house. Casey did an outstanding job of locating the points of ingress and removing the snakes, which he kept at home until spring.

Finally, a February snake call! I had to free a gopher snake from a glue trap in a basement. I had now received snake calls in every month of the year. Not every month in the *same* year, but still amazing considering the climate.

With another snake season behind me, I removed the stickers from the back window of the snake mobile, replacing them with new ones in the spring.

Many years ago, I was diagnosed with Seasonal Affective Disorder (SAD), a depressive condition resulting from the lack of sunlight on short winter days with a corresponding decrease in serotonin production in the body. I think it may also have something to do with the lack of snakes and the corresponding decrease in motivation that occurs when I can't look for them. I call it Seriously Seasonal Snakeless Affective Disorder (SSSAD). When you're a snake man, winter sucks!

During the slow time-creep of winter, Nemo the Wonder Cat would gaze pensively out the window wondering what had happened to his world. He still enjoyed going outside briefly, but he longed for green grass and patrolling for bugs in the backyard shrubbery. We both had chronic cabin fever but the cure was months away.

So what does a snake man do when there are no snakes? In my younger days, I used to ski, but my back and knees have threatened to sue me if I do it now. These days I hibernate as any good snake man should in a place with four seasons. But I still get restless once in a while.

One chilly autumn day, I drove down Highway 89, then west on I-70 to Fremont Indian State Park. I had never been there. The visitors' center had a laminated, foldout pamphlet about snakes, so I bought it. After a short hike, I continued west to I-15, then north to Meadow, where I spent a relaxing couple of hours marinating in my favorite hot spring in the middle of a cow pasture. It was always the best cure for my SAD.

While there, I met a man from Alaska who is an actual balneological therapy expert. Balneology is the belief and practice of using hot springs for the benefit of therapeutic healing, mentally, spiritually, and physically. We talked for nearly an hour before he had to leave, but I told him about a few hot springs that even he had never heard of.

Hot springs were spiritual places for Native Americans and warring tribes were required to lay down their weapons at these sacred sites. I walked around the area, picked up some litter to appease the ancient gods, and hit the road again, which led to a Mexican dinner on the way home.

One especially cold winter, my friend Mark and his 14-year-old son Ryan and I ventured out on the coldest night of the year (it was well below zero in the mountains) with a frigid wind howling down an ice-encrusted canyon as we began the two-and-a-half mile downhill trek to another favorite hot spring.

Once in the water, all was well, except that when we got hungry our fingers froze to our flashlights and to the metal zipper tabs on our packs which were within easy reach at the edge of the spring. The air was so cold it burned. Even the darkness that surrounded us was frozen solid.

We were the only humans on the mountain. After soaking for several hours in the steaming waters of this geothermal oasis, we got out in the middle of the night — an act that defied all human logic. Mark had promised his wife he'd be home by a certain time without realizing the perilous nature of our situation. And we had no cell coverage.

With steam still rising from his shivering body, Ryan slid his swimsuit off and laid it on a rock. Rummaging in his pack, he found his long john bottoms and eagerly pulled them on. It took less than a minute. In that brief time, his swimsuit froze solid. Peeling it off the rock, he held it up like a frozen flag of surrender. (We later learned that it was minus 16 degrees on the mountain that night).

Standing in the steam at the edge of the thermal pool, flashing blades of light from our headlamps stabbed momentary holes in the canyon's inky blackness. Naked and wet, with a thin layer of ice on our bodies and fingers numb beyond feeling, it took us a while to get dressed. It's hard to do much of anything when your fingers are so cold they feel like they're on fire, signaling the onset of frostbite.

On the three-mile hike out, we didn't dare stop for fear that we would succumb to the cold. (Did you know that super-cold snow squeaks like Styrofoam when you walk on it and that frigid, spiky air stings your lungs like needles?)

I wasn't sure my old 4-Runner would start once we reached the ridge, but after several reluctant tries, the engine grudgingly turned over. There was a quarter-inch of ice on the inside of the windshield which we tried to scrape off using credit cards, but to no avail. (Ice scrapers don't work on the *inside* of a windshield.)

After a half-hour or so of running the defroster full-blast, I only had two dollar-sized peepholes to peer through as I drove us down a narrow, winding road in the dark on solid ice with a steep drop-off on one side. We laugh about it now, but it was crazy cold and scary as hell at the time.

Back in civilization, we arrived at an all-night diner in the wee hours of the morning, ragged and reeking of sulfur, our teeth still chattering. We must have looked like refugees from a Siberian Gulag. The waitress asked if we were okay and plied us with cup after cup of coffee and hot chocolate.

What did we learn from that experience, you ask? Not much, because we did it again the following year.

Each year around solstice time, three or four friends and I venture into the frigid wilderness to test our mettle against the elements, soak our bones, and eat copious amounts of junk food. My posse and I sacrifice ourselves to usher in the winter season so that the space/time continuum will progress as it should. If we didn't, time would cease to exist and spring would never come. (It's a very important job!) We've been doing this for so many years that we don't know how not to do it.

In 2024, five of us, Mark, Mike, Dax, Chance and I, trekked to the land of steaming waters where we soaked under a gloomy sky and toasted each other with homemade wassail (liquid Christmas) made by Mark's wife, Dellene.

We left Salt Lake at midnight on Saturday morning, and after a three-hour drive to an adjacent state, followed by a short hike, we arrived at our geothermal destination in the wee hours.

As we undressed to enter the hot spring, the icy wind roaring up the canyon dropped the air temperature to negative numbers. The frigid gusts stabbed our bare skin with tiny daggers of airborne ice particles that stung like fragments of frozen shrapnel. After slipping eagerly into the welcoming water, the same wind skipped low across the surface, keeping our ears as cold as popsicles, despite being only inches above the steaming water. We ate with one hand at a time, keeping the other hand submerged so it would still function.

Shrouded in steam and darkness, lit only by glow sticks, a strand of LED Christmas lights, and a haloed zombie moon, we ensured that time wouldn't stop and that all was well with the universe. We soaked and talked, consuming mass quantities of junk food and submarine sandwiches as jet planes streaked smoky grey contrails across an angry winter sky.

The thought of emerging from the spring in such a wind, wet and exposed, was daunting at best. But we got lucky. The longer we stayed in the water, the more the wind died down, until finally, shortly before sunrise, it blew itself out like a spent birthday candle, leaving us alone on the silent mountain. The surrounding hills were silhouettes against a slowly rising crimson sun that squinted over the jagged horizon like a bloodshot eyeball, blinking through eyelid clouds at the pale world below.

Why do we do it? Because that's the stuff life is made of!

Even though I've spent much of my life looking for snakes, I don't always find them. Sometimes however, they find me. One of my weirdest encounters with a snake happened at a hot spring on a snow-encrusted winter night. I was about to strip down to my nuthin's when I spotted a tiny gopher snake under the arch of my boot. I had missed crushing it by a fraction of an inch. It had no business being there at that time of year.

This unlucky snake was only alive because it was trapped in the tepid void between the warm water and the snow that lie just beyond the edge of the pool. With months to go until spring, it would have surely died. I took the stranded snake home and released it after Memorial Day.

I wasn't made for winter. Still, other than snow, ice, cold feet, sneezing, flu, hypothermia, frostbite, Seasonal Affective Disorder, cabin fever, high heating bills, and the conspicuous lack of reptilian activity, winter really isn't all that bad. And yet, for some strange reason, I'm always ready for summer to return. Go figure.

A favorite winter pastime is watching other herpers' road cruising videos on YouTube. Ethan and I can sit for hours marveling at the plenitude and diversity of snakes in other places, envious of those herpers who live where the climate is conducive to year-round herping and finding snakes we may never see in person. Although we pretend not to like them, there's something deeply satisfying about living vicariously through those lucky souls cruising lonely roads in warmer climates while our own backyard lies dormant under a layer of frost. This sort of armchair herping satisfies our need for take-out food and the wintertime tendency to be lazy. It also provokes a deep longing for spring.

But no matter how long winter ensnares us in her frigid embrace, testing our endurance, spring always comes back as she has done for millennia, dancing seductively on a distant horizon with flowers in her hair.

In 2015, abnormally warm winter temperatures lured Mark, Ryan, and me on a trip to the San Rafael Swell on President's Day weekend. Even the long drive was a respite from the daily grind. We found the trailhead for Crack Canyon and made camp. Nightfall brought temps in the mid-20s, and the wind chill made it even colder. A campfire and a hot dinner kept us warm.

Monday dawned cool and cloudy. We delayed our descent into the canyon until we were mostly sure it wasn't going to rain. After a late breakfast, we broke camp and entered the canyon's mouth under somber gray skies, savoring the tranquility of the place. Satiating our need for nature, we reveled in the pristine beauty that surrounded us. Windows of blue opened and closed overhead as the sun played peek-a-boo amid ominous clouds.

Every canyoneer knows that there is a point-of-no-return — a place somewhere between safety and certain doom — when a rainstorm miles away can flood a slot canyon in a matter of minutes.

Logs and stones jammed between the walls 20 feet overhead are testament to the power of a desert deluge and its unmerciful aftermath. Although flakes of graupel fluttered down on us, causing momentary concern, the clouds departed by mid-afternoon and the sun came out to stay.

Like most desert canyons, Crack's curvy sandstone walls undulate like a giant snake, wending its way through country that is equal parts beautiful and foreboding. It alternately broadens and narrows, constricting and widening, falling 700 vertical feet over its two-and-a-half-mile length. Choke stones and drop-offs ensure that it isn't a walk in the park, and a lone hiker could have difficulty ascending some of these obstacles on their own. Fortunately, we had each other to hoist and pull ourselves over some of the more arduous hurdles.

19 | The Off-Season

As we hiked, we joked about the best places to put oil derricks in this incredible place, something the cretins in the legislature are actually proposing. We have to stop them from their greedy subterfuge of our public lands because a connection to the natural world is the panacea for what ails our species.

The greedy reprobates in the Utah Legislature are quite possibly the most obtuse mob of money-grubbing miscreants on the planet. To look at Utah's incomparable natural beauty and see only drilling rigs and dollar signs is a sure sign of insufficient character development. As part of a broader "conservative" agenda, this obtuse brand of conservatism has no connection to or understanding of conservation. Enjoy Utah's wild places while you can, even if it's only in a video. Do it before they're drilled, fracked, poisoned, and aesthetically compromised forevermore.

Of course we can have a booming economy by exploiting all of our natural resources, but is it worth the cost? Once these irreplaceable resources have been depleted, we'll be left with nothing more than a Mad Max wasteland of despoiled scenery devoid of wildlife and poisoned beyond repair. For what? A few years of lower gas prices? Is this the legacy we want to leave our children?

The potential for exponential population growth is a concept that needs to be avoided at all cost. Continued growth is unsustainable, irreversible, and in the long-run, completely detrimental to the perpetuation of our species.

Like bacteria in a petri dish, human expansion cannot continue unabated without eventually consuming everything around it, resulting in our own demise. We exceeded our carrying capacity on the planet long ago. It's time to slow down our parasitic assault on the Earth or reap the consequences.

We can't borrow our way out of debt, we can't build our way out of gridlock, and we can't overpopulate ourselves into sustainable consumption.

How many people reading this have run a wild river, hiked a slot canyon on a cloudy day, or slept on a sandstone mesa on a night so cold and still that you could almost hear the stars shining down on the sleeping desert? If you have, you know what I mean. If you haven't, you should.

The Only Good Snake . . .

America's public lands provide tranquility in an increasingly chaotic human world and satiate our need for nature by allowing us to revel in pristine, natural beauty. Keeping public lands in public hands is imperative for a civilization hell-bent on sacrificing itself to the gods of consumerism, political corruption, and the threats imposed by artificial intelligence (considering that our politicians possess little natural intelligence).

Humans need nature. We need it as surely as we need air and water. We don't need short-sighted, gluttonous, self-serving corporate shills taking America's lands away from Americans and handing them to the dirty energy industry like an extortion payment. Once destroyed, these sacred lands can never be reclaimed. You don't make a country great by destroying the best parts of it. Even sustainable energy has its downside, but fossil fuels are the biggest culprits, producing greenhouse gasses that alter the natural climate.

Reptiles and amphibians are considered "barometer species," meaning that they are accurate indicators of environmental health and stability and are often the first predictors of ecosystem imbalance.

Amphibians, with their porous skin, are highly sensitive to both airborne and waterborne toxins. In addition, sensitivity to temperature variations is not only detrimental, but often fatal for these fragile creatures.

Reptiles, with their armored scales are less susceptible to environmental toxins, but as egg-layers primarily, incubation and the ratio of male to female offspring is directly affected by temperature fluctuations caused by anthropomorphic climate change.

Negative human influence on the climate often means that we're sometimes basking under a resplendent winter sun, enjoying unseasonable, even record-breaking warm temperatures earlier and later than we're supposed to. As easy as it is to appreciate January and February weather in the 50s and 60s, it simply is not normal. Someone sent me a photo of a Great Basin rattlesnake taken on January 27. Dazed and confused, this snake was active at a time of year when it should be in deep stasis, below the frost line, dreaming of mice.

We expect behavior like this from certain species such as garter snakes and rubber boas, but this sighting was definitely unusual and potentially deadly for this snake. I have seldom seen rattlesnakes, except near den sites, earlier than April. As one of the first species to call it quits in the fall, rattlers are one of the last snakes to emerge in the spring. It's bound to get cold again, and if he's too far from his den when it happens, he will die, lured by a false sense that spring is here to stay.

After months of virtual hibernation, I crawl from my own den looking like a pallid cave creature, barely human, squinting at the light, seeking a seasonal transformation. The first 70-degree day in May finds me sprawled on sun-drenched stone, basking under a rejuvenating desert sun as its warmth rewires my winter brain.

Nearby, an exuberant fence lizard does pushups on a rock, and for the same reason. We understand each other. We are kindred spirits.

CHAPTER 20

It Takes All Kinds

"I have an unshakable belief that the entire human race (including me) is no smarter than a loose collection of lug nuts."
–Robert Kirby

The older I get, the less faith I have in humanity's ability to save itself from itself. Crowds feel like chaos in motion, too often oblivious to the damage they leave in their wake. I prefer to sidestep the human stampede with its mass delusion, mass hysteria, mass consumption — masses of humanity chasing curated joy and algorithm-approved meaning, where individuality is traded for the safety of consensus and approval.

The more people I have to deal with, the more I love snakes. Their honesty is refreshing. There's no small talk, no ego trips, no hidden agendas, no attempts to impress — just grace, precision, and a quiet defiance of everything we've been taught to fear. I prefer the solitude, silence, and company of creatures who don't pretend to be something they're not.

This chapter is dedicated to all the humans I met in the course of relocating rattlesnakes. Most of them were good, kind, well-intentioned and generous. I couldn't find fault with anyone who took the time to call me instead of killing a snake. But it takes all kinds to make the world go around, as they say, and I can tell you with certainty that there are many kinds out there.

Some people were dropped on their head as babies. Others were tossed into the air, got smacked by the ceiling fan, bounced off the wall and fell out the window. Some are dumber than rocks, a good many need the crap slapped out of them, and a finite few dwell on the far side of evil.

Homo sapiens are an enigma, and in spite of being one myself (a fact I'm often embarrassed about), I will never fully understand our species. Like anyone who works with the public, I have met all kinds of folks, running the gamut from the most compassionate and friendly to the truly angry, psychotic, and dangerous.

My background in both retail sales and government public service were invaluable training grounds for learning to deescalate even the most potentially volatile personalities and the lapses of emotional control that can occur when people get angry or scared. Most upset people merely want to be heard and understood, and the ability to listen is a powerful tool in anyone's public relations toolbox.

I am happy to say that the vast majority of people by far were good, conscientious folks who wanted to do the right thing for the right reason whenever possible. These were my favorite peeps.

The Good

"What you do makes a difference, and you have to decide what kind of difference you want to make." –Jane Goodall

Most of my calls were from homeowners — just everyday folks who were casually doing the things people do in their yards — gardening, grilling, weed whacking, playing with the kids, dog, etc., when a wayward rattlesnake changed their plans.

One sultry summer day in August, a man called to say that he discovered a rattlesnake while landscaping his yard. He had an appointment, he said, so he wouldn't be home when I got there. Anticipating this, he put the snake in his county-issued recycle bin and parked it near the curb.

Fortunately, it wasn't recycle day. (The last time I checked, rattlesnakes were not recyclable.) Upon locating the street, which was in an exclusive area of Salt Lake known as Olympus Cove, all I had to do was look for the only home in the neighborhood with its blue recycle bin out front.

Driving past the home, I flipped a U-turn and pulled up on the opposite side of the narrow street directly across from the bin. After grabbing a snake stick and bucket from the back of the snake mobile, I crossed the street and approached the bin. Was there really a rattlesnake in it, I wondered, or was this a prank on the snake man?

Upon opening the lid, I gazed into the dim blue interior of the receptacle. Sure enough, coiled loosely amongst a dozen or so pop cans and the crinkled remnants of yesterday's Tribune lay a con-genial little buzzer butt. This was too easy! I lifted her out, placed her in my bucket, drove to the nearest trailhead, and prepared to hike her away from the subdivision, wrongly assuming that this was a freebie call. The homeowner, however, whom I never did meet, had watched the whole event from his cell phone via his home security cameras and Venmo'd me my fee plus a generous tip.

A nice lady called from a private, gated community on Salt Lake's Upper East Side and a hotbed for rattlesnakes. She could see the three-foot snake on her patio from the kitchen window. I asked if she could see its tail. She said she could. "Does it taper to a point?" I asked, "or does it have a rattle on the end?" She said it was long and pointed. "Does the tail have black bars on a tan background?" I queried. "Yes, it does," she replied. She sounded astonished that I knew this. I congratulated her on having a big, friendly gopher snake in her yard and made sure she was okay with that. She assured me that as long as it wasn't a rattler it was welcome to stay.

A short while later, the same thing happened again. Just be-fore noon, I got a call from County Animal Services to pick up a rattlesnake from an opulent home and happily left work to do it. The nice lady who lived there was delighted to find out it was ac-tually a gopher snake and was thrilled to have it as a guest.

A call came from a man who swerved his car to avoid hitting a snake in his neighborhood. He pulled over, ushered the snake on-to someone's front lawn and stayed with it until I arrived about 20 minutes later. He didn't know what kind of snake it was, he just knew it deserved better than to be run over by a car. It was a gopher snake, and this guy is a hero. Thanks to all the good peo-ple who look out for the little helpless things. You make the world a better place.

In August of 2015, I received a call from a student at the Uni-versity of Utah who spotted a small snake near the dorms. The tiny serpent had wedged itself into a crack between the curb and the grass. He didn't recognize the species, but he was as con-cerned for the safety of the snake as he was about the well-being of passers-by. From his description, I knew it wasn't a rattlesnake and assumed it was a young gopher snake.

When I arrived some 45 minutes later, the guy was lying next to the curb in the sun (it was a hot day) making sure that no one stepped on the snake. He had been there the entire time, keeping it shaded from the sweltering heat. I extricated the snake, which was a hatchling Western racer, and released it near Red Butte Creek.

Just when I had almost reached the point of giving up all hope for the human species, some individual human did something beyond impressive. Thank you, sir! May the snake gods smile upon you!

A woman named Laurie shared her only experience with a rattlesnake. "Many years ago, I was a senior Girl Scout helping out at a junior Girl Scout jamboree," she told me. "At one of the events for the little girls, we were in a wooded area and there was a baby rattlesnake curled up under a tree a few feet away. My assignment was to keep an eye on the baby and make sure no one harassed it. No one did, and when the event was over it eventually slithered away. Everybody won! The end."

In an unusual turn of events, a nice lady called me to ask if I could put snakes in her yard. (I know, right?) She had voles in her lawn and wanted a couple of gopher snakes to solve the problem. To her credit, she does not use herbicides, pesticides or glue traps. I think I'm in love!

The first official snake call of 2020 came from Lori, who had more than a dozen garter snakes living near her front porch and in a crevice by her garage door. She admits to not being terribly fond of snakes, but she was worried about their safety and asked if we could move them away from her driveway.

Averi and I caught as many as we could, and Lori suggested releasing them at an organic vegetable farm near her home. Chris, the owner of the farm, was happy to have the snakes at his facility where other people release their urban snakes and where there is plenty of food for them all.

Thanks to Lori and Chris for being snake heroes!

In May of 2020, as the pandemic was raging, a nice woman named Marge called me about a rattlesnake on her patio. She didn't know me and had never heard of Wasatch Snake Removal prior to finding my website, prompting her to interrogate me like a Mafia boss.

She wanted to know where I was going to release the snake, what my credentials were, and whether I was a legitimately licensed business. Mostly she wanted reassurance that I wasn't an exterminator. She refused to give me her address until she was satisfied that the snake wasn't going to be harmed and that my intentions were above reproach. I don't think the FBI could have vetted me more thoroughly than Marge did.

I must have passed her test because she finally capitulated and told me where she lived. I arrived and caught the snake. It was a three-foot buzzer butt that was loosely sprawled out on the warm concrete like a bikini model on a sandy beach.

"Thanks for coming," she said as I was leaving. "I like you."

Marge called me several more times over the next few summers, usually to move a snake, but sometimes just to talk. We always chuckled about that first call. She even threatened her neighbors, telling them they hadn't better kill a snake or they'd have to answer to her. I got a lot of business as a result of Marge's threats. Marge is a no-nonsense kind of gal. Don't mess with Marge!

The first rattlesnake call of 2021 was for a tiny baby buzzer butt in a backyard on Devonshire Drive. That diminutive snake was born late last summer and managed to survive its first winter. Many neonate snakes don't live to be a year old because something usually eats them first.

The homeowner put a bucket over the little critter to keep it in place until Bebe and I arrived. We released it away from homes and trails where it would be safe from people. We always appreciated the homeowners who did the right thing by calling us when a rattlesnake stopped by to say "hi!"

After removing a rattler from a different yard, I emailed the homeowner to let him know that his snake had been safely and successfully relocated to habitat. He wrote back, "Thank you for the speedy service. We do like to see our wildlife preserved and appreciate the people who help with saving their lives."

I hear so much malicious talk about snakes that I hardly know how to react when someone goes above and beyond to save one.

I received a call early one morning from an amazing woman named Jennifer. After her cat mauled a little racer in her yard, leaving it severely injured and with little chance of survival, Jennifer felt an obligation to help the tiny creature. Most people would have given it back to the cat or simply left it to die. But not Jennifer. She took the injured snake to a vet where it underwent surgery for its wounds, and she bought a tank and all the necessary supplies to care for the snake during its recovery. She named him Ganesh.

When I inquired about the cost to rehabilitate Ganesh, Jennifer told me that the surgery bill was $400 and the equipment another $150, all for an animal that most people would consider expendable. I could hardly believe it.

After three weeks, with his wounds nearly healed, Jennifer called me to ask about the proper method of releasing Ganesh back to the wild. Her concern for this animal was so genuine and was such a departure from the usual disregard most people have for these lesser beings that I was genuinely moved.

Thank you, Jennifer, for reminding us that compassion and empathy still exist, and that we have an obligation to all God's creatures. You are one in a million!

After releasing a snake in Ferguson Canyon, I met a group of people as I was leaving. One man shook my hand. "It's really cool what you do," he said. "Thanks for your service." He said it as though I was a veteran or a police officer. Thank you, sir! I work really hard at this, and I appreciate it.

Someone else told me that anyone who saves rattlesnakes is, in his words, "a little off kilter." No sir, that's not true. I'm a lot off kilter. Get it right!

Thanks to the lovely woman who called me in September 2023. You made my day.

She called to say that she found an injured garter snake in the gutter in front of the house and texted me a photo. She didn't know much about snakes, but she wanted to help this one if she could, mostly as a lesson in compassion for her little boy, and because she didn't want it to suffer.

It had blood coming from its mouth, which didn't sound very hopeful from a rehabilitation standpoint. She had already called a vet clinic but couldn't afford the fee. I told her we'd pick it up for free, perform an evaluation, and do what needed to be done.

Before I could dispatch anyone to pick up the snake, it died of its injuries. I suggested that she have a little funeral service for her son's sake. She told me they already had plenty of pets buried in the yard, and that sounded like a good idea. Then she asked where she could learn more about snakes so her son wouldn't grow up to be afraid of them.

Does anyone realize how astounding this scenario is? I still get choked up when telling this story. Most people who don't like snakes have already imposed their own irrational fears onto their innocent, unbiased children, perpetuating an unnecessary ignorance and perhaps even a lifelong phobia.

You, dear lady, are my new hero.

The Bad

"Bad people don't go to hell, they are already there." –Dan Millman

In my early days of removing snakes for a local rescue, I received a call from the guy in charge. "I just got a call from a woman," he said, "and I think she's crazy. You talk to her." Sure. Why not?

I wrote down the number, and mustering my less than professional skills in dealing with the mentally unstable, I called the woman. I'll refer to her as Mrs. Jones.

"Hello!" said the loud voice on the other end. She sounded agitated but not insane. Not yet.

"Hi, Mrs. Jones. This is Dave from the rescue. What can I do for you?"

"What's wrong with you #%$@*&#&*%@$! snake people?" she screeched. Her voice instantly shifted gears, sounding like a logging truck that had lost its brakes on a steep gravel road. And she had a vocabulary like the driver. "That last guy pissed me off!"

I apologized and asked if she had a snake in her yard.

"I don't have ONE @#$%&* snake in my yard," she hissed, "I have TWO! And you had better come over and get them RIGHT NOW!"

"Do you know what kind of snakes they are?" I asked politely. "Are they rattlesnakes?"

"No, they're not @#$!%&* rattlesnakes!" Her voice was rising, cracking, becoming shrill, like a witch being burned at the stake.

"Can you keep an eye on them until I get there?" I asked, trying to be reasonable.

"What the @#$% for?" she screamed. They're not going anywhere!"

I'll cut to the chase and tell you that her husband, in his infinite idiocy had chopped up two adult gopher snakes that had been casually performing a mating ritual on the pool deck and these two geniuses didn't want the pieces of the amorous serpents in *their* garbage can. They wanted them in mine.

"You want me to come and pick up pieces of dead snakes?" I asked. I was incredulous! This woman really was nuts!

I informed her that I was a snake rescuer and relocator, not a snake resuscitator and resurrector, and what the hell did she expect me to do with two dead and desecrated snakes? The fact that a breeding pair of completely harmless and highly beneficial snakes had been sacrificed on the altar of stupidity had me seething.

Then I asked her the question that pushed her right over the edge. "Why," I inquired, "didn't you call us BEFORE your husband killed the snakes?"

I suppose logic wasn't her strong suit. She went off like an improvised explosive device. She was screaming now, and the volume of her remonstrations was deafening. I held the phone away from my ear. "You [blanking little blanker]!" she shrieked maniacally. "Why don't you go . . ."

And that's when she told me to do something to myself, which, in case you haven't tried it, is difficult at best, even for a professional contortionist, and which is probably not all that enjoyable even if you could.

Most folks were more emotionally stable than that, even if a few of them weren't the brightest bulbs in the human chandelier.

The Clueless

"Some people drink from the fountain of knowledge. Others just gargle." –Robert Anthony

One morning I received the following phone call from someone with a heavy Asian accent:

Me: "Wasatch Snake Removal, this is Dave."

Caller: "Hello, Wasatch Snake Removal, LLC."

Me: "Good morning! Who's this?"

Caller: "Thanks for the respond I really appreciate. I will like you to please do provide me with the total cost for a tree removal by my house."

Me: "Ten thousand dollars."

Caller: "This sound stupid and funny. You haven't even look at the house."

Me: "Dude! This is Wasatch Snake Removal, not tree removal."

Silence . . . call ends.

I had a panicked call from a man near a local canyon with a snake in his yard. It could have been one of several species, including a rattler, but then he texted me a photo and it was just a garter snake. I'm always happy when I can put someone's mind at ease. When I asked him how he found my number, he said he called County Animal Services (which only deals with domestic animals). He then called Unified Police (which doesn't deal with animals at all). He called three other municipal agencies before someone, probably the DWR, finally gave him my number. FYI: There's this new thing called Google. Just sayin'.

As I was returning from releasing a rattler on the Ferguson Canyon trail, a hiker named Sam told me about a snake he'd seen on the trail just moments earlier, and led me back to where he saw it. The snake had moved off the trail and into the underbrush. It was on a steep downslope pointed toward someone's backyard. There was no time to use my stick. I dove headlong toward the snake as if I was sliding into home base, reaching over the drop-off just as the startled snake tried to make its getaway down the slope. I grabbed the surprised buzzer butt by the tail, pulling her gently onto the trail and tailing her. Sam shot a video but somehow missed the capture. "Dude!" he said, looking and sounding like Shaggy from Scooby-Doo. "You're like a magician!" It seemed to me that Sam was enjoying a little magic of his own.

I got a call for a snake under a fridge on the third floor of a downtown apartment complex. Although I was skeptical, stranger things have happened.

An elderly woman saw what she thought was a snake leering at her menacingly from under the fridge. She called SLCPD who referred her to me.

The "snake" turned out to be a garlic husk with two eyeholes. But . . . I found a missing steak knife, two dog bones, and a family of dust bunnies, so it wasn't a total waste of time.

A guy who lived near the medical center asked if I moved tarantulas. It was already late in the year and male tarantulas only live about a year anyway, so I asked if he knew what sex it was. There was a pause, then he said, "It must be a female. I don't see any testicles."

In the fall of 2020, a panicky woman called me to say she had a rattlesnake in her shed next to the lawnmower, but based on her location, I knew it wasn't a rattler. I asked if she could text me a picture of the snake, which was most likely a gopher snake.

After waiting about 25 minutes for her text, I got worried and called her back to see if everything was okay. She admitted that she was too embarrassed to confess that her "rattlesnake" turned out to be a pile of pinecones, but she thanked me for following up.

A nice, seemingly normal woman named Sherry called to tell me about the snake she killed in her yard with a shovel and to ask what kind it was. She was even thoughtful enough to text me a photo of it. I think you know how I feel about people who send me pictures of dead snakes.

This was my first clue that Sherry may not be firing on all cylinders. It was another case of killing a snake and then calling the snake removal guy. That's like killing the stray dog that wanders into your yard and *then* calling the dogcatcher.

The Only Good Snake . . .

She told me it was a black snake, and even though there are no all-black snakes Utah, she wasn't entirely wrong. The snake was a melanistic garter snake, one with an excess of melanin, or dark pigmentation, and very different in appearance from a normal specimen. This one would have been highly prized by someone who breeds garter snakes, like my friend Don. Sherry not only killed a harmless snake; she killed a genetically unique individual.

I tried to be nice to everyone who called, but I told Sherry that calling the snake relocator after the snake was dead made no sense whatsoever. I also told her that killing any snake is illegal, and that killing one as unique as this was a travesty.

She was indignant. "You can chastise me all you want," she said, "but I have grandchildren, and I did what I had to do." I stopped just short of asking her if she also killed puppies and kittens with a shovel for her grandchildren's sake, but I bit my tongue.

I explained that the only venomous snakes along the Wasatch Front were Great Basin rattlers, and reassured her that she didn't live in rattlesnake territory. She vowed that she would never call me again and I assured her that it was fine by me.

I suppose I get a D in diplomacy, but I really don't care. I was nicer than I should have been. I don't think she'll kill another snake, but whether she does or doesn't, she's not going to tell me about it. Some people refuse to be educated, and I can't help those people.

A concerned homeowner sent me a photo of what he believed was a rattlesnake in his yard. It was actually a harmless gopher snake, but its tail had been injured to some degree. It was hard to tell from the photo exactly what was wrong with it. Ordinarily, a harmless snake would have a pointed tail, so I can understand how he could be confused, especially since he lived near the foothills in rattlesnake domain. I then found out that he had seen the snake several days earlier.

I'm glad I was able to put his mind at ease, but I still don't understand why people waited two or three days to call me after they saw a snake in their yard, especially if it might be a rattlesnake. They could wait for it to leave (which it would eventually

298

do), or they could call me while the snake was still there so I could find it quickly and easily and relocate it for everyone's safety and peace of mind.

I sent Jordan on a wild goose chase for a woman who claimed to have a rattlesnake in her yard. When he got there, she informed him that the snake was there five days ago — a tidbit of information she neglected to mention on the phone. And she gave him nothing for his time and trouble.

I took many calls from homeowners who asked if we wanted to come and look for the snake that was in their yard last week. No, we absolutely didn't. I actually had to start asking my customers if the snake they were calling about was in their yard at that moment.

On another occasion, two people called on the same morning, each of whom had seen a rattlesnake in their yard earlier in the week; one several days ago and one yesterday. They both wanted to know if I could find the sneaky serpents.

I could perform a yard inspection and maybe find the snake (but yard inspections weren't free), or it may have been hiding in some inaccessible place, or it may have left long ago. If they hadn't seen it for four or five days it was probably long gone. But they weren't sure, and now they were nervous because they didn't know where it was, which is why they should have called when they first saw it.

One guy wanted me to move the rattlesnake that was in his yard last week. "Well, I can't move it last week," I told him. "Is it still there today?" He hadn't seen it since, and didn't seem to comprehend the ridiculousness of his question. I can't move the snake in your yard last week if you wait till today to call me.

An almost hysterical lady called me to say that her dog told her there was a rattlesnake in the yard, but after an hour of looking, I didn't find any snakes. I should have asked more questions, such as, "Did your dog tell you how big the snake was?" What else do you and your dog talk about?" and, "Do you believe everything your dog tells you?"

Heck, what do I care? I made $12.

I sent Casey on a call in response to a worried couple who claimed to have a large snake under their water heater. Getting to the water heater meant removing a hatch from the kitchen floor and wiggling into the narrow crawlspace underneath.

Inching along on his belly, Casey aimed his headlamp at the heater in the far corner and tried to determine what kind of snake the homeowner may have seen lying beneath it. Using a snake stick, he skillfully removed the snake from its cozy lair and popped back up through the kitchen floor. He then diplomatically explained to the homeowners that their "snake" was actually a braided rug.

Our irrational fears don't always protect us from the things we're afraid of. Sometimes they just cost us money and make us look silly.

Every year I'd get a call from some whiny woman telling me that she can't have a garter snake in her yard because she has a toddler, as though an 18-inch snake is going to swallow her precious progeny whole in front of her eyes.

I told her that the snake was in far greater danger from her little yard monkey (I was more diplomatic than that) than he/she/it was from the snake, and that the snake wouldn't let the kid get close enough for either of them to get hurt. But she just kept whining.

I explained that the snake would eat any nestling mice in her yard and some of the insects in the garden. But she still kept whining.

Some people completely lack logic and common sense and you cannot help them. So I sent Casey to remove the snake and it cost her $60. She'll spend a lot more than that on mouse traps and insecticides. She should have listened to me.

This is similar to the guy who said he had a garter snake in his yard and "might need me to come over and move it." I asked him what his objection was to having a garter snake in his yard. "I have a 17-month-old child," he said. "Uh huh," I replied, waiting for further explanation. But that was it.

At least a dozen times over the years I've had people call me and say, "I have a snake in my yard, and I know it's harmless, but I have a toddler." Then I wait for them to elaborate, but they never do. Is there a question in there somewhere?

What am I supposed to say to them when I don't even understand the inference? I can only assume that they're afraid their toddler is going to hurt the snake, am I right? I didn't think so.

I've been bitten by snakes and toddlers alike, and I can tell you that I'm far more concerned for that snake than I am for that kid. Protecting children is one thing, but a parent passing their personal fears to their children is like handing them a bag of rocks to carry for the rest of their lives. Why burden them like that?

Then there was the woman who said, "I can't have a snake in my yard. I'm pregnant." (The snake was harmless.)

Me (to myself): 'Yeah? So? I'm overweight, what's your point?' Years later, I'm still looking for the logic in her statement.

I went to move a garter snake for a Chinese guy named Frank. Frank was nosy. He inquired about my marital status, where I lived, and what I did for a living. Frank said I was a great guy and he wanted to set me up with a Chinese woman who didn't speak English. Frank needed to mind his own damn business. He also needed to clean up his yard. Nobody is ever going to find a garter snake in that mess.

I once had a homeowner point to a 40-foot-long row of prickly hedges and exclaim, "The snake went in there!" She then handed me a set of pruning shears. I had to remind her that I was the snake removal guy and not the gardener. Some people will take advantage of you if you let them.

The Fearful

*"Fear controls us, but knowledge empowers us." –*Unknown

A homeowner had two garter snakes in a window well. I told him I'd be happy to send a guy down there, but that he could save himself the cost of removal by simply putting on a glove, placing the snakes in a container, and releasing them by the nearest irrigation canal. His response was classic: "I have absolutely no desire to do that." He said it with such stoic resolve that I had to bite my tongue to keep from laughing.

A winter phone call came from a concerned lady. She had a small pile of firewood in her garage that "rattled" at her whenever she got near it. "I know it's a snake," she said. "Can you come and get it?"

I was there in 10 minutes and dismantled the woodpile. Not only was there no snake, there wasn't any other critter that I could see, but there was definitely a noise coming from a tiny hole in one of the logs. Some kind of beetle? A cricket perhaps? I had no idea.

"Do you want the wood?" she asked. I told her I didn't have a fireplace. "How much do I owe you?" I told her not to worry about it.

Guess who left with $25 and a small stack of firewood?

Whew! That was close! I got another call to rescue a woman from a slithering mass of homicidal baby garter snakes. I hate to think of the carnage that could have resulted if I hadn't gotten there in time!

A woman once called me to apologize for killing a baby snake in her basement. "I just panicked," she said. "I didn't mean to."

She wanted to know what kind of snake it was (gopher), what she should do if there were more, and how she could keep them from getting in the house. I wish more people had that much integrity. Her confession made me feel like a priest. I told her that under the circumstances I would forgive her and we shared a good laugh.

We talked for a while and she thanked me for making her feel less anxious, saying she'd call again if she found another one, although after our conversation she may try moving it on her own.

I will never stop teaching others about snakes. A little education sprinkled with humor can go a long way, changing not only behavior, but lives as well.

The Stupid

"It's hard to win an argument with a smart person, but it's damn near impossible to win an argument with a stupid person." –Bill Murray

While it may be possible to silence stupid with duct tape, it won't fix the problem permanently. I suppose ignorance really can be bliss for some, but it's not a state most people care to live in.

In January 2020, I got the first rattlesnake call of the year. It was an obvious case of animal cruelty, neglect, abuse, abandonment, and possession of a protected and prohibited species without a license.

After not receiving payment for several months, the owner of a storage facility opened a rental unit to discover a crudely made wood and Plexiglas cage with two rattlesnakes inside. The snakes were intact, didn't smell, and other than not moving, appeared to be alive but possibly too cold to move.

After photographing the snakes in the enclosure, I prodded them and determined that they were dead, although they were undoubtedly alive when they were left there. Records showed that this occurred months earlier during their active season. Some cerebrally challenged cretin must have caught them, thinking it would be cool to show off for his friends. Instead, he abandoned live animals in total darkness in an uninsulated metal building and left them to die. There wasn't even a water bowl in the cage. These state-protected animals had perished under miserable circumstances after months of starvation before freezing weather finally provided them with a semi-humane death.

The DWR sent an officer to investigate. The individual responsible was already incarcerated in another state pending extradition for this crime. I was asked to freeze the snakes as evidence in the trial, if and when it ever occurred.

Most people would probably shrug it off by saying, "They're just snakes," and yet those same people would lose their minds if it had been puppies, kittens, birds or any other sentient creature. I wanted prosecution of those responsible for this heinous act, and I expected the state to bring the perpetrator to justice. Despite my attempts to follow up, I never did learn the outcome.

The soulless, subhuman sack of garbage that did this doesn't deserve to live in civilized society. People this desensitized to the suffering of animals need to be removed from the gene pool because they all too often pose a danger to society as well.

The Evil

"We cannot have peace among men whose hearts find delight in killing any living creature." –Rachel Carson

Tortoises are among the most benign and gentle creatures on Earth, and are known for being affectionate with other animals and familiar humans. I once met a wild gopher tortoise near St. George. It didn't know who or what I was, but it kept ambling toward me out of pure curiosity. I was lying on my stomach taking pictures and had to keep scooting back because it's illegal to touch or handle a wild desert tortoise. It was an exhilarating experience.

A short while later, a friend texted me a photo of a gopher tortoise he found not far from there. These creatures are harmless, helpless, and federally protected, yet some brain-dead redneck thought it would be fun to kill this one. Based on tire tracks on a dirt road, it had presumably been run over by an ATV because its shell was shattered. When it comes to the selfish, ignorant behavior of human beings, I'm not only cynical, but disgusted and pissed off as well.

Humans fear what we don't understand. Most people live in a bubble so small that nothing outside of their personal, petty problems is of any real concern to them, and demonstrating compassion for anything outside that bubble is an alien concept. Most humans won't do any more than the very minimum that is expected of them in a given situation. Many of them won't take the time to learn any more than what they absolutely need to know in order to function within their limited personal realms, using fear as an excuse for bad behavior because they're too ignorant to know how ignorant they really are, all the while believing themselves to be smart.

Most human beings are responsible for their own misery, although the social safety net is there to support them if they fail. Animals, however, through no fault of their own, are quite often the victims of human greed, stupidity, hostility, ignorance, contempt and superstition.

Someone once called me a "snake-loving, rock-licking, tree-hugging, dirt-worshiping, liberal sonofabitch." He looked confused when I thanked him profusely and told him to have a nice day.

As a human who gives a damn and wants to make amends for my species, I am more inclined to assist a helpless animal than a fellow human whose problems are self-inflicted or substance-induced. Some people don't want help and others just resent it. Some will take everything they're offered as long as it's free, never once thinking of paying it forward.

Conversely, all animals respond to kindness, even snakes. I've dealt with hundreds of snakes and I know this to be true. There are videos of forest rangers in India providing water to cobras during times of drought. These highly intelligent snakes will eagerly gulp water from a bottle held in the ranger's hand as the two species share a moment of compassionate symbiosis.

I have also seen caring individuals hold water bottles so that thirsty rattlesnakes could take a drink. I've done it myself. Kindness is its own reward, providing a connection that transcends the unfortunate restrictions we place on these animals and their ability to interpret our intentions. The kindest thing we can do for most animals most of the time is to stop persecuting them and simply leave them alone to fulfill their inherent destiny.

As for people who deliberately kill tortoises, snakes, and other harmless creatures, l can only hope that karma comes around and slaps their sorry selves.

The following story is just sad, and is in a category all its own. I am in no way making light of this situation. On the contrary. It scared the hell out of me.

The hysterical woman on the phone asked if I was the snake guy and I assured her that I was. I've dealt with hysterical people before — people with a hyper-phobic fear of snakes who could barely function in the presence of one. I asked if she had a snake in her yard.

"No!" she shrieked. "I have snakes in my body! And ants! And they're consuming me!" She was crying and screaming. I could tell from her tone that it wasn't a joke.

In that moment I was dealing with someone with a severe psychological condition and I was way outside my wheelhouse.

I called her by name and asked how the snakes got into her body. "I don't know!" she exclaimed, sounding even more agitated than before. I asked her if she had spoken to anyone else about this. "Like who?" she demanded. "Like a doctor," I said. Her reply was, "You need to help me, but you think I'm crazy just like everyone else does!"

Long story short, I found out what community she lives in and told her I'd see what I could do to help her. I placed her on hold, then called the police and told them about the conversation, thinking they might want to perform a welfare check. Instead, they referred me to a crisis intervention hotline where a nice woman named Elaine listened as I explained the situation in detail.

Elaine had me speak to the woman via a three-way call because she had initially reached out to me. Then I introduced her to Elaine and excused myself from the call.

I hope she got the help she needed, but I'll never know.

These and hundreds of other scenarios kept me ever vigilant, never knowing what the next call might bring, providing me with an open window to worlds I never knew existed, but which I was sometimes invited to visit.

As a snake relocator, I've met hundreds of snakes and hundreds of people. Despite the stark differences in appearance and behavior (with the common exception of comparing snakes with politicians), snakes and humans are both vertebrates, meaning we share many physiological traits. This single factor alone provides snakes and humans with a similar evolutionary ancestry, giving us more in common than most people realize or care to admit.

Snakes are often misunderstood or vilified in human culture — symbols of danger, temptation or evil. In many cultures, snakes symbolize deception or hidden threats. Think of the serpent in Eden or Medusa's hair. But deeper reflection suggests a tangible truth — the more we look past the surface, the more we see ourselves in the other.

In September 2022, I conducted a 24-hour poll on Uncle Dave's Reptile Page just for fun. The challenge was to complete the sentence, **"Snakes are better than people because . . ."**

I won't list the responses here, but a theme developed — namely, that snakes don't kill for sport, but only to survive, and they don't waste anything. Also, that snakes don't judge, they have better intentions than some humans, and are more trustworthy. I've always thought so too.

Unlike many humans who may resort to deception or manipulation to achieve their goals, snakes behave in a consistently instinctual and predictable manner. Their actions are driven purely by the imperative to survive and not by trickery or malice.

A famous quote, often misattributed to Albert Einstein, goes as follows: "Everyone is a genius, but if you judge a fish by its ability to climb a tree, it will live its whole life believing it is stupid."

This quote emphasizes the importance of clarity and accuracy when judging individuals by their unique strengths and not by common or irrelevant standards. In other words, it's unfair to judge any person or creature by the attributes of another. This is because every creature is endowed with specific traits and skills that make it an essential part of the ecological order.

Humans tend to embellish positive attributes in the creatures we deem worthy of our affection, usually because they're "cute" or because they reciprocate our love.

Snakes became targets of human enmity early on, and they remain convenient scapegoats for our fears and nightmares. This isn't due to anything snakes have done, but is an anthropomorphic misprojection of the human psyche based on an incomplete understanding of their true purpose.

Humans have a tendency to externalize internal fears. Snakes, with their silent movement and unreadable expressions became the perfect vessels for a fear of the unfamiliar. Although fear is essentially a learned response, their alien form and clandestine behavior trigger an automatic unease in some people.

But these fears are rarely based on actual snake behavior. Snakes don't seek out humans, avoid confrontation when possible, and bite only when threatened or provoked.

The Only Good Snake . . .

By assigning negative human attributes to creatures that operate solely on instinct, we reveal more about our own psychological architecture than about the animals. Snakes have become projections of our shadow selves, serving as symbolic aspects of our own dark nature that we fear, suppress, or don't fully understand.

Some cultures revere snakes as symbols of healing (the Rod of Asclepius), transformation and rebirth (the shedding of skin), wisdom, fertility, eternal life, and even divinity. These interpretations suggest that when fear is replaced with understanding, the snake transforms from villain to teacher.

Have you found that your personal experiences with snakes have helped you see through the veil of cultural fear? Or perhaps reshaped how you interpret other misunderstood beings, human or otherwise?

Snakes are amazing creatures that contribute enormously to the betterment of humanity and maintaining the precarious balance of nature.

Whether you love them or hate them, one fact is undeniably true: the only good snake is the one that remains alive at the end of the day. The next time you meet a snake, respect its ancient lineage and its modern boundaries, wish it well, and let it perform its vital role in nature's grand design.

EPILOGUE

"True friends are those rare people who come to find you in dark places and lead you back to the light." –Unknown

Nemo the Wonder Cat used to lie regally on my computer desk, watching me with half-closed eyes, oblivious to the words I was typing but fascinated by the process. The moment I broke contact with my keyboard, he would insinuate himself between me and my pseudo-social online life by leaping onto my lap, refusing to be ignored for long.

He was a gentle critic but a lousy editor — his soulful blue eyes blinking in blissful approval of every syllable and sentence that flowed from my brain to my fingers no matter how convoluted they might be. Cats' eyes can see into our souls, and I have no doubt that he understood the intention, if not the meaning, behind the thoughts I sometimes struggled to put into words.

As a writer most of my adult life, my work consisted mostly of informational articles, letters to the editor, opinion pieces and blog posts. The decision to write a book was slow in coming. The question is, are you really a writer if you never write a book? We all supposedly have at least one book in us, maybe more, or at least one significant story to share with the world. The difficulty lies in coaxing it out, baring one's soul, and placing it on the table for our critics to scrutinize.

Everyone's a critic, and even if they never write a book of their own, a few of them will happily find fault with this one. The same is true of any achievement. It's an odd phenomenon, but skeptics, and sometimes even the people who know us best and love us most, may resent us for having the audacity to exceed their limited expectations of us. That's okay; I didn't write this book for those people.

Coaxing this book out has been a labor intensive, soul-searching, memory-mining, deep-dive into a life that I miss terribly. Most people my age can relate to a loss like that in their own lives. Those who can't probably haven't lived long enough yet.

Like most things in life, timing is essential. For me, writing this book was a race against an invisible clock — like trying to outrun time itself. I should have started years ago, because as my sight diminished, so did my motivation. Still, things happen when they're supposed to, right? Or does that sound too much like the stilted prognostication of a fortune cookie?

Speaking of fortune cookies, I wrote most of this book in 2025, the Chinese Year of the Wood Snake, which began on January 29, 2025, and ended on February 16, 2026. This was merely a coincidence. The previous year of the snake was 2013, so we waited a long time for it to slither back around. We'll all be much older when it strikes again in 2037.

According to ChineseHoroscope.com, ". . . the Snake represents wisdom, knowledge, intelligence, intuition, and creativity. Snakes are also associated with good luck, prosperity, fertility, and longevity. In some legends, snakes are considered divine messengers or guardians of sacred places. Snakes are also revered for their ability to shed their skin and renew themselves, symbolizing transformation and rebirth."

I wasn't born in the year of the snake, a fact that may have been due to a cosmic oversight. Like most children, I blame my parents. I was, instead, born in the Chinese Year of the Pig under the sign of Aries the Ram. This is why I can sometimes be a butthead. Arians are supposed to embrace change, but sometimes life gets in the way of living, taking us down paths that lead us away from desired destinations. Change is a good thing when the changes it brings are positive, but most people resist unexpected change due to a fear of the unknown.

From my childhood throughout early adulthood, I watched as my grandfather, my mom's dad, slowly lost his sight due to an insidious form of retinal deterioration known as retinitis pigmentosa, or RP. By the time my mother reached her mid-50s, she too watched helplessly as her world grew dim. As a genetic condition, RP is passed down from generation to generation via the genetic pipeline. Fifty percent of the offspring of a carrier — those who draw the short genetic straw — will inherit the condition. My mother, as my grandfather's only child, had a 50/50 chance of acquiring it. But, as bad fortune would have it, and through no fault of her own, she drew the wrong straw.

Epilogue

RP is no respecter of persons. It attacks the very young, the very old, and everyone in between. Some victims are born blind, while others have the better part of a lifetime to see the world before RP steals most of their sight. Some, like my mother, will never see the faces of their grandchildren.

I have three siblings. Two of us — myself and my youngest sister Lisa — have RP. Julie and Gary, the sibs in the middle, dodged the genetic bullet. Two out of four. Statistical perfection. Despite ongoing research, there is no cure at the present time.

Lisa is seven years younger than me, but her condition kicked in at an earlier age and progressed faster, forcing her to stop driving in her mid-50s. Adding to her burden, Lisa and her husband adopted children at an age when other couples were having grandchildren. As an example to her children, Lisa chooses to accept her hardship with courage and conviction. With no biological connection to our family, my nephews and niece have zero chance of inheriting the condition.

People with RP are born with it. It lays hidden deep within our DNA like an ambush predator, waiting for the right moment to launch its relentless attack. By the simplest definition, it robs victims of their sight by destroying the light-sensitive receptor cells in the retina, which is the interior back wall of the eyeball. These cells send images to the brain. Although it typically starts in the periphery, slowly working its way toward the center of the visual field, mine is behaving more haphazardly, leaving me with more peripheral vision than most, which enabled me to drive until just after my 66th birthday.

I was diagnosed in my late 30s. Initially, the diagnosis wasn't devastating. My ophthalmologist called it a mild form of the disease. What little damage there was resided in the outer periphery of the retina where it was hardly noticeable at the time. The question was how long it would remain that way.

There is very little that medical science can do to prevent the progression of RP. My doctor's advice was to eat right, exercise, and do all the things I wanted to do. I continued to get regular checkups every other year, but after years of hearing the same advice, it was easier not to think about it. After all, anxiety is one of the aggravating factors. So I stopped going in for checkups and lived my life instead. Doctor's orders, right?

I didn't live a lavish lifestyle. I couldn't afford to. In addition to doing the necessary things like holding a job, I did the things that made me happy: participating in cycling events with friends, rafting rivers, climbing local peaks, spelunking mine shafts and caverns, and of course, teaching people about snakes. And I continued to write. I became a self-taught editor. Because opportunity has an expiration date, I visited the Bahamas, México, Kenya, and China. And I started Wasatch Snake Removal.

Sixteen years went by before I saw the doc again. In that time, the condition had sprinted ahead like a 50-yard-dash participant at the Olympics. It hasn't yet reached the finish line, but if I live long enough, it likely won't stop until it does. The most I can hope for is that it plateaus at some point and stays there for a long time.

I should have started writing this book long before I did, but there is a tendency to procrastinate when we think we have ample time. RP became the impetus to begin this project or I may have put it off until it was too late. The sure knowledge that my time was limited became the motivation I needed, forcing me to write my story in a 14-month burst of frenetic effort. It may be the only good thing to come out of my situation.

The disease progresses slowly and changes can be imperceptible in the beginning. As receptor cells begin to die, the brain fills in the missing data like pieces of a picture puzzle. Only after too many pieces have been lost does the brain perceive the loss of data and lose its ability to replace the missing imagery.

The first symptom was an inability to see well in the dark. For most of my life I had eyes like an owl, able to see the smallest of snakes at great distances, even on sun-bleached asphalt where the contrast was low. Later on, an extra pair of eyes was always welcome when road cruising at night, and getting to the theater before the previews started was imperative without a flashlight.

One night, on an especially dark stretch of road not far from home, I struck something with my right side-view mirror, hoping to God it wasn't a person. Fortunately, it was only a garbage can, but it scared the hell out of me. Shortly after that, on the advice of my doctor, I stopped driving at night altogether.

Over time, I started noticing deficits in my daytime vision as well. Changes can be subtle or abrupt. It's not uncommon to awake in the morning to find the world darker, foggier, or less distinct than the night before. The process can take years or even decades to run its race, but the less vision that remains, the faster it seems to sprint ahead.

The biological mechanics of retinal degeneration are well documented, yet the experience of losing one's sight is not reducible to an eye chart. The world doesn't vanish all at once, but like the stars at dawn, it fades imperceptibly until it disappears altogether.

In the spring of 2021, I noticed a persistent blurry spot on the upper right corner of my right-side monitor at work. No amount of eye rubbing made it go away, nor did cleaning the monitor or my glasses. I had planned to work a few more years, but if this thing was going to happen, I wasn't about to let it happen on someone else's clock. It was time to get out of that place. Thirty-one years at the county was more than enough to collect a pension, and at 62 years of age I could also claim my Social Security benefit, albeit at the minimum rate. Few people ever retired faster than I did.

In 2022, we were all still in the throes of Covid. In Salt Lake's booming housing market, my landlady's greedy daughter and son-in-law saw the potential to squeeze more money out of the place I had called home for 26 years. Leaving there was one of the hardest things I've ever had to do. That little bungalow on Salt Lake's eastside served as headquarters for Wasatch Snake Removal, was close to my customer base, and provided me with a comfortable bachelor abode complete with a short commute, great neighbors, ample storage, convenient access, and affordable rent in an affluent part of town where I couldn't afford to buy a house.

I did buy an old home in 2005, but I didn't live in it. It was meant to be a flip — an investment property — a handyman project that I could sink all my time and money into and sell for a reasonable profit. Well, I got the first half right. I went through a series of tenants, most of whom took adequate care of the place. But before I could fix the home's myriad defects, the bottom fell out of the housing market in 2008, leaving me and millions of other Americans underwater and nearly sinking me financially. I hung onto that house for eight more years, letting tenants pay the mortgage while scrambling to keep pace with the deferred maintenance. The tax deduction for depreciation was nice, but overall, I'd have been better off if I'd never bought the place, or if I had lived there instead.

They say everyone should move every five years just so they can purge themselves of the junk that accumulates, and to be honest, there was a fair amount of trash along with the treasures. The load today is definitely lighter and getting more so all the time. Consolidating my belongings forced me to sacrifice possessions that took me a lifetime to acquire, and it hurt. I have given away hundreds of books and mementos that simply will not fit in a one-bedroom apartment, but perhaps it's for the best.

I miss walking around that old neighborhood in the dark, with or without a snake. Today, even walking around my new neighborhood in the daytime requires a good deal of fortitude and navigational skill. It's too easy to trip over curbs, tilted sidewalk blocks, broken concrete and chuckholes. I've nearly been hit by cars while crossing major intersections, even though the pedestrian light was in my favor. Some drivers are in such a hurry that they make left turns in front of me, cutting me off in crosswalks. So much for right-of-way.

I don't embrace change and don't seek it out. Nevertheless, changes of all types have been pelting me like hailstones over the past few years, and they're likely to continue well into the future. But there can be no growth without change. Ironically, change is the only thing in the universe that's constant. Change is guaranteed. Therefore, resistance to change is not only futile; it is also antithetical to self-improvement. I hope I'm up to the challenge.

In January 2022, I moved closer to my parents and was able to help them out when dad could no longer drive. This took me miles away from my customer base just as I was curtailing my own driving, making it impractical to drive across town or interact with venomous snakes.

Epilogue

At 18-and-a-half years old, I worried about Nemo in the best of circumstances. After several months of being on a joint supplement for arthritis and a kidney diet for renal failure, he was beginning to look and feel like a younger, more energetic cat. I could imagine him enjoying a long and comfortable life indoors, perhaps even for a couple more years, but he only lived six more months in the new place, not quite sure where he was. I was resentful that we were forced to move because he should have been allowed to live out his days in the only home he ever knew.

Nemo added substantially to the quality of my life. He was the cat who insisted on helping me change the oil in the snake mobile by lying on my chest as I tried to scoot under the car. He was the cat who crouched Sphinx-like on the bed at night, watching me sleep. He was the cat who never harmed another living creature, making friends with mice, praying mantis, and katydids. He even brought home a baby quail chick once, ushering it around the house like it was his personal pet. He was the cat who would rather be on my left shoulder than anywhere else in the world. He was the cat with the unlimited vocabulary. He was the cat who slept with his back pressed against mine or on the pillow next to me for more than 6,500 nights. Nemo was my animal soulmate.

As a flame point Siamese, Nemo was a white cat with pale caramel tips, tail, and mask. He looked like a perfectly toasted marshmallow. He was a sweet, intelligent cat who loved everyone, but his prime years were behind him and his quality of life diminished greatly toward the end, which meant that I finally had to do for him what I hoped could be postponed forever. I would have given him 10 years of my own life not to have to say goodbye.

Looking back, 2022 was a helluva year. The move in January was tough. Being uprooted from the place I'd lived and loved for nearly three decades and being transplanted elsewhere was a major stressor. But I survived.

A forced move and the tentative closure of Wasatch Snake Removal made me worry about what other changes lie in store. It was a concern that was both preemptive and prophetic, because nothing lasts forever and our present circumstances are tenuous at best and subject to change without notice.

The Only Good Snake . . .

Even though it wasn't our final year in business, 2022 marked the beginning of the end for Wasatch Snake Removal, and it hurt. But I backed away from that venture with my head held high, knowing that for nine years my team and I provided a valuable public service, sacrificed personal and family time, and often spent our own money to ensure that people felt safe in their own homes and yards. I also knew that the snakes we relocated were treated with kindness, compassion, and concern for both their long- and short-term wellbeing.

I said goodbye to my involvement in a business that enabled me to make a difference in the lives of total strangers and to interact with animals that I dearly love. I miss it terribly, but I will survive. Despite the disclaimer on my website, my phone still rings with snake calls, and while Jordan and Averi still do what they can, there's not much I can do to help anyone except offer advice.

One of my long-time customers texted me about a rattlesnake in his yard. I explained to him that I could no longer relocate snakes and referred him to another individual. This was his reply:

"I'm sorry to hear you've retired, but I understand the reason why. I have always appreciated your great service to the entire community! I also appreciate your tireless service as a [county employee]. I wish you luck in the future!"

In July, I held Nemo as he transitioned to the next stage of his eternal journey. Nemo was more than a cat. He was a guru; a mystic who understood the secrets of life and the universe, but couldn't impart them due to an impenetrable language barrier. He was the only person to greet me at the end of each day. I can't wait to see him again so we can communicate on the same level. My life is diametrically different without him, but again, I will survive.

My dad died in December of the same year, leaving our family without its patriarch and a gaping hole in our hearts. It's strange how someone can be here one moment and gone in a single heartbeat, but that's the tenuous and temporary nature of life. It's hard to imagine losing a parent until it becomes a reality, if it ever really does. The hardest part was watching him suffer the debilitating effects of Parkinson's disease over many years before slipping slowly away, knowing that his departure, when it came, would be permanent. But life goes on for those left behind.

I even survived Covid in 2022 after dodging it for two years.

This is not a list of grievances, but rather, an inventory of events that combined to make me stronger than I thought I was. Isn't it amazing what we can do when we have no other choice but to face life's challenges head-on with courage and determination, and with the love and support of those around us? Sometimes all we can do is take life one step at a time — especially when we can't see the entire staircase.

Even so, as a being of light, I question my ability to live in a world of darkness. As a photographer most of my life, I painted with light. As a writer, I tried to enlighten people with my words and teach them about the beautiful world around us. I crave the glow of a summer moon, the resplendent beauty of nature, and the radiance of a child's smile.

As a creature addicted to sunshine, I can't abide being thrust into a dark and dismal void. To what end? Who benefits from this? How can I be a light for others if my own candle is extinguished, the curtains are closed, and the shutters are nailed shut? How can I help anyone else if I'm helpless myself?

I have always been a man of action and adventure. I am independent, self-reliant, and I contribute to society. I'm still pursuing unrealized goals and ambitions on all fronts. I am not a do-nothing kind of person. I need to be busily and actively engaged in worthy causes. I have a hard time asking for help because I was the one who helped others. I worked my entire life to finally break the shackles of work-a-day servitude and truly live my life to the fullest, only to have a lifetime's worth of hopes and dreams stolen from me by an invisible thief. My retirement plans were yanked out from under me like a new rug I barely had time to walk on.

On the advice of my doctor, I stopped driving in July of 2025 and sold my car. This meant I could no longer take Mom to the grocery store or out to lunch. It's funny, but I always detested grocery shopping until I could no longer do it, then it didn't seem like such an awful chore. With so many options available, I can still get around without being able to drive, but after having a car since the age of 16, giving up 50 years of independence won't be easy. I always assumed I'd drive well into my 80s like my dad did until fate sent me down a dead-end road. But for me, that day came several years later than it did for my grandfather, mother and sister. For that, I am grateful.

At the beginning of this book, I mentioned that it wasn't my place to question fate. While it would be easy to cry "Foul!" or "Unfair!" no one ever said life was fair. But knowing that doesn't change the facts or make things easier. We play the hand life deals us because there is no other game.

I told my doctor I was safer behind the wheel than I was walking because I couldn't trip when I was driving. He doesn't think I'm funny.

My grandfather stopped driving in his 50s and was forced into an early retirement. I watched him transition from a youthful, energetic man to a shuffling, cane-bearing invalid. He spent nearly 35 years in that condition, pitied by all and envied by none. Although he tolerated his situation with commendable stoicism and resolve, RP robbed him of the life that should have been his.

While no one ever heard him utter a single word of lament, I'm sure he endured many moments of private anguish. His quality of life was sabotaged by his own genetics and the same is true of my mother. I understand now the anger she manifested throughout much of her life as a result of her victimization by a cruel and insidious condition she couldn't control.

To live alone in a sunless world is the greatest punishment I can imagine. Having to transition from a dynamic, productive individual to a reclusive housebound invalid is a torture no human should have to endure. I know that many sight-impaired people lead rich and rewarding lives, but for me, to be severed from nature is to be severed from life itself. The future, which once seemed so bright, is now a bleak and interminable void that I would never choose to inhabit. We all walk blindly into the future, not knowing what awaits us. But the future is not our enemy. Our fear of it is. It's important to embrace the life we have, live in the moment, and hope the future is kind.

Whereas my path was once illuminated by sunshine, it is slowly diverging into a path that leads to an obscure dimension I can't imagine. Traveling a road in total darkness seems like a cruel and pointless journey to oblivion. It is not a place anyone would willingly choose to go. Why pursue a destination chosen for me by a sadistic condition that loves the darkness and shuns the light? What does it mean to know something without seeing it? How do we trust, imagine, or remember that which is hidden from us?

I have earnestly sought divine guidance, but those pleas have gone largely unheeded. I'm not asking for a miracle. After all, I'm no more entitled to a miracle than any other person. I'm no less entitled either. But my earnest supplications bounce off the ceiling like so many errant Ping-Pong balls.

There were moments when I was hesitant to bend a humble knee, even in times of great need. It wasn't that I didn't believe help was there; it was because I was always convinced I could help myself. I suppose it was a matter of prideful impertinence deeply rooted in self-sufficiency — a result of living alone for so long — the one mistake I wish I could undo. Other than that, my regrets are few, stemming more from things I didn't do than from anything I did wrong.

I don't blame God for my situation, although He could have waited 10 years to impose it on me. I'd rather suffer a fatal condition and know that my days were numbered than to speculate on how long I may have to linger behind a black curtain. Why would God allow a healthy, vital, and productive person to be sidelined long before their useful years were spent?

If it sounds like I'm playing the victim card, I don't mean to, but I'm too young and too healthy to spend the rest of my life in a dark place surrounded by bitter thoughts of better days, unable to perceive the world beyond the length of a cane. What am I supposed to learn from that? It would be easier if I had a companion, because humans were never meant to be alone. I would have made a great dad, too, but by not having children, I avoided passing this condition to another generation. It ends with me.

The fact that I'm alone today was not intentional on my part. No one should go through this life alone unless it's by choice. I didn't choose singleness, things just worked out that way. Bad luck, misplaced trust and betrayal left me jaded and a little cynical I suppose. Perhaps I should have tried harder but it's too late now. It wouldn't be fair to drag someone into my life at this point.

Most people would rather lose a limb than lose their sight. Count me among them. No one wanders willingly down a dark and dismal path from which there is no return, and I'm not going passively. It's easy to be angry, but it's hard to know where to aim that anger when there's literally no target and no one to blame. And while it may garner me nothing in the end, at least I will have resisted because there's no virtue in passively rolling over and playing dead.

I have the greatest family and friends in the world. With their help and assistance from technologies that weren't available to my grandfather, I'll face this ordeal head on, confident that I'm not taking this journey alone and knowing that it won't last forever.

To lose the gift of sight is to lose a way of seeing, but not the capacity to perceive. It is a profound shift and a loss greater than or equal to losing anything precious. It is a source of mourning — a cause for grief. But it is also a portal. Through it, I hope to discover new dimensions of empathy, creativity, and resilience. In the absence of light, other senses awaken. And in the darkness a new kind of clarity may guide the way.

In an unattributed quote, someone said: "One of the recurring truths about the human psyche is that those who face the darkest moments of their lives with courage, loving acceptance and surrender, always experience massive growth and a blossoming thereafter. Confront the dragon; get the gold."

No one gained more insights from this book than I did. If you learned something too, we'll consider it collateral knowledge. I wish you all lives filled with opportunities for peace, growth and happiness.

Life is for living. Don't squander it. If you're young, take advantage of it. Grab life by the tail and yank it till it squeals! Make your journey count. Live your dreams while you can because time isn't always our friend. Confront whatever dragons may stand in your way. You will not only survive, but I'm counting on you to thrive.

ACKNOWLEDGMENTS

Books like this don't just happen. This book resulted from the wisdom and support of all those who helped shape my journey. None of us stands alone in our achievements. Rather, we borrow from the influences, guidance, and insights of those around us.

Countless teachers, mentors, friends, and even passing acquaintances all contributed to the sum of my collective understanding. Those who encouraged my love of snakes in any way (or at least didn't discourage it), especially in my formative years, are too numerous to mention. The same is true of those who encouraged me to write a book. While I can't possibly name all of you in this limited space, your impact lives within these pages, and for that I am profoundly grateful.

To my team at Wasatch Snake Removal: Thank you for your tireless dedication and hard work. I couldn't have done it without you.

Thanks to my brother Gary for the times we spent catching snakes and lizards together, and for reading and recommending changes to the manuscript. It's better because of you.

Thanks to D. Russon for his technical savvy in preparing the manuscript for publication, and for his many years of friendship and adventure.

Special thanks to Jessica Lee Anderson, my editor, publisher, mentor and friend, for helping me navigate the perils and pitfalls of the publishing world. Your knowledge, expertise, and support were invaluable.

ABOUT THE AUTHOR

David E. Jensen is a freelance writer, copy editor, educator, environmentalist, former owner of Wasatch Snake Removal in Salt Lake City, Utah, and an enthusiastic advocate for scaly creatures everywhere. While he has never met a snake he didn't like, he has met a few that weren't too fond of him.

Photo by Rindy Richins

www.ingramcontent.com/pod-product-compliance
Lightning Source LLC
Chambersburg PA
CBHW022044020426
42335CB00012B/535